DATE DUE

Smoot's Ear

Smoot's Ear
The Measure of Humanity

Robert Tavernor

Yale University Press
New Haven and London

Designed by Sarah Faulks

Printed in China

Library of Congress Cataloging-in-Publication Data

Tavernor, Robert.
Smoot's ear: the measure of humanity / Robert Tavernor.
p. cm.
Includes bibliographical references and index.
ISBN 978-0-300-12492-7 (cl : alk. paper)
1. Mensuration--History. 2. Metrology--History. 3. Mensuration--
Standards. 4. Metric system--History. I. Title.
QA465.T38 2007
530.809--dc22
2007010417

A catalogue record for this book is available from The British Library

To my parents

Contents

Acknowledgements

We measure ourselves in relation to the world about us from the day we are born, so I have many people to thank for helping me develop the ideas contained in this book. They may remember some of the key moments – vivid to me – to which they were party:

- As a child, building a garden den with friends to accommodate the size of our bodies, and from that secure position to spy on an adult world;
- As a teenager, being taught at school to prepare for decimalisation (which was introduced officially in 1971 in the UK);
- Studying architecture the following year and designing rooms and furniture in relation to my body dimensions, but having to refer to meaningless numbers using metric conversion tables;
- Living and studying in Rome in the late 1970s and being told not to measure the ancient buildings in metres, but in feet and inches if I wanted to understand their true proportions (in fact, I soon realised I had to find the specific measures that each building had been designed with, depending on its age);
- Designing a modest extension to my home in the Georgian city of Bath in the late 1980s, while thinking and designing with my body in feet and inches (as my eighteenth-century predecessors in Bath had done), translating these into the metric system, and then listening to local builders on site converting the metric dimensions back into feet and inches according to the sizes of timber and block they were handling; and

- Encountering otherwise intelligent and capable individuals who claim that the measures we use are entirely rational and objective.

It was Joseph Rykwert who taught me to judge the present through an experience of the past and, in the context of this book, it is of course no coincidence that I co-edited *Body and Building: Essays on the Changing Relation of Body and Architecture* (Dodds and Tavernor 2002) in his honour. His writings, in particular *The Dancing Column* (1996), provide a constant point of reference for all such studies. The main structure and much of the content of my book was in place by early 2000. Indeed, I conceived it as a companion volume to the collection of essays that comprise *Body and Building* and the expansive scholarship it celebrates. Distractions – including the editing and presentation of those essays with George Dodds – conspired against such synchronicity.

An earlier version of my introductory chapter here, 'Measure and Meaning', was presented at the Nexus 2002 conference in Óbidos, Portugal (Tavernor 2002b), and I am grateful for the encouragement I received from Kim Williams and the other conference participants on that occasion. My former colleagues and students at the Department of Architecture and Civil Engineering at the University of Bath patiently listened to sections of other parts of the evolving book after 1999 and provided insightful comments. Joseph Rykwert, Alan Day and Andrew Ballantyne read the first full manuscript version in 2004, and Vaughan Hart, Richard Padovan and Mark Wilson Jones also commented on aspects of it. I am grateful for their scholarship and time, and only sorry it has taken still longer to be turned into a book: a delay caused by the challenges of firstly becoming Head of Department, and then my subsequent move in early 2005 to direct the Cities Programme in the Department of Sociology at the London School of Economics (LSE). My colleague at LSE, Richard Sennett, wrote *Flesh and Stone* (Sennett 1994), an inspiring history of the western city told through bodily experience. I am grateful to Richard, and Niall Hobhouse, for encouraging me to make the move to the LSE, where I have been introduced to new ways of measuring the world in relation to people, and where I have a group of bright graduate students with whom to discuss such ideas.

During the time that the manuscript has been languishing on a shelf, the scholarship on and around the subject has continued to grow. Initially, two excellent unpublished PhD theses provided me with impetus and direction: Ruth Champagne's 'The Role of Five Eighteenth Century French Mathematicians in the Development of the Metric System' (Champagne 1979), and Edward Franklin Cox's 'A History of the Metric System of Weights and Measures' (Cox 1957). More recently, the more mature scholarship of Karsten Harries's *Infinity and Perspective* (Harries 2001) and Ken Alder's *The Measure of All Things* (Alder 2002) helped me to evaluate what I had written. The books that inspired me at the outset, however, were Arthur Koestler's *The Sleepwalkers: A History of Man's Changing Vision of the Universe* (Koestler 1959), which bridged effectively what he referred to as the gulf separating the Humanities and Science (which Koestler termed 'the Philosophy of Nature'), and Julian Barnes's iconoclastic and entertaining novel, *A History of the World in 10½ Chapters* (Barnes 1989), which linked the ancient world with the near recent so poetically. To all these distinguished authors I owe a debt.

I am indebted most to my wife, Denise, who conspired to sacrifice holidays so I would complete this book eventually, and to Joanna, Faye and James, who were children when I set out on this particular journey, but are now adults measuring the world according to their own standards. As an errant and dilatory author, I could have not received more understanding and support than that provided by Gillian Malpass and her colleagues at Yale University Press in London. Finally, I am delighted to have been able to make contact with Oliver R. Smoot in recent months – a famous living measure – and thank him for his corroboration of the material in the preface that follows.

Preface: Smoot's Ear

> This plaque is in honor of THE SMOOT which joined the
> angstrom, meter and light year as standards of length,
> when in October 1958 the span of this bridge was
> measured, using the body of Oliver Reed Smoot, MIT
> '62 and found to be precisely 364.4 smoots and one
> ear. Commemorated at our 25th reunion June 6, 1987
> MIT Class of 1962.
>
> Commemorative plaque on the Harvard
> Bridge, Massachusetts, USA

Oliver R. Smoot was a newly arrived freshman at the internationally renowned centre of technological excellence, the
Massachusetts Institute of Technology, in 1958.[1] His body was
chosen as a 'sacrifice' with which to initiate his class into the MIT
chapter of the fraternity, Lambda Chi Alpha, whose creed
embraces the notions of 'service, sacrifice, and even suffering
and humiliation before the world, bravely endured if need be'.[2]
No doubt mindful of these standards, Tom O'Connor, the fraternity's 'pledgemaster', contrived a task for the initiates of measuring Harvard Bridge. Smoot, at 5 feet 7 inches tall, happened
to be the shortest initiate, and was selected by O'Connor as their
living measure. The token suffering he would endure at the
hands of his classmates would soon compound the humiliation
of having been singled out for his diminutive height.

In the intellectual spirit of the great institution of technology
they had entered, the initiates planned their task practically and
efficiently. They measured his height as one 'smoot', and created
a 10 Smoot-long unit with string and then proceeded north
across Harvard Bridge from the Boston side towards Cam-

bridge. Using the stretched-out length of string, they marked the ends of each 10 Smoot unit on the ground with a painted line and number. Not too much hardship in the pledge so far, as Charles M. Annis, a second-year student (sophomore) in the fraternity, was quick to point out when he caught up with the group on his bike. Disapproving of their methods, he instructed the initiates to use Smoot's actual body, rather than the simplified standard they had derived from it. Smoot was duly required to lie down – placing his feet on the edge of the last chalk mark – so that his fellow initiates could make a mark above his head. He then pushed himself up, walked forwards and stretched himself out again, placing his feet on the preceding marker. Harvard Bridge is the longest to span the Charles River, and Smoot would be required to repeat this feet-to-head, press-up, forward-march process more than 360 times to traverse its entire length. Herein

1a   Oliver R. Smoot being lowered towards the 71 Smoots chalk mark by Peter S. Miller (dark hair, left) and Gordon W. Mann (light hair, right). Harvard Bridge, MA, USA, October 1958. Photograph courtesy of O. R. Smoot

lay Smoot's true 'suffering', which he was to endure for two hours, with the assistance of his classmates.

Smoot eventually became fatigued from his physical exertions, and his classmates were forced first to drag him, and when that became too painful, to carry him horizontally – like a log (fig. 1a) – towards the Cambridge end of the Harvard Bridge, pausing to calibrate as they went (figs 1b and 1c). Temporary respite came three-quarters of the way across the bridge when a police patrol car drew up, causing the initiates to scatter. Fortunately for the history of metrology, the officers left the scene, permitting the initiation – and Smoot's suffering – to continue.

1b   Oliver R. Smoot being upended for the next Smoot, October 1958. Photograph courtesy of O. R. Smoot

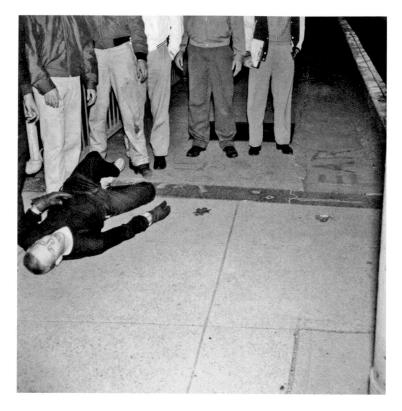

1c   Oliver R. Smoot collapsed at the Cambridge end of Harvard
Bridge measuring 364.4 Smoots ± an Ear, October 1958. Photograph courtesy of O. R. Smoot

As the commemorative plaque demonstrates, the actions of
the class of 1958 have achieved lasting fame through Smoot's
person. Harvard Bridge measures precisely 364.4 Smoots
plus/minus an ear. Indeed, it is difficult to find a conventional
measurement for the length of the bridge, either in feet and
inches (the official standard measuring system of the United
States) or in metres, except by conversion of the Smoot (364.4±
Smoots × 5 ft 7 in.).[3] When Harvard Bridge was rebuilt in the late
1980s, the Smoot calibrations were repainted, and successive

Lambda Chi Alpha initiates refresh them twice yearly. More tangibly, the contractors, the Modern Continental Construction Company of Cambridge, produced Smoot-length slabs for the pavement sidewalk that were each 5 feet 7 inches, rather than 6 feet, in length. It is reported that the local police have used the Smoot markers to fix the positions of road accidents when filing their reports. The Smoot has retained human and practical value for four decades.

Nor does the story end there for Oliver R. Smoot. Fame as a measuring standard set him on a career path. After graduating in Economics at MIT, Smoot moved to Washington, DC, to read law at Georgetown University: on qualifying, he became an active participant of the American Bar Association. But it appears that measurements were ingrained in his being, and he later participated in the American National Standards Institute, becoming its chairman. Even more prestigiously, on 1 January 2003 he began a two-year term as President of the International Organization for Standardization (ISO), an international body intended 'to facilitate the international coordination and unification of industrial standards' using the metric system.

ISO had come into existence as an organisation just eleven years before Smoot calibrated Harvard Bridge. In 1946 delegates from twenty-five countries met in London, and ISO officially began operations on 23 February 1947. Its name is derived from the Greek word *isos*, meaning 'equal', a more neutral acronym for *Organisation internationale de normalisation* than 'OIN', which was preferred by the representatives of France, where the metric system was born. The ISO is now a network of the national standards institutes of 153 countries, and has its headquarters in Geneva, Switzerland. How curious that Smoot, a standard of local measure in his youth, was to preside over global standards using the metric system in later life. How ironic, too, that Smoot, famous as a youthful body-measure, should mature to become the leader of standards activities based on quantities pointedly lacking in human qualities.

Different types of measures form the subject of this book, from body-related measures to the abstract scientific measures of non-physical derivation. I shall introduce the principal standards of measure, from those that once referred to the feet and inches of ideal bodies, to Enlightenment attempts at creating a truly scientific system of measures, the metric system, based on the dimensions of the earth. Metrification is regarded by some (as we shall see) as a malformed progeny of the French Revolution, and counter-reactions will be provided of attempts – by artists, architects and philosophers – to humanise its being. My book concludes with another beginning, humankind's journey into outer space, and the first direct encounter with the unfathomable measure of the universe.

My approach to this subject is historical and non-technical. I shall provide an account of measure in the Western world that is integral to cultural history, and not – as is more usual – as if it were a pure science divorced from ordinary (and extraordinary) human concerns. The MIT Class of 1958 reasoned, wisely, that the apparent precision that the recorded length of 364.4 Smoots suggests is a delusion. The significance of Smoot's ear is that it is a built-in error; it recognises that fallibility is ever-present in human affairs. I would argue that it is an essential quality of human nature, and is at the root of human creativity. As an explanation of Smoot's ear, this book is concerned with human measures and measuring; scientific quests for precision divorced from human experience and artistic – and human – attempts at balance; of certitude, and irony its close companion.

Introduction: Measure and Meaning

Measure: *mens* (Latin: 'mind'), *mensurare* =
                 measuring/measure
Metre: *metron* (Greek), *metrum* (Latin: 'measuring
                 rod'), *mètre* (French) = metre
Irony: *eironeia* (Greek: 'simulated ignorance'),
                 eiron ('dissembler and simulator of power')
                 = irony

Measure is as old as language and both have influenced the
development of civilisations.[1] The origins of language and
measure are simple and immediate, having their roots in the
practical and useful. Language and measure are necessary parts
of everyday experience, so much so that we take them for
granted – until, that is, attempts are made to regulate or impose
change, and so wrestle the familiar from popular consent.

Grammar, spelling and the form of the written word define
ideas and speech. They combine to give language shape, rhythm,
power and authority. There is an official language regulated by
lawyers, teachers and governments, and a conventional everyday
language of the street and marketplace. We define language, and
then language defines us. Through the popular media, novels,
newspapers, television and Internet, there are constant challenges to the value and purpose of regional and national language. The unconscious and deliberate breaking of rules, the use
of slang and the formal inventions of poets and writers modify
the official language as new exemplars enter usage. In short, we
express ourselves through language – individually and in groups,
locally, regionally and nationally.

Until the globalisation of standards, weights and measures had
a voice too – local, regional and national. They were usually

characterised in relation to our daily activities and to the form of our bodies. Conventionally, I might say that something beyond me 'is about my height'; or I may gesture, hands apart, to indicate the size of a smaller object. In as much as language defines human speech, measure also has its own official structure of agreed interrelationships: being calibrated and subdivided into parts that relate to a governing idea or set of principles, organised around a primary unit length of measure.

Industry and government would argue that measure cannot be as fluid as language because, like any medium that affects the monetary value of the trade and exchange of commodities, nationally and internationally, there is a need to agree and control the quantities involved. The modern – post-Enlightenment – world has worked to achieve a strictly regulated international language of exchange, based on the metric system, that allows for the effective global communication of lengths, weights, volumes and related measures. The metric system is truly international. It is in use everywhere, but belongs to no one. Originally, it was meant to relate to the dimensions of the earth. In fact, its length is defined by a light wave in gas; it does not represent anything physical; and it is intangible and unrecognisable.

The metric system is meant to be as neutral as Esperanto, which was also invented, in the late nineteenth century, as a universal, non-nation-specific language. Esperanto did not catch on, however, and English has become an unofficial international language. The present dominance of the English language resulted from an expansion of power and authority around the world through British colonisation, empire and trade, and it was then perpetuated by the subsequent global commercial empire of the USA. Similarly, the ancient Romans had provided the Western world with the Latin language, which still underpins many European languages. They also, however, introduced standards of weights and measures across Europe from which the Anglo-Saxon standards of measure – of feet and inches, gallons and pounds – were adapted, regionalised and nationalised. Across the breadth of the British Empire the Imperial system of weights and measures acquired true global influence. As that empire waned, so did the authority of its weights and measures. The USA has to some extent rationalised its mensural inheritance from the mother country, and – unlike any of the world's other major nations – still uses feet, inches, gallons and pounds on a daily basis. Elsewhere, a scientifically (artificially) constructed system of metric weights and measures has gained general acceptance and official sanction. Unlike Esperanto, the metric system has become a required method of communicating. Yet, as individuals, we continue to measure the world around us through and in relation to ourselves.

Herein lies the dilemma I will explore in this book. The metre length and associated weights and volumes are based on the assumption that measurement can be reduced to quantities, and that these quantities are applicable to any discipline within the arts and sciences, and to any nation. Yet, as the standard Smoot suggests, measures are much more than quantities. They have symbolic as well as practical value. History demonstrates that measures have embodied (literally) and signified the potency of their creators: the ancients attributed the creation of measure to gods, the Egyptians to Thoth and the Greeks to Hermes. Judaeo-Christian literature associates measure with Cain – the first offspring of Adam and Eve – and thus the very beginnings of Western civilisation.[2] Eminent mortals, too – great heroes, warrior-kings and queens – were elevated above the ordinary and, as the earthly representatives and personifications of the gods, were correspondingly idealised and idolised. They were often presented as divine beings in communion with the heavens, and as channels of heavenly power and authority they bore gifts from the gods that would benefit their subjects. Their likeness – their physicality – was captured in physical artefacts, in statues and paintings, works of art that sought to equal or surpass the perfection and beauty of their subject. As we shall see, their idealised forms, along with the staffs and rods that defined their office, provided the basis for the earliest recorded linear standards. Weight and capacity were frequently derived from these.[3]

Fundamental Measures

Ancient measures were neither as precise nor as finely subdivided as the modern scientific measures used today because they did not need to be. At first, local surveyors marked out territories with their own strides; builders and craftsmen sized and shaped materials using the best hand tools available. As tools became more precise and durable, so the objects they made were capable of greater refinement. But as trade between different communities increased, as regions coalesced into sovereign states and nations, mensural agreement was sought.

Whatever the actual physical lengths adopted, the human form provided the practical and familiar names of customary measures. It is important to clarify why this should be so, and architecture is a useful medium by which to explain the particular relevance of the body to the spaces we inhabit. Buildings are the largest man-made constructions, intended for human use and occupation. They frame ordinary and extraordinary activities, and give shape and meaning to human actions. It should be no surprise that furniture, rooms and entire buildings usually relate to the size of the human body – to the needs of differently shaped humans. In the classical tradition, even the arrangement of the body has relevance to buildings, which have a 'face', with a primary, centrally located aperture – like a mouth – for the door, while unsightly activities and spaces are kept to a building's rear. Whole cities have been designed to resemble the human form.[4]

When designing an internal enclosure such as a room, a decision has to be taken about its size, as well as the dimensions of openings in its walls and the sizes of the beams supporting its floor and ceiling. The more an architect is aware how a space will be occupied, the more likely it is that the outcome will be satisfactory, spatially and structurally, for its users. Again, in the classical tradition, the better the proportions of the spaces – like the body – the more beautiful they are considered to be.[5]

To set out a particular kind of room, ensuring that corners are square to one another, and walls parallel and of equivalent length (in a square or rectangular room), requires careful measuring. In the absence of an official measure, individuals will use their bodies – their foot, hand or arm – with which to measure and design enclosures. This may be done physically, at full-size, by pacing out a space, and using hands, feet and arms for smaller dimensions: the body and ear of Smoot provides evidence for this. But a collective endeavour, particularly in an organised society, requires more universal agreement as to the measures appropriate. The body may then be idealised according to the conventions that prevail, perhaps as general, even 'perfect', bodily proportions among the group, which are represented using standards accepted and regulated by the community at large. To avoid confusion, falsification and corruption, agreed measures will be defined as a standard. This standard will be carefully controlled, and then preserved for comparison with the products of the measures in daily use.

Builders and craftsmen, who make spaces and handle materials directly, experience the physicality of materials of different sizes. Complex and significant building enterprises of grander conception demand an appreciation of size and scale. Starting remote from the building site, and usually without the same degree of direct, hands-on contact with different materials, architects spend their formative years drawing and modelling simple and complex spaces to scale before an accurate comprehension of size becomes second nature to them. Once the mental prefiguring of size is complete, the dimensions of the design proposal need to be communicated to the builder and craftsman, and by the builder to the material supplier. Drawings are the principal means by which the architect transmits this information. Architects make drawings to scale, sometimes accompanied by three-dimensional models, and annotated with numbers representing quantities or lengths. The measurements they indicate must be accepted as standard by all those in the chain of information and instruction, and – when materials are imported from a distance – they must have validity beyond the immediate locality of the project. To facilitate easy application, the smallest measure is set in relation to the largest.

Western measures inspired by the human body commonly use the finger – or digit (the breadth of the middle part of the first joint of the forefinger) – as the smallest element in the system. The digit is related to the palm (which equals 4 digits and a hand-breadth), the foot (16 digits or 4 palms), the cubit (the forearm equals 24 digits, which is also known as the *braccio* or 'ell' of 1½ feet), the body height, span or fathom (6 feet, and the distance between the tips of the fingers of arms outstretched) and the pace (of 2 strides equals 80 digits and 5 feet).[6] Sets of linear relations of this kind were usually calibrated on rigid linear rods and defined as the official standard. Replicas were displayed in public places and distributed for general use and benefit, while the original standards were stored safely in the treasuries of temples.

When other measuring standards were required that were considerably smaller or larger than body-related standards, they still usually related to its proportions. Commerce uses standards set by precious metals such as gold, agriculture by grain size, and land surveying by the size of fields and related property. In Roman times the *uncia* or 'inch' was introduced as one-twelfth part of the foot measure. During the reign of Edward II (1307–27) of England, an inch was defined through the lengths of 'three barley corns, dry and round' laid end-to-end.[7] Alternatives to a body-centred system are rare. Although any familiar and conveniently sized items may be related to one another to create a coherent system, they will not necessarily make for useful or memorable comparison. There can be no doubt that Western culture would have difficulty comprehending the ancient Indian scale of measures in which the *yôjana* (yu-shen-na, a day's march for an army) variously equals multiples – 16 or 30 or 40 – of a unit called a *li*, which is also

equal to eight *krôśas* (keu-lu-she): a *krôśa* is the distance that the lowing of a cow can be heard; a *krôśa* divided into 500 bows (*dhanus*): a bow is divided into four cubits (*hastas*): a cubit is divided into 24 fingers (*angulis*): a finger is divided into 7 barleycorns (*yavas*): and so on to a louse (*yûka*), a nit (*likshâ*), a dust grain, a cow's hair, a sheep's hair, a hare's down [. . .] and so on for seven divisions, till we come to [. . .] an excessively small grain of dust (*anu*): this cannot be divided further without arriving at nothingness [. . .][8]

Coherence comes through a single form or an over-arching concept. Nothing is more readily accessible in everyday experience than the human body and its constituent parts, and – once – nothing was more meaningful. In the ancient world, the body symbolised the qualities of the intangible universe.

Perfect Measures

It was the ancient Greeks who realised that quality could be described not only with words, but also through the application of numbers. Pythagoras (582–496 BC) defined the properties of certain numbers, and he considered the integers 6 and 10 to be perfect because they were extraordinary numbers exhibiting specific qualities. They can be regarded as the sum of their parts: 6 is the sum of 1 + 2 + 3, and 10 the sum of 1 + 2 + 3 + 4. In the *Timaeus*, Plato (427–347 BC) used Pythagoras' perfect numbers as a means of describing the perfection of the natural harmony that existed in the world and universe. He combined language and number to define what he called the measure of 'the world soul', using a pattern of ten numbers derived from the powers of 2 and 3, and arranged in the form of the Greek letter lambda (λ):

$$
\begin{array}{ccccc}
& & 1 & & \\
& 2 & & 3 & \\
4 & & & & 9 \\
8 & & & & 27
\end{array}
$$

They represent the monad, the first even and odd numbers, their squares and cubes (1, 2 and 3, 4, 8), and point, line, plane and solid (1, 3, 9, 27).[9] The mathematical canon of united numbers and qualities that both men described is consequently known through a resolution of their separate conclusions as the Pythagoreo-Platonic number system. Knowledge, Plato argued, begins with observation, which leads to insight. Measure – passive and active – leads to facts.

Aristotle (384–322 BC) developed a non-Platonic theory of form and a system of deductive reasoning in his treatise on *Categories*. For Aristotle, number and speech are discrete quantities, and have qualities that relate to 'habit' (the various kinds of knowledge and virtue). To be described and defined fully, qualities need to be measured and compared with established standards, such as what is beautiful and ugly. Artists in antiquity imitated the physical objects of the natural world: this approach was valued because accurate imitation reveals and represents truth, which Aristotle discusses in his *Poetics*.

Accordingly, the sculptor Polyclitus (or Polykleitos) of Sikyon (or Argos), who was active in the fifth century BC, gave form to the Pythagoreo-Platonic system of numerical perfection. Famously, he created sculptures of a man and a woman whose forms expressed perfection, such that the parts of the body corresponded harmoniously with the whole. This perfection was not only visible to the Platonists, it was also set out in a written and tabulated form that described relations of ideal numbers. In relation to the Pythagoreo-Platonic universal numbers, this system subsequently became known as the 'canon' of perfect proportions.[10] The qualities of Polyclitus' sculpture and number canon were regarded as a natural symbol of earthly and heavenly perfection. Simultaneously, the body of man (and of woman) was regarded as a symbolic microcosm of the harmonious universe.

The source for Polyclitus' canon is uncertain, but it probably reached back to Egyptian antiquity. Whatever its precise origins, the body analogy permeated many aspects of ancient thinking, including language. According to Plato, it was Socrates who had compared the structure of speech to that of a living being, 'with a body of its own as it were, and neither headless nor feet-less, with a middle and with members adapted to each other and to the whole'.[11] Following in this tradition, the great Roman orator Cicero, writing in the first century BC, stated a similar belief to Socrates: that verbal delivery should be composed like well-formed bodies.[12] Marcus Pollio Vitruvius, a Roman architect working and writing about the time of Cicero, also absorbed this tradition and stated – what was probably a commonly held belief – that the finest buildings of antiquity reflected in their form the human proportions of the Greek canon.[13] Since these proportions were derived from Pythagoras' and Plato's numerical definition of the universe, Vitruvius was aware that the measuring units he used to design buildings – the finger, palm, foot and cubit – and the perfect number relations between them were a combination derived from the measures of the universe and of the idealised body of man.

This notion was reappraised 1,500 years later by Italian Renaissance artists and architects, who referred to the classical ideal body once again. Leonardo da Vinci memorably represented the idealised Vitruvian man graphically as *Homo quadratus*, a naked figure with outstretched limbs bounded by a circle and a square (fig. 2). They also made this analogy of universal perfection relevant to their own times, by conflating this essentially pagan and anonymous figure with the primary symbol of Christianity, the crucified body of Christ. As the Son of God, Christ's body reflected in its form and proportions the order of God's universe, and so personified heavenly and earthly perfection.[14]

This association of the quality and quantity of measure with a sacred body contrasts starkly with the bodily detachment towards measure – intellectually and physically – of the modern era. Modern science does not recognise that the human body has relevance to a universal system of measures. Instead, a new system was conceived based on the much vaster (and even less precise) girth of the earth, a conception that proved faulty and was eventually abandoned. The metre is defined instead by light waves in gas produced in a science laboratory. Measure has been dehumanised. It has been reduced to a practical tool deliberately stripped of human association.

2   Leonardo da Vinci, *Homo quadratus*. Galleria dell'Accademia, Venice

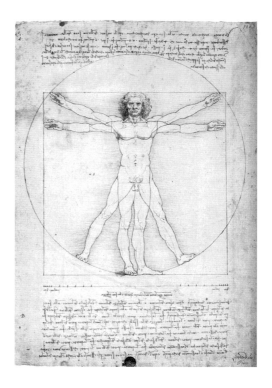

The ancient union of mathematics and words is at the root of this approach. By using numbers and symbols as the principal language to relate abstract and concrete ideas, the sciences during the last two-and-a-half millennia have become increasingly mathematical and reductive: that is, differences in quality have been reduced to unitary differences of quantity. As qualities have been turned into abstract scientific quantities, so everything can be dissected into ever-smaller units of measurement, into measures incomprehensible to and remote from everyday human experience. Consequently, modern measures are as meaningless and – in the qualitative sense – as valueless to most of the world's population as is the ancient Indian scale referred to above.

Enlightenment Reason and the Metric

Sir Isaac Newton, the father of seventeenth-century Enlightenment science, unwittingly sowed the seeds of this dilemma in the second edition of his *Principia* (Mathematical Principles of Natural Philosophy) of 1713, even though he believed in a universe of qualities in which God permeated everything, from earth to the limitless boundaries of space.[15] Being everywhere, however, Newton's God was necessarily incorporeal and lacked the identifiable body granted to mortals. Newton's friend, the philosopher John Locke, extended this reasoning to society and politics in an age when monarchies were still regarded as divinely appointed authorities, that kingship was a God-given right. Locke rejected the notion of a divine origin for human government and argued instead that sovereignty resides not in any one individual, but in all the people. Locke's reasoning is encapsulated in two books, *An Essay Concerning Human Understanding* and *Two Treatises of Government*, both published in 1640. They provided the intellectual basis for social and political revolution in Britain.

More emphatically, Locke's writings contributed to the uprooting of the French monarchy, destroying the symbolic validation of political power through the king's sacred body. The execution of Louis XVI in 1793 was both sacrilegious (as regicide always is) and, through the implementation of the recent invention of the guillotine, intentionally impersonal. At the Revolution, an elected (but still undemocratic) body of the nation's representatives – its citizens – were to rule in place of the divine authority of a solitary monarch. The committees they constituted failed to unify the nation, however, but a charismatic leader, Napoleon Bonaparte, filled the void as national hero and provided the leadership that the Revolution had attempted to destroy. Napoleon became emperor of the French, their surrogate king.[16] His was a modern reflection of the king's majesty and dominion, though (officially, at least) not his divinity.

Notions pertaining to the divinity of kingship have since been mostly expunged from modern thinking. Instead, we place our faith in democracy (another ancient Greek concept), elected leaders – rarely superior models of humanity, moral or physical – and an advanced technological society, a value system shaped by the dispassionate objectivity of modern science. Rationality is usually held in higher esteem than subjectivity in this system, and rational science is preferred to what is regarded as the subjectivity of art – which is consequently poorly understood and mistrusted.

This modern imbalance is very evident in the changed response to the representation of human proportion in art and architecture. In the classical tradition the body was regarded as expressly beautiful, as something tangible – to be touched – as well as being a reflection and embodiment of universal harmony, a balance of quantity and quality. Since the Enlightenment, scientists, in tandem with philosophers, have scrutinised the human body with detachment. It is now something to be abstracted, quantified and dissected into ever-smaller microscopic and atomic detail. Similarly, the measurements of the internationally controlled metric system are precisely calibrated abstract quantities, verified scientifically. The metric system is not representative of the body; it is a product of modern scientific thinking, propelled by the rationalism of the French Revolution in particular.

The metric system developed from Enlightenment concerns for precision, and from political demands (in the name of 'the people') for an equitable system that would provide uniformity across the civilised world.[17] In the search for measures appropriate for all nations on earth that would be 'rational' – quantifiably natural – the metre rod, which is at the root of the metric system, was conceived as a fractional representation of the physical dimensions of the earth. It was determined in relation to the mechanical laws that were understood to be controlling the forces of nature and the universe.

In fact, a rational scientific conception was never delivered, and was doomed at birth. As Newton first hypothesised, the earth is not a pure sphere and therefore the metre rod could never be the precise fraction of the earth's circumference that

French scientists had intended.[18] Nor have metric measures proved to be finite, or any more ideal than the standards derived from the idealised human form. Since the metric system first came into being in the late eighteenth century, its standards have been refined several times and are now defined by the insubstantial elements of the universe itself, of light and gas, using technical apparatus of scientists' contrivance.[19] The metre has become a measure without relation to corporeal form or even common human experience; it is an abstract measure without tangible value. It is, as Le Corbusier – one of the most influential architects of the twentieth century – pronounced, 'a mere number without concrete being'.[20]

The Metre Reconsidered

I have introduced measure here as an essential part of the history of ideas, as something shaped by social and political concerns, because it is more usually presented one-sidedly, as a catalogue of quantities of quasi-scientific status in relation to advances in scientific understanding. Indeed, metrology is ordinarily defined as a 'science or system of weights and measures'.[21] Numbers are calibrated with decimal-point precision in comparative tables and accepted as verifiable truths around the globe. Neither scientists nor historians have considered measure as an *art*: as a commentary on changing social and political conditions, or as a potent instrument of creativity in the hands of artists, painters, sculptors and architects, who provide cultures with their tangible imagery and physical legacy. Yet, the relevance that nations attach to one kind of measure over another is the most succinct and precise statement of the dominating forces within a civilised society; measure is always an expression of ideas and creativity, deriving from science *and* art.

While practicality has been a constant root of measures for five millennia, it will be evident from this introduction that the idea and reality of what measure represents has been transformed in that time. It is the *idea* of measure – what it purports to be and actually represents – that is the focus of this book.

Measure, I will argue, needs to be recognised as more than a specialised, abstracted, physically remote, calibrated dimensioning of inert material. Measure is a deliberate consequence of human thought – in Latin, *mens* (the root of 'measure') – and the dissembler – in Greek, *eiron* (the root of 'irony') – and simulator of power. Indeed, because of its changing and irrational character, the modern metric system based on the metre rod might be better understood as the measure of all irony. For although it was designed to be rational, in the process of its scientific refinement and adoption internationally the metre has become disembodied, non-figurative and abstract – terms that, perhaps more than coincidentally, have also been applied to the art and architecture of the twentieth century.

I am not alone in the belief that a reconsideration of measure has the potential to reunite art and science. During the twentieth century, two leading French-speaking artists questioned the scientific search for precision through abstraction, of separating body from measure. They challenged what the metric system represented and its appropriateness for their own disciplines. The French artist Marcel Duchamp was concerned in his work to challenge the absolute value of the metre, to create 'a new image of the unit of length [. . .] the meter diminished'. He contrasted the certitudes of the metre rod – its logical linearity – with metre-long curves that he created by chance. The Swiss-French architect Le Corbusier was also highly critical of the metre and he designed a new measure for architects, the Modulor, with which they might modify the metric system by combining modern anthropometrics with a classical regard for measure. He incorporated the Modulor in the design of some of his most famous and influential post-war buildings.

The human body remains a primary point of reference as humans venture beyond the earth. The first man-made object to escape the pull of our sun, the NASA spacecraft *Pioneer 10*, was dispatched into outer space in 1972 with a plaque on its exterior bearing pictograms as messages. These included an idealised naked male and female body, should intelligent extraterrestrial life forms stumble across the spacecraft and question its origins. These bodies figure prominently on the plaque, as do the forms of the spacecraft, the planets and the sun. But the dominant measure of science – the metric system – was not identified so explicitly.

In order to explore the changing attitudes to measure, this book has three parts, each with its own chronology and theme, which aim to describe – like a perfect body (its feet, torso and head) – the whole. The first part is concerned with the traditional relation of body and measure, the second its replacement with 'rational' or scientific measure, and the third with creative attempts to redress what artists, architects and writers regard as a modern imbalance in attitudes to measure. Historical facts concerning the evolution of modern measure will be linked by threads of narrative to reveal the human story of the individuals and groups who influenced reform: their aspirations and disappointments, even their personal sacrifices. It will chart an aspirational journey through Western civilisation, from the construction of the Great Pyramid to the first manned flight to the moon – epoch-defining artefacts and events, ancient and modern, achieved without reference to the metric system. In parallel, it will record the negative and alternative responses to the metric system, from individuals and entire nations. Their reactions, as I shall describe them, were profound and ironic.

1. Body and Measure

There is no such thing as primitive man; there are
primitive resources. The idea is constant, in full sway
from the beginning.[1]

We interact with each other and the world around us through
our bodies. Before humankind became airborne and penetrated
the earth's atmosphere to enter outer space, it was necessary to
speculate about the form and extent of the globe while remaining firmly rooted to the surface of the earth. The first philoso-
pher-scientists naturally gauged its extent in relation to their own
physicality and to the heavenly bodies, particularly the sun and
the moon, and their effects on the earth.

Thales (*circa* 624–546 BC) made an important step in this
direction at the end of the sixth century BC. A rich olive-oil merchant turned natural philosopher, Thales came from Miletus in
the Greek colonies of Ionia in the eastern Aegean, just south of
Ephesus on the Mediterranean coast of Asia Minor (modern
Turkey). Pythagoras was born on Samos, an island nearby. The
region had been fought over by the Babylonians, the Egyptians,
Persians and Greeks, and each conquering nation had brought
with it new forms of learning. Scholars of the area assimilated
Egyptian geometry and Babylonian and Persian astronomy, and
went on to provide the foundations of Western arithmetic, geometry and physics. Thales of Miletus proved to be as successful a
scholar as he had been a merchant, and is regarded as the father
of Greek and Western natural philosophy: 'science' was not yet
regarded as a separate discipline. He was the first to predict a
solar eclipse, which he calculated would occur some time in 585
BC. Its occurrence on 28 May of that year, during a great battle

between Lydia and Media, was taken as an omen by both sides, and the confrontation was abandoned. Thales is also famous for having determined the height of the great Egyptian pyramids according to the shadow they cast from the sun. Undaunted by their mystery and phenomenal scale, he treated the pyramid as if it were a gnomon of a sundial, not pyramidal in shape, but a simple vertical shaft. According to Greek historians, Thales measured the shadow of the pyramid at that moment in the day when his own shadow matched his body height: he used his body-scale to determine the height of the pyramid.

Thales was helped in his calculations because he assumed that the earth was flat, that it was disk-shaped and floated on a sea of water, the fundamental natural element. The idea that it was spherical derives from Pythagoras, whose reasoning was based not so much on observation but on the conviction that the most important objects in the universe would display the qualities and characteristics of pure natural geometry – the circle and sphere. Thus, not only the earth, but also the sun, moon and planets, *had* to be spherical. In the second half of the fourth century BC, Aristotle confirmed Pythagoras' hypothesis through observation. He noticed that ships vanished hull-first on the horizon in whichever direction they travelled, and that during a lunar eclipse the earth's shadow on the moon was always curved. It took four centuries and the wonderful imagination of the poet Eratosthenes to extend Thales' principle of measuring using the shadow cast by the sun to calculate the size of the earth.

Eratosthenes (*circa* 276–196 BC), a North African born in Cyrene (modern Shahhat in Libya), had been taught by the great Greek poet and sculptor Callimachus (reputed to be the originator of the ornamental Corinthian capital), and he made his mark as a geographer and librarian of the Library in Alexandria, the greatest repository of existing scholarship. Eratosthenes came to prominence in Egypt when he initiated the science of mathematical geography, locating places on the earth's surface using coordinate lines of latitude and longitude. His mapping led him to ask questions about the earth's total extent, and with the resources of the Alexandria Library at his disposal, Eratosthenes thought laterally. Astronomers had already concluded that the sun moved around the earth each day in a 365-day cycle; the Babylonians had earlier calculated, by the third century BC, this cycle as 360 days, which is how circles came to be subdivided into 360°. Also, recognising the earth as a sphere, they observed that the sun has a constant relation to a central band wrapping the earth – the Equator – and that the sun turns in a snaking pattern, from about 24° south of the Equator to the same distance north, before retreating over the same course. This zone of 'turning' – *tropos* in Greek – marked the limits that the sun moved to in relation to the Equator and the Tropics of Cancer and Capricorn.

Eratosthenes assimilated these observations in his *Geographia*, where he also set out his calculation of the circumference of the earth. He based the circumference on the difference in latitude between the Egyptian cities of Syene (the Greek name for the southerly city of Aswan) and Alexandria. It had been observed at Syene that sunlight was directly overhead at the summer solstice – since it penetrated the shaft of a deep vertical well – a phenomenon that did not occur in Alexandria, where walls of buildings always cast a slight shadow at this time. Based on the assumption that the rays of the sun were parallel, and the earth was a perfect sphere, Syene was understood to be on, or very close to, the Tropic of Cancer (in fact, it lies about 60 km/40 miles north). It was also believed that Syene was located due south of Alexandria (actually, it is 3° 3′ to the east of Alexandria), and Eratosthenes calculated that the two cities were 5,000 *stades* apart (approximately 800 km/500 miles, a *stadion* being the official Egyptian standard for geographical distance). Thus, when the sun was directly overhead at Syene (at 0°), the angle of light cast by a gnomon 5,000 *stades* away at Alexandria would indicate the fraction of a 360° circle being covered. Armed with these 'facts', Eratosthenes calculated that the sun's shadow at Alexandria has an angle of 7° 12′, or one-fiftieth of the circumference of a circle. Multiplying fifty times Alexandria's distance from Syene of 5,000 *stades*, he made the circumference of the earth 250,000 *stades*.

Eratosthenes realised that precision in his calculation depended on synchronicity, knowing the exact time of the summer solstice, and that his calculation could be only an approximation. He therefore considered it legitimate to increase fractionally his calculation of the earth's circumference to 252,000 *stades*, since then the result could be subdivided by the numbers 6 and 60 (which related to the perfect Pythagorean numbers 6 and 10), and the length of 1° of the earth's surface would equal 700 *stades*, a figure that would be easy to use and yet sufficiently precise for practical navigation by land and sea.

The ancient Romans also had a convenient idealised dimension for the circumference and diameter of the earth. For the Romans, a *stade* equalled 125 paces (625 Roman feet) and 1,000 paces (*mille passus*) equalled a Roman mile. Consequently, when writing in the first century BC, the architect Vitruvius presented the earth's circumference as 31,500,000 Roman paces (252,000 *stadia* × 125 paces), or 31,500 miles.[2] For the Romans, the earth's diameter was consequently 10,000 miles, a better number still (as Vitruvius noted, 10 is a perfect Pythagorean number, as is the number 6, which relates to the ideal body height of 6 feet). It had been possible to calculate the diameter of a circle since Archimedes, a contemporary and correspondent of Eratosthenes, had provided three propositions in *The Measurement of the Circle*. His third proposition is that 'The ratio of the circumference of any circle to its diameter is less than $3\frac{1}{7}$ but greater than $3\frac{10}{71}$', a ratio that we have known since the seventeenth century as *pi*. In modern decimals, Archimedes' range for *pi* is between 3.141 and 3.143. However, if *pi* is approximated at 3.15, it clearly has a direct relation to the Romans' circumference for the earth of 31,500 miles, and the diameter of 10,000 miles.

Vitruvius interpreted the size of the earth through perfect numbers relating to the idealised body. Its physical dimensions were understood through the strides that humankind made upon its surface, and its great extent was understood relative to the size and upright actions of our bodies. More directly still, Thales' physical interaction with the Egyptian pyramid, where his body provided the gnomon, enabled Eratosthenes, with minimal

means, to define the size of the earth. Great civilisations came
and went, yet after two millennia Thales' and Eratosthenes'
body-measure method was to underpin the idealised concept of
the modern metre rod: 252,000 *stades* is the modern equivalent
of 39,690 kilometres, which is very close to the eighteenth-
century estimate for the earth's circumference of 40,000 kilometres,[3] the metre rod being one forty-millionth ($^1/_{40,000,000}$) of
that dimension. Both measuring systems idealised their measures in relation to the earth's size, but the ancient systems had
the additional advantage – a given of natural philosophy – that
the earth should be comprehended in relation to the size of the
human body.

Setting the First European Standard

The ancient Greeks provided the Romans with the basis for their
measures, and the Romans spread their influence across Europe
as far north as Britain. They imposed their system of law and
order on each nation and region they conquered, building roads,
bridges and new settlements. Their system of measures became
the most widely used in the known (Western) world, yet its
origins are poorly understood. A fundamental measure in this
system was the Roman foot (*pes*), which was most probably
derived from the Greek foot (*pous*), and was retained by the
Romans as an official measure of the eastern half of their empire.
The Romans called it the 'Greek royal foot', the *pes Philetaereus*,
after Philetaeus, the founder of the kingdom of Pergamum,
which was bequeathed to Rome in 133 BC. It appears in the
Greek metrological tables of Heron of Alexandria, where the
length of the Greek royal foot is related proportionally to
the Roman foot for ease of trade between the fractured halves
of the empire.[4] Thus, 5 Greek feet were equivalent in length to
6 Roman feet,[5] a ratio of 5:6, which were subdivided by 16 digits
or fingers (Greek *dactyloi*, Roman *digiti*).[6] It would appear that
these standards enjoyed equal status in Rome's dominions.
There is considerable scepticism, however, as to how universally

adopted these particular measures were, or whether their lengths were regulated with much precision across the empire.[7] Nonetheless, the 'idea' of the Roman foot is at the root of most pre-metric European measures, and the English foot was less than half an inch shorter.[8] The Roman foot of 16 digits was also composed of 12 *uncia* (meaning 'one-twelfth part'), the source for the English words 'ounces' and 'inches'. The English word mile derives from the Latin for 1,000: there were 5 English feet to a Roman pace, and 1,000 paces (*millia passum*) to an English 'mile'.

The subdivision of the foot into 12 *uncia* was a practical expedient. The Roman foot of 16 digits did not lend itself well to calculations of areas, an essential requirement when laying out building designs and determining areas of land. Vitruvius described the process of doubling plan areas geometrically and as a calculation by 'squaring'.[9] Since Pythagoras, this has involved drafting out the square to be doubled and measuring the length of its diagonal to produce the side of the next square, or multiplying the length of its side by the square root of 2 ($\sqrt{2}$). Before the precise numerical value of the square root of 2 was found in relatively recent times, it was described approximately through pairs of numbers, such as 5:7 and 12:17, something that the Greeks had learnt from the Babylonian mathematician Hammurabi (*circa* 1750 BC).[10] The foot of 12 *unciae* was introduced some time in the late second century BC, perhaps – it has been suggested – because of the convenience of the 12:17 approximation.[11]

Land surveying required units larger than either the foot or the cubit, and Greek precedent influenced the Romans again. A *pertica* of 12 Roman feet equalled the older Greek *akaina* of 10 Philetaerean feet, and the Roman *actus* of 120 × 120 Roman feet was equivalent to the Greek *plethron* of 10 × 10, or 100 Greek square feet.[12] The interconnectivity of measuring systems is apparent in the nomenclature, the English 'perch' being derived from the Roman *pertica*.

Pagan Embodiments of Perfection

Examples of the principal measuring standards used by the Greeks have survived in the form of stone reliefs, shallow sculptures on slabs of stone that depict the upper part of a male figure.[13] The most famous of these is a metrological relief now in the Ashmolean Museum, Oxford (fig. 3). Another was found recently in Salamis, a small settlement west of Athens. They are fascinating objects visually since they represent the standard measures – of foot, cubit and fathom – in relation to human form: the compact between body and measure made explicit. The Ashmolean metrological relief was probably carved in the Ionian lands during the mid- to late fifth century BC, the great age for Greek sculpture and architecture. Although the relief is slightly damaged, the top half of a man is clearly recognisable, his head in profile. A section of his left forearm has been lost, but it is clear that his outstretched arms demonstrate a fathom length, which the Greeks called *orguia*. Above the intact arm are the imprinted outline of a right foot and the imprint of the ball of the foot.[14] It is likely that the relief bore all the crucial measurements in use in that region, from the fathom to the width of a finger and associated anthropometric dimensions. The fathom is measured between the fingertips of outstretched arms, and is equivalent in length to an idealised human height of 6 feet. However, the length of the fathom represented here is seven

3   Metrological Relief. Ashmolean Museum, University of Oxford

times the length of this foot, not six. There are hypotheses why this may be so, but as yet nothing conclusive.[15] The Romans appear not to have made use of this Greek measure, and preferred to use its dimensional equivalent, the *passus* (pace) or double stride of 5 feet: the 5:6 ratio prevailed.[16]

It is therefore unlikely that there was a single standard of measurement in ancient Greece. The surviving Greek reliefs show discrepancies in standards, the same members of the human body being provided with different lengths, and metrologists have identified variations in the ancient Greek foot of 8 centimetres, ranging between 27 and 35 centimetres. Yet, precise measurement is a fundamental principle that defines the acclaimed art of ancient Greece. Measuring had significance for Greek philosophers too. Plato argued that art is composed of appropriate relations that describe the perfect mean – a standard removed from the extremes. Harmony is represented by that which is neither too big nor too small, neither fat nor thin, such that its parts are in proportion to the entire form.[17] Polyclitus composed his canon of human proportions at around the time that the Ashmolean metrological relief was being carved. The Polyclitan canon is three-dimensional and is incarnate in his sculpture of *Doryphorus*, who is represented as a naked male spear-bearer (fig. 4). The *Doryphorus* had a female counterpart, the *Amazon*.[18] These were to become the most copied of ancient sculptures in stone and bronze, although most surviving examples are Roman copies of Greek originals. They were frequently copied because they were judged to be beautiful – perfect – representations of the natural human form. Polyclitus had matched the verse of the poets to his sculptures, idealising the male figure through number and proportion.

A written account – or canon – of ideal human proportions probably accompanied Polyclitus' statue of *Doryphorus*, but only fragments survive.[19] There are explicit references to it in the later writings of Plutarch, Philo of Byzantium, Galen and Lucian.[20] Galen (AD 129–200), the son of a wealthy Greek architect, and court physician to the Roman emperors Marcus Aurelius (AD

4 *Doryphorus.*
Museo
Archeologico,
Naples. © Fratelli
Alinari

161–80) and Lucius Verus (AD 161–9), refers to the relation of physical beauty and symmetry, which

> should link finger with finger, all the fingers with the palm, the palm with the wrist; these to the ell or forearm [cubit], the forearm to the upper arm, and every other part to every other, just as it is written down in the canon of Polyclitus.

More detailed is Vitruvius's description in his treatise on architecture, which may also derive from Polyclitus, although Vitruvius fails to mention him by name, and lists instead less well-known Greek artists who had probably used it subsequently. Vitruvius writes:

> It is not possible for any building to be properly designed without symmetry and proportion, that is, if its parts are not

precisely related, as are those in the figure of a well-made man. Since nature composed the body so that the face, from the point of the chin to the top of the forehead [or hairline] should be a tenth part of it, which is also the length of a spread hand from the wrist to the end of the middle finger; the head from the chin to its very top an eighth; the distance from the top of the breast bone, where it joins the neck, to the bottom of the hair is a sixth; [from the middle of the breast] to the crown of the head is a fourth. As for the face, a third is from the point of the chin to the underside of the nostrils, and the same to the line of the brows; from that line to the hair of the forehead takes up another third. The foot goes six times into the height of the body, the cubit four times, the breast is also a quarter. The other members have their appropriate measurements: by making use of them famous painters and sculptors of antiquity gathered glorious and lasting praise.[21]

This rendering of the canon of ideal male proportions by Vitruvius exerted a considerable influence on successive generations on the notion of what constitutes physical beauty. Beauty was important to Vitruvius when describing the design of buildings. As with a well-shaped man, he wrote, the design of a temple depends on the fundamental principles of symmetry and proportion, and 'Proportion is a correspondence among the measures of the members of an entire work, and of the whole to a certain part selected as standard'.[22] Columns were crucial components in the composition of ancient buildings, and were regarded as sculptural representations – significations – of the most essential of human characteristics, and thus of human proportional perfection. As Vitruvius relates, the ancient Greeks defined three main types of column, the Doric, Ionic and Corinthian. The Doric is the stockiest, imitating the figure of a man; the Ionic and Corinthian are increasingly slender, in imitation of the graceful proportions of a mature woman and a young woman, respectively.

Vitruvius stated that 'the finger [digit], palm, foot and cubit' were the measures that architects should adopt when designing

buildings, because they were associated with the ancient
Pythagorean perfect numbers of 6, 10 and 16.[23] The Greeks
valued them for philosophical and mathematical reasons, as both
Pythagoras and Plato had explained. They are also embodied in
the parts and proportions of the human canon that Vitruvius was
accepting as the norm. Thus, a foot is one-sixth of a man's
height, the hands are composed of 10 digits (fingers and thumbs)
and the foot is 16 digits long.[24] Vitruvius describes in detail his
own design for a building, the basilica at Fanum (modern day
Fano) on the Adriatic coast. Its plan was made in the form of a
rectangle, exactly 60 feet wide and 120 feet long (a ratio of 1 :
2). It had low surrounding aisles 20 feet wide and high (1 : 1),
and a tall central space with columns 5 feet thick and 50 feet
high (1 : 10).[25] And so on. Vitruvius was demonstrating that he
had designed the entire building with symmetry and proportion,
like the idealised human body, so that the proportions of the
parts of his building relate to the whole through multiples of the
perfect numbers 6 and 10.

As well as embodying perfect numbers, the idealised human
form was also circumscribed by the primary geometries of the
circle and the square. The geometrical diagram of the perfect
male figure, known as *Homo quadratus*, was famously reinter-
preted 1,500 years after the time of Vitruvius by Leonardo da
Vinci, when he depicted a naked man with his limbs outstretched
to create two figures in one (see pl. 2): with legs together and
arms outstretched to create a square, and with legs apart to
define the boundaries of a circle. Leonardo was following Vitruvius's description of the geometric properties of the 'well-shaped
man', whose

> central point is naturally the navel. For if a man be placed flat
> on his back, with his hands and feet extended, and a pair of
> compasses centred at his navel, the fingers and toes of his two
> hands and feet will touch the circumference of a circle
> described therefrom. And just as the human body yields a cir-
> cular outline, so too a square figure may be found from it. For
> if we measure the distance from the soles of the feet to the top

of the head, and then apply that measure to the outstretched arms, the breadth will be found to be the same as the height [. . .].[26]

Christian Embodiments of Perfection

Vitruvius was a near-contemporary of Christ. The success of Christianity, and the imperial sanctioning of this religion by Emperor Constantine in the fourth century AD, encouraged the conflation of long-standing 'pagan' beliefs with the new dominant Christian orthodoxy. Of relevance here is the identification of Christ with the idealised male body of antiquity. Christians regarded the body of Christ, the Son of God, as a microcosm or symbol of heavenly perfection.[27] A principal advocate of this viewpoint was the fourth-century Church Father, St Augustine. Augustine took his authority from the scriptures, where Christ is presented as the model of perfection, as 'the mediator between God and men'.[28] The Old Testament states that God provided Noah's Ark for the Flood, and the New Testament that Christ was sent by God to earth for the salvation of humankind. The potency of an idealised body is manifest in both vessels of salvation. As Augustine makes plain:

> It was to Noah [perfect in his generation] that God gave instructions to make an ark in which he was to be rescued [with his family] from devastation of the Flood [. . .] Without doubt [the ark] is a symbol of [. . .] the Church which is saved through the wood on which was suspended 'the mediator between God and men, the man Christ Jesus'.[29]

Augustine continues by making a direct relation between the perfect dimensions of the ark and the perfect body of Christ: even the door into the side of the ark is associated with the piercing of Christ on the Cross:

> The actual measurements of the ark, its length, height and breadth, symbolise the human body, in the reality of which Christ was to come, and did come, to humankind. For the

length of the human body from the top of the head to the sole of the foot is six times its breadth from side to side, and ten times its depth, measured on the side from back to belly [. . .] That is why the ark was made 300 cubits in length, 50 cubits in breadth and 30 in height.[30]

The subtlety of Polyclitus' canon of human proportions was apparently lost to Augustine. Yet he could still recognise the value of such a system. Writing in *The City of God* (*De civitate dei*), Augustine urged that the 'harmonious congruence' between the parts of the body, 'a beauty in their equality and correspondence', should be examined, for they would be 'more apparent to us if we were aware of the precise proportions in which the components are combined and fitted together'.[31] As far as we know, his suggestion was not pursued at that time.

Eleven centuries were to pass before a canon of human proportions was redefined along classical lines. Leon Battista Alberti (1404–1472), a scholar, artist, architect and antiquarian, who studied classical texts and the fragments of ancient sculptures and buildings with method and precision, was prompted to do so because of a contemporary concern for representing nature accurately. Alberti wrote books on painting and sculpture in the classical manner, and Vitruvius influenced his treatise on architecture.[32] The idealised human form is central to all three disciplines. Alberti made an effective link between Augustine's deliberation on the Christian scriptures and Vitruvius's artistic statements about the perfect body and ancient architecture. He effectively related human form, the columns of buildings and the ark of the Old Testament:

When they [the ancients] considered man's body, they decided to make columns after its image. Having taken the measurements of a man, they discovered that the width, from one side to another, was a sixth of the height, while the depth, from navel to kidneys, was a tenth. The commentators of our sacred writings also noted this and judged that the ark built for the Flood was based on the human figure.[33]

Between Vitruvius and Alberti – between the decline of classical ideals and their Christian rebirth – the culture of Byzantium was dominant in eastern Europe. Measures through the Middle Ages acquired new names and definitions. Byzantine artistic canons differed from their Greek and Roman precursors. Rather than the foot, the face and nose length provided the primary module for art – and these had also been important components of Egyptian art.[34] Vitruvius, while stressing the importance of 'the cubit, foot, palm, inch and other small parts', refers indirectly to this more ancient tradition when describing the proportions of the human face. He divides the face into three parts, from chin to base of nose, the nose length, and then the bridge of the nose to the hairline; each face-long unit constitutes one-tenth of the overall height of the body, a head-long unit one-tenth.[35]

The other main difference between ancient classical art and that of Byzantium was that Byzantine artists were not concerned to imitate the naked human form naturalistically. Instead, their art relished an abstract pattern-making, which expressed a body's character.[36] Partial canons are described in Byzantine manuscripts written between the ninth and fourteenth centuries by Elpios Romaios and the historian Nicephoros Gregoras. An unknown artist called Panselinos, who was probably active during the fourteenth century, provides the most detailed account of a human canon. Panselinos describes the face as the fundamental module. He subdivides it into three equal horizontal bands, as in the Vitruvian description, and adds a fourth, the nose length, for the top of the head.[37] Panselinos provides general rules for a standing, seated and mounted figure, and precise instructions for the proportions of the heads of men (young and old), women (similar to young men's) and the Infant Christ, when seen frontally, slightly inclined and – the most common representation in Byzantine art – in three-quarter profile.[38]

Important aspects of Byzantine art were absorbed into Italy and provided the principles from which Renaissance art developed. In his *La composizione del mondo* (1282), Ristoro d'Arezzo set out a proportional description in the Byzantine manner. This text is thought to have influenced Cimabue (*circa* 1240–1302), the father of modern Italian painting.[39] In his *Lives of the Artists* (1568), Giorgio Vasari restates the tradition that Cimabue had been taught by Byzantine artists, but notes that he 'vastly improved the art of painting and raised it far above their level'.[40] When Cimabue passed his learning onto Giotto (1266/7–1337), the foundations of the classical renaissance in art were being laid in Florence.

The Classical Renaissance

Charlemagne (742/7–814), who was crowned 'Emperor of the Romans' by Pope Leo III in 800, and is regarded as the father of Europe, brought some order to weights and measures throughout the Carolingian Empire, which lasted until 888. Measures proliferated again, however, during the later Middle Ages, reflecting the fragmentation of political and administrative regions. One very positive outcome of this diversification in the Italian peninsula was that the arts prospered: as certain cities thrived commercially, communities and individuals attempted to outshine each other through the media of literature, art and architecture. During the fourteenth and fifteenth centuries Florence emerged as the pre-eminent centre not only for banking and trade, but also for art and architecture. The recovery of ancient knowledge and practical skill is associated in particular with early to mid-fifteenth-century Renaissance Florence. It was led by scholars, artists and architects and encouraged by the sponsorship of wealthy patrons, who were mostly merchants and bankers. They sought to revive the perceived grandeur of their Roman inheritance and to rediscover and revivify the culture of antiquity. Consequently, painters, sculptors and architects redefined their art in relation to ancient exemplars, using newly refined drafting techniques based on perspective and proportion. A rediscovery of the precise lengths of the ancient Roman measures was essential to their quest to understand antique art and architecture more completely.

The Florentine artists Donatello and Brunelleschi searched for the lost measures of ancient Rome by measuring fragments of sculpture and ruined buildings, literally uncovering the units used in their composition.[41] Brunelleschi went on to become the leading architect of his generation, completing Florence cathedral with a magnificent dome, the largest to be built in Italy since Roman antiquity. Alberti was influenced by his example, and records in his treatise on architecture that he 'never stopped exploring, considering, and measuring everything, and comparing the information through line drawings'. This practice enabled him to construct a picture of a ruined ancient building in its original, pristine condition, and so reveal its measurements and proportions.[42] He was also able to describe the idealised perfections of the human body in the manner of Polyclitus' canon. Alberti tabulated the dimensions of the ideal male body (*Tabulae dimensionorum hominis, circa* 1443–52) as an appendix to a treatise he wrote on sculpture: 'I wish this work of mine to be familiar to my painter and sculptor friends, who will applaud my advice, if they take heed.' His straightforward intention in compiling this table was to demonstrate that dimensions could be taken and recorded 'from a live model in order to make a figure artistically and methodically'.[43] Alberti states that he

> proceeded accordingly to measure and record in writing, not simply the beauty found in this or that body, but, as far as possible, that perfect beauty distributed by Nature, as it were in fixed proportions among many bodies; and in doing this I imitated the artist [Zeuxis of] Croton [. . .]. So we too chose many bodies, considered to be the most beautiful by those who know, and [. . .] we took the mean figures.[44]

The tables that Alberti compiled provide a set of proportional relations of the parts of the human body to the whole that probably resembled the level of detail found in Polyclitus' written canon.[45] Alberti lists body widths, progressively from foot to head, concluding with the palm of the hand. Throughout this description, however, Alberti does not refer to actual dimensions but to proportions of the overall height of the body. He reiter-

5 Male figure
with dimensions
overlaid, after
L. B. Alberti.
Bodleian Library,
University of
Oxford, MS
Canon. Misc. 172,
fol. 232*v*

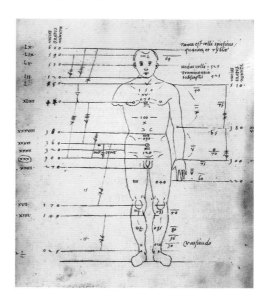

ates in the final *Tabulae* Vitruvius's proportional schema in general: a foot is one-sixth of a man's height, etc.[46] The perfect numbers are distributed throughout the body, as a sketch of a male figure appended to a manuscript of his *Tabulae* illustrates (fig. 5): when looking at an upright male figure in elevation, the proportions of the sections – from the base of the pelvis and wrist to the navel; from the knee joint to the tip of the hand; from the hips to the waist; and from the waist to the nipples – are all one-tenth of the whole; and the foot, of course, is one-sixth of the body height. Other proportions are fractional multiples of these numbers, such as one-twentieth and one-sixtieth of the whole. Alberti described through proportions only, and did not link them to a particular measuring scale; he was stressing the universality of his findings, that they were relevant for an adult body – male and female – of any height.

As archaeology developed ever more exacting methods, the issue of precise measurement gained increasing importance. Defining the exact length of the Roman foot was a fundamental starting point for those uncovering Roman remains. Angelo

Colocci, who lived on the Quirinale Hill in Rome in the early sixteenth century, made some useful studies into ancient weights and measures. He recorded the length of the ancient Roman foot from reliefs on the tomb of an ancient architect near the aqueduct of the Aqua Virgo. He later found evidence of this same measurement on a column near the Lateran Basilica, and on a block built into the façade of a shop in the Jewish ghetto.[47] Others followed his lead. When the French architect Philibert Delorme was in Rome during the 1530s, he was urged by antiquarians (proto-archaeologists) to examine examples of the Roman foot in different collections, and to abandon his habitual survey of the Roman ruins using the French *pied du Roi* (the 'king's foot'), a measure that had not, of course, been used by Roman architects to design buildings.[48] Only the original measures they had used would reveal the perfect number sequences that Vitruvius had explained were essential if a building was to be truly beautiful.

At a commercial level, the diversity of weights and measures across Europe made trade more difficult to transact between regions, states and nations, and a return was sought to the unified system that the Romans had provided. Giangiorgio Trissino (1478–1550), an important early mentor of the architect Andrea Palladio, was sufficiently concerned that currency, weight and measure ought to be systemised throughout Italy that he addressed Pope Paul III on this subject in 1541. Although the pope did not act on his advice, several European monarchs did succeed in shaping and coordinating the weights and measures of their nations – to their political and economic advantage, and the furtherance of their authority.[49]

Measure and Kingship

The Christian monarchs of Europe had a special claim to authority. While Christianity teaches that all men are made in the image of God, the king is the primary secular representative of the will and authority of God on earth. Thus, in the eighth century, Charlemagne was appointed king 'by the grace of God', and as the archbishop of Mainz declared when consecrating him: 'The grace of God hath this day changed thee into another man, and by the holy rite of unction hath made thee partaker in its divinity.'[50] The authority of Church and State (through the medium of the king) was entwined. The Church was regarded as the mystical body of Christ, while the king was thought during the Middle Ages to represent the body politic. In the fourteenth century the Italian jurist Lucas de Pena had confidence in the statement: 'And just as men are joined together spiritually in the spiritual body, the head of which is Christ [. . .] so are men joined together morally and politically in the *res publica*, which is a body the head of which is the Prince.'[51] The union of mystery and authority in one body was essential to the survival of kingship, and measure was a physical manifestation of both.

While the Church was inextricably linked to kingship, their partnership was not equitable, and there were recurring battles for supremacy. Pope Gregory VII (1073–85) asserted the primacy of the Church over secular powers. He disputed the notion that coronation enabled the king to emerge as a priest-king. Instead, Gregory and his successors insisted that the king was a mere layman, and that the pope was the true representative of God on earth. Nonetheless, the kings of England and France continued to demonstrate their divine authority from the Middle Ages until their respective demises in the seventeenth and eighteenth centuries. As James I of England declared:

> kings are justly called Gods, for that they exercise a manner or resemblance of divine power upon earth. For if you will consider the attributes of God, you shall see how they agree in the person of a King.[52]

The body analogy was of paramount importance to this equation. Society was described as a vital, living body, a product of nature rather than the human imagination, and the king its natural head. Biologically, the head is connected organically to every other part of the body, and head and body are interdependent until death. As the source of authority, the head disciplines the limbs, mouth and eyes to interact with the world and

with other individuals. The body needs just one head: power
shared will create a two-headed monster. The body is obviously
reliant on the authority that the head provides, and the natural
superiority of the head over the body is such that while limbs
may be lost, decapitation inevitably results in death. This
dependence was made very evident in the public decapitations
of the kings of England and France in 1649 and 1793 respectively.[53] Kingship was to be the most potent victim of rational
and enlightened logic.

Kings were also the source of a nation's measuring standards.
The mensural system established during the Carolingian Empire
of Charlemagne formed the basis of many customary French
and English standards. The Carolingian royal foot (*pied du roi*)
was about an inch longer than the Roman foot (*pes*).[54] It was
subdivided duodecimally into 12 *pouces* (inches), a *pouce* of 12
lignes, and a *ligne* of 12 *points*: 6 *pieds* made a *toise* or fathom.[55]
There was also an *aune*, known variously as the cubit, ell, *virga*,
verge, *ulna* and *aulne*, which had developed from a double Roman
cubit.[56]

Derived from a combination of Roman, Carolingian and
Saxon measures, the customary measures of England were systemised by the Saxon ruler of England, Edgar the Peaceful (*reg*
959–75). He decreed:

> And let one money pass throughout the king's dominion; and
> that let no man refuse; and let one measure and one weight
> pass; such as is observed at London and at Winchester [. . .].[57]

Royal ownership of England's measures was restated a century
later, in 1101, when Henry I decreed that the Saxon *gyrd* – the
girth of the male body – the yard, should equal the length of the
royal arm and replace the 'ell'. Henry defined the royal yard and
arm as 3 feet, and an inch as the length of three barley corns.
These measures are referred to in Domesday Book (1086) and
Magna Carta (1215), though the earliest complete statement of
the English system appears in a statute issued by Edward II in
1324:

three barley corns, dry and round, make the inch; and 12
inches make 1 foot; and three feet make the yard; and five
yards and a half make a perch; 4 perches in width and 40 in
length make 1 acre of land.[58]

The process of redefining measures (and weights) by the separate nation states of Europe in this period led to marked national
differences. The English foot of 12 inches became more than an
inch shorter than the Belgic or Saxon foot on which it was
based.[59] International trade was affected accordingly. While it
was still possible to trade, by relating the different weights and
measures of separate nations proportionally,[60] rival kingships
were undermining the unity the Romans had brought to Europe.

The differences in standards escalated over the next 500 years,
until an international body of scientists sought a new unity. Ultimately, they tried to establish a common measure that would be
both natural and scientific, one that could be defined objectively
and would provide the sole medium for the exchange of ideas
for all nations around the world. It was not the human body as
the microcosm of natural harmony that was their preferred
medium, as it had been since ancient times. Instead, they selected a measure without body, one that related directly to the
invisible forces that controlled the universe that modern science
was revealing. The resolution, acceptance and widespread implementation of their new measure became possible only through
the social and political revolution that Enlightenment rationality engendered.

2. Science and Measure

Human beings are, understandably, highly motivated to find regularities, natural laws. The search for rules, the only possible way to understand such a vast and complex universe, is called science. The universe forces those who live in it to understand it. Those creatures who find everyday experience a muddled jumble of events with no predictability, no regularity, are in grave peril. The universe belongs to those who, at least to some degree, have figured it out.[1]

For 2,000 years, natural philosophy was dominated by Aristotelian categories and the analogy between the cosmos and an organism. The new sciences of astronomy, mechanics and optics that emerged in the sixteenth century questioned the fundamental premises that Aristotle and his successors had taken for granted, and his natural analogy was replaced by the image of the mechanical universe. Rational thinking, and the apparent certainties of quantity and quantification, would provide the substitute for what our visual senses tell us about the qualities of the physical world.[2]

The publication of Nicholas Copernicus's *De revolutionibus orbium coelestium* (*On the Revolutions of the Heavenly Spheres*) in 1543 (the year of his death), marks the beginning of modern science. His recognition that the earth and the heavens were in motion broke with the ancient notion that the earth was still and that the sun and stars rotated around it. He recognised that the earth rotates about its axis and makes an annual journey around the sun; therefore, the sun, not the earth, is at the centre of our solar system. What Copernicus failed to realise was that the traditional ancient Greek notion that the planets traced a circular path around the sun was wrong. It was left to Copernicus's disciple Johannes Kepler (1571–1630) to demonstrate in *Astronomia nova* (*A New Astronomy*, 1609) that the orbital paths were in fact elliptical rather than heliocentric.

These momentous discoveries stimulated astronomical interest in the exact shape of the earth, whether or not it was a perfect sphere, as tradition held. The Dutch mathematician Willebrord van Royen Snell (1580–1626) made the first accurate triangulation of the earth's surface in 1615, measuring the length of a degree of a meridian near Leiden as 55,100 *toises*.[3] The first step in triangulation is to provide an accurately measured base line, since this forms the side of the first triangle of the land being surveyed. A series of triangles are then surveyed from the first, the side of each successive triangle having a side the same length as the preceding and adjacent triangle. This system works well even on undulating land, and relies on basic trigonometry and standard surveying equipment for success. Geodetic triangulation became the usual method thereafter (fig. 6).

In the same year that Kepler's *Astronomia nova* was published, Galileo Galilei (1564–1642) first used a telescope to scrutinise the heavens and to chart the visible surface of the moon. He set the scene for the science of mechanics. Initially, Galileo reverted to Copernicus's cosmic heliocentric system, since Kepler's ellipses seemed to him to run counter to common experience. His comparison of the Ptolemaic and Copernican systems in the *Dialogo sopra i due massimi sistemi del mondo* (*Dialogue on the Two Chief World Systems*) of 1632 appeared to demonstrate that Copernicus's system of circular orbits remained valid. The principle of motion was at the root of his defence of Copernicus. The Greeks, most notably Aristotle, had believed that motion grew from within a body, an acorn growing into an oak tree being his famous proof. By observing objects in motion, Galileo realised that the motion of a ball dropped vertically accelerated uniformly towards the ground; that a ball thrown has a parabolic trajectory; and that a ball rolled cannot start or stop its motion of its own accord.

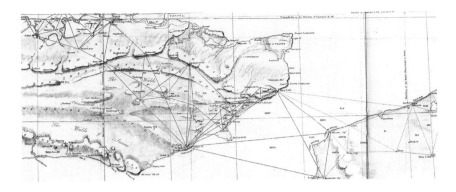

6   Triangulation between Greenwich and Paris by General William Roy in 1783. National Maritime Museum, London

Galileo is supposed to have observed the motion of falling objects from the leaning bell-tower adjacent to Pisa cathedral. Inside the cathedral he watched the regular oscillations of a large lamp swinging from the high vault. By timing its oscillations against the beat of his pulse he observed that the time of each swing was constant no matter the distance travelled by the lamp. Galileo extended this finding to an examination of the pendulum. In 1581 he discovered that the duration of a pendulum's oscillation depended upon its length, and that the time of oscillation was constant for a pendulum of given length. He also found that the length of the pendulum varied as the square of the time of oscillation. This interaction of time and size in a pendulum is known as the isochronism of the pendulum. Based on Galileo's pioneering experiments and mathematical descriptions, the French musicologist and mathematician Marin Mersenne (1588–1648) defined the length of the seconds pendulum: that is, the length of a pendulum that swings one way – as in a beat – every second, and therefore completes thirty full oscillations in one minute.[4] The pendulum relates acceleration, velocity, distance and time, and was to become crucial in defining the new system of scientific measures.

Mechanics and the Pendulum

In his *Meditationes de prima philosophia* (*Meditation on First Philosophy*) of 1641, René Descartes (1596–1650) provided the philosophical framework for the newly emerging science by elevating rational thought – reason – over common sense, which, he argued, is unreliable. Descartes reasoned that the qualities our senses detect may be very different from the true nature of the physical world, and that through first principles the physical world may be examined afresh. His reasoning had a fundamental bearing on the way that the new science regarded the physical world, and scientific reason demonstrates certain facts, that the universe is made only of quantities of particles of matter, having different sizes, shapes and motions. Any quality we derive from matter is a product of our unreliable senses; therefore, quantity is a more reliable measure than quality.

Descartes took a giant step further for the new science in his *Principia philosophae* (*Principles of Philosophy*, 1644), in which he describes the natural universe as mechanical and independent of our being. He reasoned, after Galileo, that the physical universe was composed of inert matter in which an object at rest would remain at rest, and an object in motion would remain in motion. He coined the term 'inertia' for this. Also, that the universe performed like a relentless machine independent of thought (*res extensa*); and that an independent Creator summoned the matter of the universe.[5] The ability of the human mind to think (*res cogitans*) controls our individual bodies and minds. This separates us from the matter of physical nature, over which the mind has no control, and leads to a fundamental dualism. In an independent universe composed of matter and quantity with its own laws, the concept of God as a constant spiritual influence on the actions of humankind had to be irrational.

What rational thought had yet to demonstrate conclusively was how the heavenly bodies were suspended in motion, what attracted and what repelled them. There were ideas about heavenly fluids and vortexes, but it took the genius of Isaac Newton

(1642–1727) to describe the fundamental laws on which motion is based. His *Philosophiae naturalis principia mathematica* (*Mathematical Principles of Natural Philosophy*, 1687; revised 1713 and 1726), commonly known as the *Principia*, describes the mathematics of orbital motion around centres of force, and the role – though not the cause – of gravitation. Newton was also able to explain, through computation, the forces exerted by the sun and moon on earth: the ebb and flow of tides and the procession of the equinoxes.

To formulate the laws of gravity – the force needed to hold the moon in its orbit, the centripetal force needed to hold a stone in a sling, and the relation between the length of a pendulum and the time of its swing – Newton extended the experiments of the celebrated Dutch astronomer, mathematician and physicist Christiaan Huygens (1629–1695). Huygens had found a new method of grinding and polishing lenses for telescopes in 1655, which enabled him to discover a satellite of Saturn and to give the first accurate description of the rings of Saturn. His observations demanded not only precision instruments but also precise measures. To find an exact measure of time for observing the heavens, Huygens refined Galileo's observations and Mersenne's experiments, and determined the true relation between the length of a pendulum and its period of oscillation, which he set out in *Horologium oscillatorium* (1673). Huygens's pendulum was formed from a light rod or wire held by a low-friction fulcrum at its upper end and a mass at its lower end. With this mechanism he calculated that the time, or period, that a pendulum took to swing to and fro was relative to the length of its rod and the mass, and that its swing increased in proportion to the square root of the length from the fulcrum to the centre of mass. The period is also inversely proportional to the square root of the gravitational acceleration at the location where the pendulum is swinging. With these finite natural laws of mass, time and gravitational acceleration, Huygens considered that the length of an oscillating pendulum could form the basis for a system of measures.

Space, Incorporeality and Individuality

John Locke (1632–1704) was fascinated by the scientific leaps and bounds being made by Huygens and Newton. This exiled English philosopher was living in France between 1675 and 1679 and in the Netherlands from 1683 to 1688, where Newton's *Principia* was published in 1688. While not a mathematician, Locke had befriended Huygens, and enlisted his support in his determination to comprehend Newton's *Principia*. Locke returned to England in 1689 and struck up a profitable intellectual relationship with Newton, corresponding on an array of matters that included alchemy, religion and the place of God in the universe.

Newton differed from Descartes. He did not separate science from religion, and he considered God to be an essential element in creation: a 'Being, living, intelligent and omnipresent'.[6] Evidence for his 'Being' was in the phenomena of nature. What is significant here is Newton's belief (expressed in the second edition of his *Principia*) that this Being is incorporeal: 'utterly devoid of all body and bodily figure, and can therefore neither be seen, nor heard, nor touched; nor ought he to be worshipped under the representation of any corporeal thing'.[7] It is assumed that Newton's all-pervading, bodiless God stemmed from his belief in Arianism, which denied the orthodox teaching concerning the Holy Trinity: of Father, Son and Holy Spirit. According to Arius (*circa* 256–336), the originator of this heretical belief, Jesus was a supernatural creature who stood between earth and heaven, who was neither human nor divine, and was therefore neither co-equal nor co-eternal with the Father. Newton's science took this heresy a stage further. If God is omnipresent and incorporeal, He is without dimension, and the Christian commonplace, that Christ embodied the dimensions of His Father and the universe, lacks reason. Instead, Newton believed that God was distributed in a medium, or *sensorium*, without measure and boundary. Through this *sensorium* God 'sees all things intimately in themselves and perceives them throughout, and in its presence embraces all things present in it'. Humankind possesses its *sensoriolum*, a reduced version of the *sensorium* that can perceive only the image of things.[8]

This was an evolving thesis. Newton later changed his mind about the existence of the *sensorium*, but maintained the notion that space and time were absolute and real entities, and existed independently of the human mind.[9] He explains this again in the *Principia*: 'As a blind man has no idea of colours, so we have no idea of the ways in which the most wise God senses and understands all things.'[10]

God was a remote being for Newton: while essential to the workings of the universe and the source of everything, He had become a distant cause of causes. What should concern the enlightened individual was his or her place in, and relation to, the natural world, to Nature.

Locke expanded Newton's notion of the universal *sensorium* into politics. As a philosophical empiricist he held that all knowledge, other than deductive reasoning, must be based on experience gained through the senses. Thus, a child gains knowledge only through experience, and at birth its mind is as a blank slate, which is ready to receive knowledge. In *Two Treatises of Government* (1690), Locke argued that since God had designed human beings and given them reason, they were able to know natural laws. He did not believe in a divine origin for monarchical government, a commonplace still being promoted by Sir Robert Filmer in his *Patriarcha* (1680), which states that the Divine Right of monarchs had been handed down from God via Adam. In the first of his two treatises, Locke countered Filmer's patriarchalism directly, arguing that such governance forged 'Chains for all Humankind'.[11] Instead, he took the stance that man was born free; that sovereignty resided in the people; and that humankind was fit and able to make decisions for its own governance. Since government gains its legitimacy and authority only by the consent of those it purports to govern, a transfer of individual rights is granted by means of a social contract. The role of government is therefore defined very specifically: it exists only for the security and liberty of the people. If it no longer serves this purpose, and becomes oppressive, then it is justifiable for the people to remove it by force. His political theory provided the basis, in the next century, for revolution in France and the American War of Independence.

The revolution in measure that was to take place in France in the late eighteenth century also derived from Locke's notion – after Newton – of space and time, which Locke had put forward in his second treatise. Newton had defined space as 'absolute' and 'relative' in the *scholium* to Definition VIII of the *Principia*. He states that absolute space 'remains always similar and immovable', while relative space is 'some movable dimension or measure of the absolute spaces'. We sense relative space in the context of what appear to be static bodies, and which are perceived to be immovable, but are in fact in motion: 'For it may be that there is no body really at rest, to which the places and motions of others may be referred.'[12] Locke interpreted the 'idea' of space through the senses of man, and described it as if it were composed in stages. He writes about the 'expansion' of space, which he defines through the repetition of dimensions, from short to long: from inches, feet and yards to miles and the diameter of the earth, and from there into the immensity of the universe:

> Each different distance is a modification of space [. . .]. Men, for the use and by the custom of measuring, settle in their minds the ideas of certain stated lengths [. . .], which are so many distinct ideas made up only of space. When any such stated lengths or measures of space are made familiar to men's thoughts, they can in their minds repeat them as often as they will without mixing or joining to them the idea of body or anything else; and frame to themselves the ideas of long [. . .] amongst the bodies of the universe, or else beyond the utmost bounds of all bodies; and by adding these still one to another, enlarge their idea of space as much as they please.[13]

In a similar vein Locke explains that time, or 'duration', 'is another sort of distance, or length, the idea whereof we get not from the permanent parts of space, but from the fleeting and perpetually perishing parts of succession'.[14] Time increases through the repetition of seconds, minutes and hours to days, months and years.

The Disembodiment of Measure

According to Locke's reasoning, the human senses are incorporeal, and – in this system of thought – space and time should not be defined through the experience of an embodied mind. Measure, he argues, is abstract from human experience and exists independently of humankind. Thus, space is not measured by or in relation to the body directly, and is not perceived from the perspective of an individual at all, just as time cannot be moderated by the emotions of the individual.

French scientists were ready to receive this line of reasoning, which emphasises the quantitative measurement of space and time. Treatises by French mathematicians had been describing visual perspective abstractly since the early seventeenth century,[15] though it took Locke, through his direct understanding of Newton's *Principia*, to conceive of measure in universal terms through 'the idea of infinite space'.[16] European scientists in general were also acutely aware of the need to abstract measure from the idea of the body and the complex customary measures in current usage in Europe. They spoke a universal scholarly language of Latin, a surviving legacy of Roman Europe, but without Roman mensuration there was no common language for quantities. When linear measurements relating to scientific discoveries were channelled through the Royal Society in London and the Academy of Sciences (Académie des sciences) in Paris – the principal centres of European scientific excellence – it was necessary to exchange information using the Parisian *pied du Roi* and the English foot.[17] Although the Parisian foot was only very slightly shorter than its English counterpart (in a ratio of $1:1.068$), exact equivalence would eliminate errors in translation in the interests of scientific precision. When Huygens made accurate measurements of the swing of the pendulum, he did so, as a member of the Academy of Sciences, in Parisian feet (*pieds*), inches (*pouces*) and lines (*lignes*). Since Newton worked in English feet and inches, he had to translate the *pied du Roi* in order to refine his calculations for the gravitational pull of the moon, and when validating other experiments conducted by his counterparts in Paris. The Royal Society began to address this issue soon after its foundation in 1660, once Charles II had returned from exile. Charles granted the society its royal status by incorporation in 1662. Louis XIV granted the Academy of Sciences its royal status much later: although founded in 1666 it did not become the *Académie royale des sciences* until 1699.[18]

Sir Christopher Wren (1632–1723), a gifted mathematician and astronomer as well as an eminent architect, provided an important focus for the idea of a learned scientific society in London.[19] His lectures at Gresham College, Oxford, in the late 1650s, drew together distinguished scientists and students, thirty-eight of whom were to form the nucleus of the Royal Society. These founding members of the Royal Society were concerned to 'make faithful records of all the works of nature or art which can come within their reach' to lay 'a philosophy of humankind'.[20] Wren prepared papers on shipping, solar eclipses, longitude and associated instruments in support of this grand mission. In the summer of 1665 he visited Paris for the first and only time. There he met the French architect François Mansart (1598–1666) and the Italian architect and sculptor Gian Lorenzo Bernini (1598–1680).[21] In that same year Wren – in the spirit of Huygens and Newton – suggested a natural standard of weights and measures based on a seconds pendulum,[22] although it is unknown whether this idea came before or after his visit to Paris.[23] No matter, measure was a principal concern of the Royal Society, and technical apparatus was collected at this time to provide a 'universal standard or measure of magnitudes by help of a pendulum', which Bishop Thomas Sprat referred to in his prematurely titled *The History of the Royal Society* (London, 1667).[24]

Dr John Wilkins, Wren's former tutor at Wadham College, Oxford (he was later appointed bishop of Chester, and was married to Oliver Cromwell's sister), proposed a decimal metrological system based on the seconds pendulum. He named the length of the seconds pendulum a 'foot', which he subdivided into tenths an 'inch' long, each inch subdivided by tenths to define a line: 10 feet would make a perch, 10 perches a furlong, 10 furlongs a mile, and 10 miles a league. He also proposed a cubic 'foot' to determine weights and volumes.[25] This was the earliest natural system to combine weights and measures and metric multiples and subdivisions, and used nomenclature familiar to the British populace. This made sense. Compared to the French system of weights and measures, the British system – while not in perfect conformity – was at least well regulated across the nation. In France, measure was a source of utter anarchy.

The Needs of the French

On the Continent Charlemagne, as we have seen, provided the first rational standards since Roman times, and, as one French Enlightenment commentator observed in 1780: 'All measures were equal in the days of our earliest kings.'[26] However, for the 1,000 years that separated Charlemagne from the outbreak of Revolution in France in 1789, French weights and measures were far from standardised. Charles the Bald had vainly attempted to maintain a royal standard across France in 864, as had Philip IV and Philip V in the fourteenth century, Louis XI in the fifteenth, and Louis XII, François I and Henri II in the sixteenth.[27] These kings had legitimised certain weights and measures by public and official decrees, but it was rare that they were able to enforce their will nationally, even though it was enshrined in law that the king of France had supreme authority to impose royal weights and measures throughout the kingdom. In practice, as a magistrate acknowledged in 1758, this authority was delegated to regional and local governance: 'all edicts and decrees touching this matter emphasise particularly that His Royal Highness has no intention of harming the *seigneurs* who enjoy the right of weights and measures in their lands'.[28] This was because the old system of measurement was not confined to commerce and extended to the legal tenure of land.[29] Each feudal lord could introduce

> in his lands usages conforming to his interests. Consequently, most of the customs attributed to the lords, as high justices, the right to keep the standards and to verify the weights and measures employed in the administration of their jurisdiction.[30]

French monarchs sought uniformity without success. At the beginning of the sixteenth century Louis XII issued an edict that 'weights and measures in the kingdom ought to be standardised'.[31] Yet in 1540 François I was compelled to reassert that 'the supreme authority of the king incorporates the right to standardise all measures throughout his kingdom, both in the public interest and for the sake of promoting commerce', explaining that 'We wish that all abuses, swindles, speculations, and mistakes made because of the diversity of measures, ells, and methods of measuring should cease.'[32] It was decreed that the basic units of length would be the *toise*, *aune* and *pied du Roi*, the last at one-sixth of the *toise*. In 1554 the standard *aune* was preserved as an iron bar at the Bureau des Marchands Merciers. Subsequently, Henri II issued a decree in 1557 that aimed to proscribe the rights of his lords (*seigneurs*):

> those who hold the privilege of measures, are obliged to furnish the names of their weights and measures, from the largest to the smallest [. . .]. Old standards, not harmonising with our measures, shall be broken up [. . .]. All shall be required to regulate their measures according to ours.[33]

In fact, seigneurial authority retained its grip on the cities and regions of France. Their right to regulate measure in the localities under their control – a right held also by parish priests, even in Paris – ensured that the diversity of measures in France was maintained. The resulting confusion led to abuses by merchants, and the opportunity to vary the so-called customary standards (*coutumes*), almost at will, added to the profits of the *seigneurs* – usually at the expense of the peasants.[34] Constant reminders of the official standards were required, and in 1688 at the Grand Châtelet – a fortress gateway into Paris, now destroyed, but once the headquarters of the Provost of Paris – an official *toise*, made of iron, was embedded into a wall at the foot of the main stairs.[35] While this helped to regulate standards in Paris, Louis xiv's Controller-General of Finance, Jean-Baptiste Colbert, later concluded that total reform in France would be impossible.[36]

Reason demanded change: maintaining the chaotic status quo was not an option for the French. An English agriculturist, Arthur Young, spent several years in France during the late eighteenth century and experienced the woeful state of weights and measures at first hand:

> in France, the infinite perplexity of the measures exceeds all comprehension. They differ not only in every province, but in every district, and almost in every town; and those tormenting variations are found equally in the denominations and contents of the measures [. . .]. The denominations of French measure [. . .] are almost infinite, and without any common standard to which they can be referred: the number of square feet in the contents is the only rule to adhere to: yet the foot itself varies [. . .]. In France, they have no common denomination [of bushel and acre, and . . .] to this confusion of measures is added the almost universal ignorance of the people in the provinces, who often know nothing of their own measures, and give information totally erroneous [. . .] the labour, perplexity, and vexation [. . .] both in travelling and writing, has much exceeded anything I could have conceived before I went abroad [. . .].[37]

Nor did Young find the leading metrical authorities of France reliable. The tables supplied in A.J.P. Paucton's *Métrologie* (1780) 'would lead us astray as often as they would guide us. By going through the country, I have found, from five to ten different measures in a province, where he has noted only one – I suppose the legal one of the capital cities.'[38] The French Royal Society of Agriculture made similar complaints in 1790 to the National

Assembly: across France 'the measures differ although they are designated by the same name; that these differences are very considerable, not only from one province to another, but in the same city, in the same borough, in the same village'.[39]

It has been estimated that there were as many as 800–900 customary units of measure in use in France during the eighteenth century.[40] In the north of France there were eighteen kinds of *aune* (varying in length from 0.620 to 0.845 of a modern metre).[41] The French legal system was similarly complex. The southern and eastern regions of France were under Roman law (*droit écrit*), while the remainder was under customary law (*droit coutumier*), which was essentially Germanic and was open to interpretation by each province and district.

This state of affairs was hampering France economically at a time when European trade was on the increase: it is estimated that the value of England's exports trebled between 1600 and 1700, and increased by more than sixfold over the next 100 years.[42] The lack of a precise and uniform system across Europe was a pressing concern, and the need for a rational system in France was much the greatest. It is hardly surprising, therefore, that the first purposeful steps towards metrical reform were French in origin.

Tentative Early Steps Towards Reform

Two years after Dr John Wilkins had moved for a system of decimal weights and measures derived from the 'foot' pendulum arranged metrically, Abbé Gabriel Mouton, priest of Saint-Paul in Lyon, formally presented in his *Observationes diametrorum solis et lunae apparentum* (1670) a rational and natural system derived from the dimensions of the earth.[43] Unlike Wilkins, Mouton proposed new names for his units, which would distinguish them from measures already in existence and would therefore be more likely to appeal to the intellectual neutrality of the international scientific community. His primary length would be the *milliare*, equal to one minute of an arc on the great circle or circumference of the earth.

Mouton based his estimate for the length of the *milliare* on a measurement of one minute of the arc that had been defined by the Italian Jesuit astronomer Giambattista Riccioli in 1665. Riccioli had found it to be equal to 5,363.58 Bolognese *piedi* (1,855.3 metres and so almost twice the length of a modern kilometre).[44] Mouton divided the *milliare* into seven sub-units, each progressively one-tenth smaller than the *milliare*. At the midrange of one of these was the *virgula*, which approximated conveniently to the size of the standard Parisian *toise* of 1.949 metres.[45] The *virgula* was refined as the length of a pendulum making 3,959.2 oscillations in thirty minutes at Lyon.

Mouton's approach to finding a universal system of measurement was immediately acknowledged by Jean Picard (1620–1682). Picard was one of the nation's foremost astronomers and mathematicians, and as an academician at the Royal Academy of Sciences, he was presented with the task of determining the true dimensions of the earth. He took two years, between 1669 and 1671, to survey the earth near Paris, between Amiens and Malvoisine. He refined the triangulation methods established by the Dutchman Willebrord Snell earlier that century, using a telescope to sight distant points on hilltops, and he calculated the length of a degree of the earth's surface as equal to 57,060 *toises*, or just over 69 English miles (121,652 yards/111,210 metres): this was nearly 2,000 *toises* longer (3,814 metres) than Snell's calculation.[46] His calculations, however, were based on the flawed assumption that the earth was perfectly spherical. To universalise his findings, Picard then related this distance to the oscillations of the seconds pendulum, and he called his measure the *rayon astronomique*. He determined that one-third of its length would be the *pied universel*, its double the *toise universel*, which would approximate to the Parisian *toise* 'as 881 is to 864'.[47]

A disadvantage of the seconds pendulum as a base for a constant international standard was that its frequency varied according to latitude, height above sea level and temperature. At Lyon in France, at sea level at latitude 45° N, halfway between pole and Equator, Mouton and Picard had found the seconds pendulum to be equal to 36 *pouces* 8.5 *lignes* (39.112 inches/0.993 metres).

Further north, however, in London, Huygens and the Irish mathematician William Brouncker, the first President of the Royal Society, had measured the seconds pendulum in 1666 as fractionally longer (39.25 inches/0.997 metres).[48] Undeterred by these variations according to location, Huygens set out in his *Horologium oscillatorium* of 1673 the rationale for the seconds pendulum as the source of a universal unit of length, calling one-third of its length the *pied horaire*.[49] However, his proposal appeared simultaneously with the discovery of a far greater discrepancy. This was identified by Jean Richer in 1674 when he recorded that a pendulum clock regulated to beat seconds in Paris had lost two-and-a-half minutes daily in Cayenne in South America, and to keep time its pendulum had to be shortened by one and one-fourth *lignes*.[50] Global variations in the seconds pendulum were described by Newton in Book III of his *Principia* (1687). He attributed them to the gravitational pull being exerted on the pendulum's weight. Since gravitational force varies on the earth's surface, according to the distance to the earth's centre (such as height above sea level), there can be no universal length for the seconds pendulum. To be used as a standard, it would have to be defined according to a particular latitude and altitude on the earth's surface, and be identified with a fixed place and country.

Without an accurate figure for the circumference of the earth, Newton had been unable to announce his general theory of gravitation to the world. With Picard's accurate determination of a degree of latitude there existed a scientifically verifiable refinement of Eratosthenes' calculation: Eratosthenes had estimated a circumference equivalent to 39,690 kilometres, while Picard made it only slightly larger at 40,035.6 kilometres. Newton, however, was aware that both circumferences were idealised, because they were based on the assumption that the earth was a perfect sphere, which Huygens's studies of centrifugal forces had brought into question. Newton reasoned that because the earth spins on its north–south axis centrifugal forces would cause the earth to be an oblate sphere – to bulge at the Equator – and be correspondingly flattened at the poles. In his *Principia* he estimated that this would cause a degree of latitude to be shorter nearer the poles and longer near to the Equator.

Newton's theory was the cause of a scientific controversy that centred on Picard's contemporary Jean-Dominique Cassini (1625–1712), who initiated the first accurate topographic map of France. Cassini headed a family of French astronomers, surveyors and mapmakers – father, son, grandson and great-grandson – who dominated cartography in France for a century. A native of Italy, he had been baptised Giovanni Domenico, but his reputation brought him to the attention of Jean-Baptiste Colbert, Louis XIV's influential controller of finance. In return for his services he was made a French subject, and he dutifully Gallicised his first names. Cassini was appointed specifically to map France, and by 1682 its boundaries were properly defined for the first time, causing Louis XIV to jest: 'Your work has cost me a large part of my state!'[51]

Picard died the same year, and Cassini took over his role of surveyor of France. Aged well into his seventies, he was commissioned by the French Royal Academy of Sciences to test Newton's flattened earth theory, which he undertook with his son Jacques. Together they extended Picard's survey north to Dunkirk on the English Channel, and south to Perpignan, close to the Pyrenees and the Spanish border. Their results did not support Newton's theory, and suggested that a degree of latitude was shorter north of Paris and longer southwards towards the Pyrenees, and that the earth was more likely a prolate sphere, bulging at the poles and flattening at the Equator. The Cassinis did not reveal this fact to the Academy of Sciences, however, since they were aware that the terrain and distance they were covering might have caused an accumulated error. After the death of his father in 1712, Jacques Cassini retraced his steps north of Paris, and this confirmed their earlier findings.

Whether the earth was oblate or prolate, there was general acknowledgement among scientists that it was not a perfect sphere. Still, Jacques Cassini devised – in the spirit of Mouton – a system of measures derived from the earth's surface as if it were perfectly spherical. He defined the *pied geométrique* as equal to $\frac{1}{100}$ of the arc of one second of a meridian (360,000 would equal 1°), and 6 *pieds* as equal to 1 *toise geométrique*.[52]

Desiring a Natural and Scientific System of Measures

While scientists were exploring systems of mensural reform in France, an intellectual framework for change was also being examined. The *philosophes*, a new breed of enlightened seekers of wisdom and knowledge in France – *savants* – debated the reform of weights and measures at meetings and through published pamphlets. A *philosophe* is defined in the *Dictionnaire de l' Académie française* as 'a man who [. . .] places himself above the duties and ordinary obligations of civil and religious life. [. . .] who denies himself nothing, allows himself to be constrained by nothing, who leads the life of Philosophy'.[53] They venerated Nature and Reason with an equal passion, and demanded an entirely new conceptual framework for weights and measures that would break free of the irrational prejudices of tradition. They reasoned that a new system should be universal, constant and eternal, and derived from the essential being of Nature.[54]

Voltaire (François Marie Arouet de, 1694–1778) epitomises the persona of the *philosophe*. An aristocratic man of letters, rather than a scientist, Voltaire was well informed about the significance of recent scientific discoveries, and he sought the advancement of science as well as arts and letters. He was a decided Anglophile. He had been resident in England for three years in enforced exile from 1726, and he found England sympathetic and congenial, and he immersed himself in the work of English scientists, philosophers and religious and political free-thinkers.[55] In his pioneering *Lettres philosophiques; ou, Lettres anglais* (*Letters Concerning the English Nation*, 1733) he glowingly described England as a 'nation of philosophers'. The *Lettres* make clear his admiration for the enlightened progress made by English society during the seventeenth century, such that king-ship and political and governmental liberty could coexist in harmony: 'The English are the only people on earth, who have been able to prescribe limits to the power of Kings by resisting them [. . .] where the People share in the government without confusion.'[56]

Voltaire's admiration of England proved influential for Denis Diderot (1713–1784), a *philosophe* of the next generation. He too admired the nation where 'philosophers are honoured, respected', whereas in France 'they are persecuted'. He went on to claim that 'without the English, reason and philosophy would still be in the most despicable infancy in France'.[57] Parisian *philosophes* contracted this enthusiasm. The most ardent of them met informally to drink tea and absorb English culture through readings of English literature.[58]

Voltaire admired Isaac Newton in particular. His understanding of Nature was characterised by the 'world-machine' of Newton, a synthesis of scientific knowledge and universal order expressed in terms of mathematics. In his *Éléments de la philosophie de Newton* (*Elements of Newton's Philosophy*, 1738) he explained the theory of gravitational attraction to his French readers. Newton, aided by Voltaire's promotion of him as a modern intellectual hero, became a primary source of inspiration for the *philosophes*. Following Voltaire's lead they adopted the Newtonian view that Nature was mechanical, orderly and rational, and accordingly they believed in the unlimited power of Reason as the key to comprehending Nature in all its glory, and that such knowledge would provide the panacea for every human ill. Nature and Reason had the power to eliminate all that was irrational, including the unnatural customs of humankind.

Achieving rationality in weights and measures was a primary objective that the *philosophes* – especially Voltaire – shared with scientists. Voltaire began a campaign for a uniform system of weights and measures in 1751, and he upheld the English commercial model as the one to follow, stating (in error) that Henry I (*reg* 1100–35) had introduced it for the benefit of the whole nation.[59] Voltaire was not supported with any great enthusiasm. There were even divided opinions in France as to the value of standardising weights and measures. Philosophically, Diderot doubted whether measurement was an essential part of knowl-

edge – a romantic, anti-analytical viewpoint he shared with
Rousseau. Practically, too, he doubted whether standardisation
was feasible. The entry on *Poids* (weights) that Diderot edited
with D'Alembert for the *Encyclopédie* (1751–65) concludes that
not only will nations never agree to adopt the same weights, but
that standardisation of different weights by a single nation would
be impracticable. With regard to *Mesure* (measure), they con-
ceded that unity 'can be achieved within one country with a
single ruler', as the English model demonstrated,[60] but that it
would take extraordinary optimism even to imagine that France
might be unified around a single system of weights and measures. Voltaire was not short of optimism, and in his *Essai sur les
Moeurs*, 1756 (*Essay on the Manners and Mind of Nations*, 1759)
opined 'that reason and industry will always bring about new
progress'.

A. R. J. Turgot (1727–1781; also known as the Baron de
l'Aulne) was a founding father in the philosophy of progress; he
has even been described as the 'Newton of a new social philosophy'. In 1750, while a young theology student at the Sorbonne,
he wrote   *Sur le progrès successif de l'esprit humain (A Philosophical Review of the Successive Advances of the Human Mind*). His
thesis was that every civilisation had its barbaric beginnings, and
that: 'The whole human race, through alternate periods of rest
and unrest, of weal and woe, goes on advancing, although at a
slow pace, towards greater perfection'.[61] For Turgot, progress
was an all-pervasive and all-powerful motive force in history.

Turgot made considerable personal progress in his career, succeeding politically as well as intellectually. He was appointed
Minister of the Navy and Controller-General of Finance by
Louis XVI. In the latter role he took a radical and highly con-
troversial economic standpoint. Turgot's ambition was for a
national economy based on laissez-faire principles that could
be achieved by freeing the archaic restrictions linked to the
seigneurs. He identified the nobility as a legitimate target for tax-
ation, reasoning that since they owned the land that was the principal source of wealth in the nation, they should pay the dues
they could afford. At the same time he attempted to neutralise

their authority, and so undermine the restrictions and variations they imposed between localities, which served only to restrict trade nationally and internationally; and he urged that the nation's weights and measures be reformed. As Inspector of the Mint (*inspecteur des monnaies*) from 1775, he made some valuable early decisions that would influence subsequent reform.

Perhaps the most influential individual to initiate a reform of weights and measures in France was the Marquis de Condorcet (Marie-Jean-Antoine-Nicolas de Caritat, 1743–1794), who was by nature a reformer. Condorcet had established his name as a *philosophe*, and in later life wrote biographies of Turgot (1786) and Voltaire (1789), indicating for posterity his political admiration for those who promoted reform and progress. Condorcet also wrote a telling eulogy on the death of Charles-Marie de La Condamine in 1774. La Condamine had led an Academy-sponsored expedition to Peru in 1735 to measure an arc of longitude about 3° south of the Equator, while Pierre-Louis Moreau de Maupertuis (1698–1759) led a parallel expedition to Lapland in 1736 to measure a degree of northernmost latitude. Their common mission was to determine once and for all whether the earth was an oblate or prolate sphere – whether Isaac Newton or Jacques Cassini had been correct.

Both La Condamine and Maupertuis had been appointed academicians while in their early thirties: La Condamine was a geographer, and Maupertuis the foremost Newtonian in France, who enjoyed an early friendship with Voltaire. Although his expedition left France a year later than La Condamine's, Maupertuis was the first to complete his survey: he reported his findings to the Academy late in 1737, seven years before La Condamine even returned from South America. Maupertuis measured the northern arc as equivalent to 111.094 kilometres, La Condamine the arc of the Equator as 109.92 kilometres. There were more than 1,000 metres difference in the length of the arc, which confirmed that the degree was shorter near the Equator, and that the earth was an oblate spheroid, as Newton had predicted.[62] Maupertuis was held in great esteem for his achievements, so much so that he was later made President of Frederick the Great's Academy

of Sciences in Berlin. This was before it surfaced that the degree
he surveyed was 360 metres longer than in fact it is: that the difference between the degrees was not so great. Whether or not
his speed relative to La Condamine had led to errors, Voltaire
quipped that his old friend had done enough to 'flatten both
poles and the Cassinis': that Newton was correct.[63]

Since the earth is not a pure sphere, La Condamine concluded
– contrary to Jacques Cassini – that it could not provide the
natural universal measure that was being sought, and that scientists should revert to the seconds pendulum as the more reliable standard. However, he knew the seconds pendulum was not
the perfect standard either. Pierre Bouguer, an expert hydrogra-
pher who had accompanied La Condamine on the Peruvian
expedition, made observations of the frequency of a pendulum
while at the Equator and found that the higher level of gravity
in the mountains slowed it further, even allowing for altitude.
This was the first indication of specific gravity, that the density
of rocks affects gravitational pull, as Newton had also predicted.
Also, La Condamine's personal preference was to use a pendulum length defined on the northern parallel of 45°, taken at Bordeaux or Saint-Flour in France. This was more readily accessible
than the equatorial measure, but he acknowledged that 'the
philosophe and the citizen of the world' would prefer the neutrality of the Equator. Therefore, conscious of the need for universality, he selected the seconds pendulum as the preferred
universal standard, and the neutrality of the Equator as the ideal
location for defining its length. He characterised two lengths of
the seconds pendulum as the *toise du Perou* – the Peruvian *toise*,
which he defined as 36 *pouces* 7.15 *lignes* (or 0.974 metres). He
presented his standard to the Royal Academy of Sciences in
1747, alongside a supporting document in which he urged for
consideration a universal and invariable measure based upon the
length of the seconds pendulum at the Equator: one that was
'constant [. . .] unalterable, verifiable through all time, capable
[. . .] of obtaining [. . .] the consent of all peoples and of uniting
all voices in its favour'. The Academy were supportive of his reasoning for a universal measure and the *toise du Perou* was adopted

in 1766: it remained the official standard for nearly thirty years, until the metric system was devised and sanctioned.[64] In 1766, at the request of the Ministry of Finance, the Academy made eighty copies of this standard, which were distributed to provincial parliaments.

Within a year of penning La Condamine's eulogy, Condorcet was working in Turgot's ministry on a uniform system of weights and measures.[65] Condorcet, in line with La Condamine, proposed that the new length should be derived from the seconds pendulum, and that it should be divided 'into twelve feet, the foot into twelve inches, and inch into twelve lines'. This would have allowed the new measure to be compatible with the customary measures of France, since Condorcet was not proposing replacing them, but rather developing a precise system by which the customary measures could be regulated. Condorcet got as far as drawing up guidelines for the scientific measuring of the length of the seconds pendulum. Again, his preference was for a universal measure derived from its length at the Equator. However, the greater convenience of latitude 45° N was persuasive enough for him. Approving of Condorcet's guidance, Turgot approached the astronomer Charles Messier on 3 October 1775 to measure the seconds pendulum at sea level at Bordeaux, the only major French city on that latitude. Messier, however, was unable to fulfil his mission immediately because the precision timepiece he required was broken. It took six months to construct a replacement, by which time Turgot had been dismissed from office and his successor, Jacques Necker, was unconvinced that Condorcet's vision could be realised. He dropped the proposals for reform:

> I have occupied myself with an examination of the means [. . .] to render the weights and measures uniform in the whole kingdom; but I doubt still whether the utility which would result would be proportionate to the difficulties of all kinds that this operation would involve [in] the changes of evaluation [. . .] in a multitude of sales contracts, of yearly payments, of feudal duties, and other acts of all kinds.[66]

It would take political and social revolution in France to provide the required impetus for change. Indeed, metrological confusion played its part in the revolution that soon befell the country. Inconsistencies led to numerous cases of litigation in the courts and general unrest. The *seigneurs,* however, were regarded as the villains, not the king, and there was an outpouring of support for the monarch in the summer of 1789, when Revolution finally broke out. The *cahiers de doléances,* grievances that the regional authorities wished the monarchy and Constitution to address, frequently refer to the need to remedy the anarchy that weights and measures engendered. More than 700 complaints about the existing system of weights and measures were reported, the overwhelming majority demanding that standardisation be nationwide, and mainly for commercial and anti-feudal reasons, though the avoidance of litigation was certainly a major concern.[67] These demands came from all walks of life – from grocers to lawyers. The grocers of Rouen believed that 'The hallmark of the perfection of our Constitution will be, above all, the integration of all *coutumes* into one whole.' From the uniformity and the universal adoption of customs 'will follow a conversion of all measures in the kingdom to the same dimensions and names': a belief that resonated around the provinces. The lawyers of Orléans urged the king's judiciary 'to remeasure particular measures and to determine their relations to the royal measure, and thereafter the *seigneurs* shall be forbidden to use [. . .] their own measures, either in the market or in collecting their dues'.[68]

The popular perception was that the king should symbolise the reformed, uniform national measures and represent a new social unity: 'one king, one law, one weight and one measure'. The *cahiers* of Rennes in Brittany urged:

Friends! Long live God and our King Louis xvi! May his reign continue forever for the happiness of the nation, for which he is a true father [. . .] We beg them to join with us in checking the abuses being perpetrated by tyrants against that class of citizens, which is kind and considerate [. . .] and now we call upon the King to mete out justice, and we express a most sincere desire for but one king, one law, one weight, and one measure.[69]

Politically, however, a different rationale persisted. There had to be a new beginning that would sweep away the elitist sectional interests of the *ancien régime*. Monarchy had to be replaced, and revolutionary thought and deed demanded that the authority of Reason and Nature, not the body of the monarch, represent the new standards.

One of the first acts of the Revolutionaries, on 4 August 1789, was to dismantle the monopoly of the weights and measures held by the landed nobles.[70] Condorcet was by then in an influential position as perpetual secretary to the Royal Academy of Sciences (a position he retained from 1776 until its closure in 1793). He had the backing of the National Assembly (which had been reconstituted on 9 July 1789 as the 'National Constituent Assembly') and the support of his brilliant fellow academicians. They enabled him to carry forward his vision of a unified system of weights and measures, and under his leadership the Academy formed a committee to undertake their study on 27 June 1789.[71] Suitable allies were sought in the National Assembly, and Condorcet found a very willing advocate in Talleyrand. The question remained, which option should the State adopt in their place, one derived from the seconds pendulum or the earth's circumference?

3. Defining the Revolutionary Metric System

> The National Assembly has ordained the work
> necessary to fix an invariable unit of length and weight.
> [. . .] It wants to ensure that in the future all citizens
> can be self-sufficient in all calculations related to their
> interests; independence without which they can be
> neither really equal in rights [. . .] nor really free [. . .].[1]

Talleyrand (Charles Maurice de Talleyrand-Périgord; 1754–1838), the recently appointed bishop of Autun, was a leading political figure in the new regime. He proposed to the National Assembly on 9 March 1790 that, while reform was necessary because 'of the confusion born of the diversity of the existing measures, of the embarrassment that it constantly makes in honest commerce, by reason of the truly astonishing differences which exist between the measures of the same denomination', the National Assembly should not take any decision on this issue, 'without first consulting the Academy of Sciences to whom, by all rights, belongs the authority to settle all opinions on such matters'.[2] The Assembly supported Talleyrand in the interest 'of reason, of justice and of honesty',[3] and his proposal was referred to the Committee of Agriculture and Commerce led by the Marquis de Bonnay.

The scholar and politician Prieur-Duvernois, aided by the chemist Guyton de Morveau, had already presented a plan for a system of weights and measures based on the length of a seconds pendulum to the National Assembly on 9 February 1790, which, they suggested, should be defined at the Royal Observatory in Paris. A standard made of platinum would then be deposited at the Hôtel de Ville at a constant temperature, and a 'natural' or 'French' foot (*pied naturel* or *pied français*) would be defined as one-third of its length. This foot (*pied*) would be subdivided decimally into 10 inches (*pouces*), and each inch into 10 lines (*lignes*); 10 feet would make the 'national perch', and 10 squared perches an area, to be called the *arpent nationale*: the cubes of these units would define a coherent system of capacity, and coinage would be decimalised too.[4] Bonnay's report on behalf of the Committee of Agriculture and Commerce similarly favoured a universal standard derived from the seconds pendulum.

On 8 May 1790 the seconds pendulum was accepted in principle by the National Assembly as the basis for the new measuring standard. They determined that the matter should be delegated to the formidable and wide-ranging scientific expertise of the Academy of Sciences, which was instructed to 'determine at the latitude of forty-five degrees, or any other latitude that might be preferred, the length of the pendulum, and to deduce from it an invariable model for all measures and weights.'[5]

In response to the National Assembly's official request, the Academy of Sciences formed a new committee on 19 May to consider 'the scale of division that it believes most suitable, for weights as well as for the other measures and for money'. It comprised Condorcet and astronomer-academicians with evident mathematical expertise: Jean-Charles de Borda (1733–99), Joseph Louis, Comte de Lagrange (1736–1813), an Italian educated at the University of Turin and former director of the Berlin Academy of Sciences; and Pierre Simon, Marquis de Laplace (1749–1827), best known for his successful application of Newton's theory of gravitation to account for all planetary motion in the solar system. The remaining members were Charles Augustin de Coulomb (1736–1806), an experimental physicist and pioneer in electrical theory; Mathieu Tillet (1714–1791), a botanist and anatomist; and the famed chemist Antoine Laurent Lavoisier (1743–1794), who is usually considered the founding father of modern chemistry. Lavoisier explored the four elements listed by Aristotle (fire, water, earth and air) and famously discovered and named the gas 'oxygen'. He was also interested in ancient anthropomorphic standards and their subdivision.

The committee reviewed the recent arguments in favour of the seconds pendulum, as well as the earlier experiments of 1735, which had demonstrated that the natural rhythm of the pendulum could be an integral part of a larger conception for a measuring standard. They concluded that a geodesic measurement – a measure related to the physical dimensions of the earth – would be an all-embracing symbol, but that the pendulum provided greater precision. By fixing its swing on the 45th parallel, earth and pendulum would be united, and at this location its frequency could be related simply to the length of a year subdivided into a constant number of 86,400 seconds for every day. Scientific impartiality was being contorted by politics, since it was by now standard scientific knowledge that the earth does not have a regular curvature between the extremities of North Pole and Equator. Condorcet presented their arguments to the National Assembly in early June 1790. He suggested that science should guide the National Assembly and that whichever mensural system they settled on, the seconds pendulum should remain at its heart.[6]

The Academy and science were major beneficiaries of the support granted by the National Assembly. Scientifically, this new strategy would also enable previous surveys of the meridian to be verified, which was of value to the astronomers and geographers.[7] It is possible, however, that Condorcet's diplomacy in this matter was not entirely impartial and that the academicians' motives in favour of the arc of the meridian were not wholly scientific; that convenience and self-interest were involved in this decision. Anxious to avoid such accusations and – within the broader scientific fraternity – chauvinism, Condorcet proposed that the latitude of 45° N should not be related to a particular place in France (such as Bordeaux). Instead, it should be referred to more neutrally, and the time intervals of a seconds pendulum defined by an international mean position or line.[8]

Talleyrand's crucial motion of 9 March 1790 proposing that the National Assembly should seek an independent standard 'derived from nature' and independent of nations was undoubtedly influenced by Condorcet, who – it is thought – probably wrote an initial draft of the paper that Talleyrand delivered to the Assembly.[9] Talleyrand certainly proved to be an effective and persuasive political mouthpiece for the Academy. However, scientists and politicians appreciated the magnitude of the task that lay ahead, and the National Assembly sought international allies, also stating in their declaration of 8 May 1790:

> that the King [of France] be equally treated to write to His British Majesty, and to beseech him to engage the Parliament of England to concur with the National Assembly, in the determination of the natural unit of weights and measures; that consequently under the auspices of these two nations, commissioners of the Academy of Sciences of Paris shall be able to unite in equal numbers with the chosen members of the Royal Society of London, in the place which shall be respectively judged to be the most convenient.[10]

During the latter part of the 1780s, Sir John Riggs Miller MP had begun investigating the problem of the diversity of weights and measures in England and Wales for a Select Committee of the House of Commons. He was charged to investigate and report 'on the best means for adopting an uniformity of weights and measures', based on the length of a seconds pendulum in London and decimal subdivisions of it. There were influential supporters for reform in Britain at that time, from the inventor and manufacturer James Watt (1736–1819), who in 1783 proposed a universal system derived either from the English foot, a pendulum oscillating 100 times a minute, or the Amsterdam pound, 'being the most universal in Europe'. He demonstrated that either source would equate well with the weights and measures currently in use at home, and advocated that the new system should be decimalised.[11]

Miller was sympathetic to France's search for a more natural measure. In a speech to the House on 6 February 1790, he saw potential in a 'general standard from which all weights and measures might in future be raised, being itself derived from something in Nature that was invariable and immutable', and that this new system should be based on 'simple and self-evident principles'.[12] Ironically, his sentiment echoed the quest for nationhood enshrined in the American Declaration of Independence from Britain of 4 July 1776. Miller was concerned, however, to establish a system that would be above the arbitrary declaration of any ruler, and any one nation:

> The essential qualities which every Standard should possess are, that it should be taken from Nature, or connected with something in Nature and not from any work of Art, which must necessarily decay, nor from anything that is merely arbitrary and which has no other right to be a standard than that it is kept in [. . .] the Exchequer or Guildhall and which has certain marks upon it and a certain name given to it.[13]

Four days after the decree of the National Assembly on 8 May 1790, Talleyrand, as French minister for foreign affairs, wrote to Miller urging a bilateral reform of weights and measures by England and France: 'For too long these two nations have been divided by vain pretensions or self-interest, it is time these two peoples freely combine their efforts and labours towards research useful to humankind.' Following the instructions of the decree, Talleyrand proposed that the French Academy of Sciences should join forces with the Royal Society in London, because this project was 'by its nature, in the domain of the sciences' and these groups were 'the two most scholarly societies of the scientific world'. While Miller supported Talleyrand's proposals, the deteriorating political climate in France and the fear of cross-contagion (that revolution in France might also infect Britain) meant that he was unable to convince the British government to collaborate. After six months of deliberation, the British government responded officially and negatively on 3 December 1790.[14]

Initially at least, political obstacles were ignored by leading scientists. The Royal Society had been considering new ways of constructing linear measures since its foundation, and it had already responded objectively to French interest in combining forces on new standards. The Royal Society's *Philosophical Transactions* of 1742 were translated and presented to the French academicians on 17 April 1790 to inform the report that Bonnay was preparing for the National Assembly. The following spring, on 28 May 1791, Condorcet read a letter from Lord Stanhope (1753–1816), a fervent British supporter of the French Republican ideal, and a member of the Royal Society, on ideas for a unit length derived from nature.[15] Undeterred by the British government's official rebuff, the French government sent Talleyrand in person to London in 1792 to conduct informal negotiations for an Anglo-French political alliance. But the overthrow of the French monarchy in September of that year, and the consequent outbreak of hostilities between France and Britain in 1793, terminated any immediate hopes of a Franco-British alliance on an international system of weights and measures.[16]

As the earliest and most positive action of the Revolution, the moves to reform the nation's system of weights and measures were repeatedly upheld as a primary example of the potential of science for modern France.[17] National prestige and convenience rather than pure scientific rationale and impartiality led to the selection of an arc of the meridian running north–south through Paris. Indeed, it was of paramount importance to French scientific prestige that the Paris Observatory was regarded nationally and internationally as the datum for the survey of France: designed by Claude Perrault, the Observatory was completed in 1672 and located on the left bank of the Seine at the southern end of an axis with the Palais du Luxembourg (fig. 7). It would connect to Dunkirk (or Dunkerque) at its most northerly point, and Barcelona at its most southerly. In fact, the arc aligning Dunkirk–Paris–Barcelona is not a true meridian, Dunkirk being located 13' west of the longitude of Barcelona (Dunkirk is located at 2° 23' E, the Paris Observatory at 2° 20' 14.025" E, and Barcelona at 2° 10' E). Nor was it an easy arc to survey. The terrain for one-third of the arc is mountainous, and the surveyors would be required to traverse the Massif Central and the

7   Louis XIV being
shown by Colbert
the Academy of
Science, with
Claude Perrault's
Paris Observatory
under construction
(completed in
1672) in the
distant view.
Frontispiece of
Claude Perrault's
*Mémoires pour
Servir à l'Histoire
Naturelle des
Animaux*, Paris,
1671

Pyrenees. On more level terrain to survey is the meridian
running through Greenwich, to which Le Havre in the north and
Lourdes in the foothills of the Pyrenees are closely adjacent, with
Bordeaux at 45° N also close by. But then the main man-made
coordinates of the world would originate from London – not
Paris – which the French would not accept: Greenwich Observatory, founded to the southeast of London by Charles II in 1675,
was the principal rival of the Paris one.[18] The fact that the arc
the academicians chose to survey is not a true meridian and runs
through difficult and foreign terrain must surely have been influenced by the political desire to associate the French capital with
the new unit of measure, physically and intellectually. Thus,
the new unit of measure would symbolise both France and
its exalted position within the international scientific community. Politics and chauvinism would ensure that the new

standards would not be a neutral statement of Enlightenment rationality.

Although Christiaan Huygens had been made an early Fellow of the French Academy of Sciences in 1666 (he had been a Fellow of the Royal Society in London since 1663), Condorcet wished to claim him – the foreign originator of the pendulum – more emphatically for the French Republic of Science and the new measure. As Condorcet informed the government on 12 June 1790:

> Since its establishment, the Academy has always seized and even sought to use knowledge acquired by meditation, or by the study of nature, for the welfare of men: it was in its midst that an illustrious foreigner [Huygens], to whom a profound theory revealed the means of obtaining a natural and invariable unit of length, formed the first plan to relate all measurements to it, thereby rendering them uniform and unchanging.[19]

Assimilated within the bosom of French science, the pendulum offered a legitimate apparatus for determining the new measure. But there were powerful contrary views. Mathieu Tillet (1714- -1791), on behalf of the French Royal Society of Agriculture, was the co-author of a report criticising the seconds pendulum in Paris in 1790. The report cited the practical problems associated with this piece of apparatus: that the length of its swing varies according to temperature, the gravitational force applied to it (i.e. its position relative to sea level and the nature of the terrain locally) and air resistance. There were ideological objections too. The second is a non-decimal fraction (it equals $\frac{1}{86,400}$th part of a day) and is determined by astronomical and mechanical considerations. The Agricultural lobby prefered a geometrical unit derived from the physical body of the earth for the new system.[20] But on which dimension – rationally – should the scientists base their earthly measure, when the true shape of the earth was not spherical?[21] Nor was the Southern Hemisphere of the earth well charted, let alone accurately surveyed. So although the latitude of 45° N represents the mean between the North Pole and the Equator in the Northern Hemisphere, there was no absolute proof that 45° s would be midway between the South Pole and the Equator. There is so little landmass – only the mountainous tips of South America (Chile and Argentina) and New Zealand – that an accurate terrestrial survey at this latitude was out of the question.

The academicians had the benefit of Jean Picard's survey near Paris and the subsequent surveys in Lapland and Peru. They also had a recent Anglo-French survey of 1787 that had measured the distance between the observatories at Greenwich and Paris.[22] From these surveys, it was already feasible to arrive at an appropriate unit of measure equivalent to one forty-millionth of the earth's meridian, or one ten-millionth part of the earth's quadrant. Determining the earth's quadrant as precisely ten million units provided a dimension that would equate well with the decimal system that was to divide the unit. Certainly, the ultimate decision to select the earth's quadrant as the base unit of measure probably resulted from the academicians' growing conviction, over the summer and autumn of 1790, that the decimal system ought to structure the new weights and measures.

Simon Stevin (1548–1620) had mooted the benefits of decimalisation some 200 years earlier, when he proposed a primitive form of decimal fractions as an alternative to common fractions. Stevin presented his ideas in a seven-page pamphlet, which was immediately translated into French in 1585 as *La Disme, L'Arithmétique de Simon Stevin de Bruges*. In the same work he had proposed that weights, measures, currency and the division of the circle by degrees could be unified and systematised with a decimal base. Stevin's pamphlet was translated into English in 1608.[23] French metrical reformers recognised the benefits of decimalisation. In 1754 D'Alembert proposed under the entry for 'decimal' in the *Encyclopédie* that 'It would be very desirable that all divisions [weights and measures], the day, the hour, etc. would be from tens into tens', as opposed to the duodecimal system common to Europe.[24] This view was officially sanctioned in the academicians' report of 27 October 1790, in which they concluded that:

The decimal scale should serve as the base for all the divisions, and that even the success of the general project on weights and measures rests in large part on the adoption of this scale.[25]

The move to decimalisation reflected a change of heart by Condorcet. In his report for Turgot of 1775 he had argued for a duodecimal scale for the new standard on the grounds of compatibility with existing systems:

This division would have the advantage that the new *toise* would be divisible three times by four and six times by two which will give the facility of having very convenient fractions in commerce.[26]

Fifteen years on, while acknowledging in his report 'the advantages of duodecimal arithmetic' for contemporary commerce, Condorcet reasoned that the long-term advantages of the decimal system were considerable if the current – decimal – arithmetical scale was to be preserved.[27] He wrote a pamphlet to promote the decimal system entitled 'Ways to Learn to Count Confidently and with Ease' (*Moyens d'apprendre à compter sûrement et avec facilité*).[28] Lavoisier had earlier adopted a metricised system of weights for his experiments, and he commissioned the manufacture of nine brass cylinders in 1788: the largest was a pound in weight, the remainder decimal subdivisions of it. He – and Laplace – similarly decimalised the existing customary measures.[29]

There was popular resistance to Condorcet's recommendation of decimalisation, and the *Moniteur* complained a few months later in its issue of 9 January 1791 that while science would benefit, the general public would surely be inconvenienced. Petitions followed in support of a duodecimal system, and the National Assembly's Committee on Education (Commission exécutive de l'instruction publique) requested formally that the academicians explain their reasoning.[30] The academicians argued that reason dictated overall uniformity, and they urged for the wholesale decimalisation of weights and measures, as well

as currency, temperature and – largely for the practical benefit
of astronomers – the measurement of time and angles. These
proposals were doomed to fail because different international
accords for these standards existed already. Public opinion
would prove even more difficult to redirect.[31]

A second committee was named in Paris on 16 February 1791
to select an appropriate natural unit of length. This comprised
most of the mathematicians from the earlier committee: Condorcet, Lagrange, Laplace, with Jean-Charles Borda in the chair.
The aged Tillet was replaced by the mathematician Gaspard
Monge (1746–1818) – an expert surveyor who is also credited
with inventing descriptive geometry – who represented the
mechanical arts and complemented the expertise of the others.
Monge was well connected politically and was a naval attaché.
He eventually became Naval Minister.[32] Lagrange and Laplace
were also members of the Advisory Board for Arts and Trades
(Bureau de Consultation des Arts et Métiers) from 1792
onwards. Their activities in the Bureau were complementary to
the concerns of the weights and measures committee, since they
were judging practical inventions and studies that would benefit
the verification of the new standards. Lagrange and Laplace were
also founding members of the Bureau des Longitudes when it
was created in June 1795, their mathematical expertise inform-
ing judgements relating to astronomy and navigation.[33] This
spread of appointments permitted the academicians to deliberate how best the new measure should reflect the new understanding of the mechanical universe – the natural rhythm of time
as the earth rotates daily on its axis, and annually around the
sun. They acknowledged that while an existing national measure
might provide an appropriate length, its very nationality would
deter universal acceptance of it, and they referred instead to
rational criteria for a new universal measure 'taken from nature'.
Condorcet presented their collective recommendations to the
National Assembly on 19 March 1791. He reiterated their
primary objective, the need to establish 'a system of uniform
weights and measures in all parts of France [. . .] which, having
a natural unit for its basis, can merit adoption by all nations'.[34]

Separately from the deliberations of the academicians, a Republican calendar had also emerged as an overly enthusiastic attempt by revolutionaries to de-Christianise time. It was inaugurated before it was institutionalised, when people began dating Bastille Day (14 July 1789) the first day of Year I of Liberty in the new calendar. While this was undoubtedly a momentous date in recent French history, the introduction of a calendar based on national events was at odds with the principles of universality underlying the reform of weights and measures. The Legislative Assembly (which succeeded the National Constituent Assembly on 1 October 1791) debated the inconveniences of an exclusively national Republican calendar on 2 January 1792, and it was agreed that January should begin the year. This reversion to the customary system led to renewed confusion. It meant that while the first two years of liberty had run from 14 July to 13 July (from July 1789–90 and July 1790–91), in the amended Republican calendar January once again became the start of year in 1792. In a flawed attempt at clarity, it was decided to call 1792 Year IV of Liberty and not Year III: there was consequently no Year III of Liberty. Confusion was compounded further when 10 August 1792 was deemed to have inaugurated the age of equality: thus, Year I of Equality would also be Year IV of Liberty. And when the Republic came into being on 22 September 1792, and the Legislative Assembly was replaced by the National Constitution, it was decided to rename Year I of Equality Year I of the Republic, with Year II of the Republic beginning on 1 January 1793.[35]

At the end of 1792 the National Convention approached the Committee on Education, which controlled the Committee on Weights and Measures on behalf of the Convention, to find ways of harmonising the 'common' (or Christian) calendar with the Republican reordering of time. C.-G. Romme (1750–1795) was Secretary to the Committee on Education, and its membership included the mathematician and academician A.-M. Legendre (1752–1833). Legendre became the unofficial director of the Committee on Weights and Measures on 3 October 1794 and was the guiding force that implemented the metric system of weights and measures. Nine months later, after consulting the Academy of Sciences, this committee recommended a new calendar enshrining four objectives: rationalisation, commemoration, purgation and replacement. The proposals for rationalisation were to be linked to the reforms of weights and measures. Accordingly, the year was to be decimalised to ten months, with weeks of ten days, and each day ten hours long. The natural cycle and the complexity of recent French history would be synchronised by a year beginning on 22 September, the autumnal equinox and the day of the Republic. A significant date as Romme happily declared, when 'equality of day and night was marked in the sky [. . .] and civil and moral equality were proclaimed by the representatives of the people'. Romme believed that the rationalised calendar had a 'natural' logic in its divisions – since humankind counts with ten fingers, the year should be organised similarly. This selective logic was less obvious for those living outside Paris: those who worked the land in harmony with the natural seasons, and the twelve-monthly, four-weekly, lunar cycle.[36] The proposed calendar reform was abandoned by Napoleon on 1 January 1806 following a report by Laplace, an influential academician and member of the weights and measures committee.[37]

Laplace believed that the new metric system of weights and measures was founded on sounder logic than the Republican calendar. Voyagers were accustomed to fixing their position on earth by astronomical observation, and the combination of a terrestrial measurement and the decimal system would usefully unite maritime navigation, cartography and land registry. Laplace explained the benefits of this coherent system to students at the École Normale in Paris:

> It is natural for man to relate the units of distance by which he travels to the dimensions of the globe he inhabits. Thus, in moving about the earth, he may know by the simple denomination of distance its proportion to the whole circuit of the earth. This has the further advantage of making nautical and celestial measurements correspond. The navigator often needs

to determine, one from the other, the distance he has traversed from the celestial arc lying between the zeniths at his point of departure and at his destination. It is important, therefore, that one of these magnitudes should be the expression of the other, with no difference except in the units. But to that end, the fundamental linear unit must be an aliquot part of the terrestrial meridian [. . .]. Thus, the choice of the metre was reduced to that of the unity of angles.[38]

The academicians were convinced that the geometric system had compelling advantages over one based on the seconds pendulum, which was merely a symptom of terrestrial authority and could not be used to unite line, area, capacity and weight, as science had demonstrated the earth could do. With the terrestrially based system there existed a seamless relationship between the angular observations of astronomy and the linear measurements of the earth's surface, using a simple interchange of units. Units of area and capacity are related to linear units in this system through squaring or cubing, and to units of weight according to the principle of specific gravity. The mathematical expertise that dominated the weights and measures committee had ensured that a coherent and viable system could be realised.

The interconnection of measures would have been more seamless still if proposals to decimalise the circle had succeeded. Instead of the ancient divisions of the circle into 360°, 100 or 1,000 parts were suggested, and even 400°.[39] The last division would have been particularly complementary to the new system, since the unit of measure recommended by the academicians was to be one forty-millionth of the earth's circumference (or one ten-millionth of a quadrant of a meridian arc).

Ancient Precedents: Mystical and Alchemical

History lent its support for the earth as the source of the new system of weights and measures. Eighteenth-century studies of ancient civilisations and their monuments revealed evidence that coherent measures had been employed based on the dimensions of the earth. For this reason, Jean-Dominique Cassini (1748–1845), the fourth member of the Cassini family to direct the Paris Observatory, and referred to as Cassini IV, had also encouraged the reconstruction of Egyptian, Greek and Roman measures.[40] Earlier still, Newton had urged that the ancient measures be recovered.

Newton was admired in France for his studies of antiquity as well as his contribution to science. Two posthumous publications – *The Chronology of Ancient Kingdoms Amended* (1728) and *Observations upon the Prophecies of Daniel and the Apocalypse of St John* (1733) – established his reputation as a rational enquirer into theology. His *Chronology* of the Fathers of the Christian Church attempted to reconcile Greek mythology and record with the Bible, while his *Observations* on Judaeo-Christian prophecy demonstrated that decipherment of the sacred texts was essential in order to understand God's message. Newton venerated the Bible and accepted its account of creation and God's providential role in nature. He also believed that it would provide answers about the principles that structure the universe through the designs that God had communicated to Noah (the Ark for the Flood) and King Solomon (the Temple of Solomon). Newton left a mass of manuscripts on the closely related subjects of alchemy and chemistry, again believing that they would provide clues to a clearer understanding of the nature and structure of all matter that God had created. He published an incomplete theory of chemical force, carefully concealing his exploration of the alchemists: it became public only a century after his death.

More specifically, Newton was concerned to understand the ancient measures that had been used to determine the earth's circumference, before Picard's precise measurement of a degree of latitude was available to him. Newton anticipated that the cubit of the ancient Egyptians would enable him to determine the length of the stadium referred to by Eratosthenes, and to evaluate the accuracy of Eratosthenes' calculation of the earth's circumference against more modern estimates. This would have provided him with useful parameters with which to check his general theory of gravitation. One route to this end was to define and refine the length of the sacred cubit used to build the Temple of Solomon at Jerusalem, following biblical descriptions. The Jewish historian Josephus had described the circumference of the columns at the Temple (the third to be built on that sacred site), and Newton deduced the probable range of the sacred cubit as between 24.80 and 25.02 inches. Newton's account of this search was published posthumously in the original Latin, and translated into English and incorporated into a two-volume work by John Greaves, of 1736–7, as *A Dissertation upon the Sacred Cubit of the Jews and the Cubits of several Nations: in which, from the Dimensions of the great Pyramid, as taken by Mr John Greaves, the ancient Cubit of Memphis is Determined.*[41]

John Greaves was a mathematician, astronomer, physician and an ardent Newtonian. Aged 26, he had already published Newton's *The Chronology* (1728). A decade later, supported by the financial patronage of William Laud, Archbishop of Canterbury, Greaves journeyed to Italy and Egypt in order to verify the lengths of the ancient measures himself.[42] He took with him a precisely calibrated 10-foot-long measuring rod, made of brass and subdivided by 10,000 equal parts, with 2,000 lines to each English foot. The measures he encountered en route were recorded by calibrating them precisely against this standard. In Rome, he 'spent at least two hours' measuring one ancient example of the Roman foot, which he found to be equal to 1,944 lines and so sixty lines shorter than the English foot. His next stop was Egypt, where he attempted to determine the measurements used to design and build the Great Pyramid at Giza. His findings were published in *Pyramidographia; or, A Description of the Pyramides in Ægypt* (1736). They were as well received as his expedition had been supported, and Greaves was appointed Savilian Professor of Astronomy at Oxford on his return.

If Newton had succeeded in his quest, if he had found tangible and precise evidence of the biblical measures, would scientists have developed an anthropometric system in preference to a terrestrial measure? The answer would probably have been no. Short of finding the actual measuring rod used to build the first Temple of Jerusalem (on which its successors were based), the outcome is unlikely to have yielded much satisfaction, since the various measures used by the ancients varied too much in size: no definitive standard has survived. Nonetheless, even though the authority of nature and the physicality of the earth would provide scientists with their model for the new universal system of weights and measures, the measures of antiquity remained a valuable source of reference and comparison. Paucton's compendium of measures, *Métrologie; ou, Traité des mesures, poids, et monnoies des anciens peuples et des modernes* (published anonymously in Paris in 1780), focused on the physical properties of ancient monuments, finding in the dimensions of their walls a permanent record of the ancients' systems of measurement. Furthermore, he argued that the measurement systems of many ancient civilisations were based on the dimensions of the earth, and he cited the measurements of the Great Pyramid as proof of this assertion: the Egyptian royal cubit was understood to be $1/500$ of the length of the Great Pyramid and $1/400,000$th of the polar axis of the earth.[43] Support for these conclusions came from the astronomer Jean-Sylvain Bailly (who has the largest distinct crater on the moon named after him), as formidable a politician as he was an astronomer, who was appointed the first mayor of Paris, the chemist Lavoisier and mineralogist Jean-Baptiste Louis Romé de l'Isle. Their enquiries confirmed that the Babylonians derived their measures from a seconds pendulum measured at the latitude of Babylon, and that eighteenth-century man was only reinstating a system of universal measures based on the dimensions of the earth, which had already been formulated by earlier civilisations.[44]

Inducing the measuring standards from ancient monuments remained popular into the next century, as in W. M. Flinders Petrie's *Inductive Metrology; or, The Recovery of Ancient Measures from the Monuments* (London, 1877). Petrie was a respected professor at the University of London, and he explained that inductive metrology relied on an assumption that the monument being surveyed was built accurately and precisely, and that the intervals between columns, the column and wall widths, or crucial lengths of a geometrical form – such as the base of a pyramid – would reveal the measuring unit used by the original designers and builders. It is important that the surveyor knows the full extent of the original building; otherwise the dimensions and modules induced will be incomplete and misleading. Apparently, John Greaves had come unstuck in the early eighteenth century when attempting to induce the Memphis cubit, because the Great Pyramid was surrounded by debris and he had not measured the true base length of its four sides which lay beneath.

While there was a common concern among French *philosophes* and scientists to find a universal system of measurement independent of nations, there is clear evidence of potentially two quite different paths to achieving this goal. Scientists, particularly the mathematicians of the Academy of Sciences, sought universal measurements detached from ordinary human affairs: their emphasis was on number as quantity that would interrelate mathematically and geometrically. The other group is more difficult to define simply. They had scientific training and displayed scientific rigour in their method, while also taking a broader cultural, socio-historical view that interpreted ancient customs, sought continuity with this tradition and looked for numbers of human significance. In short, they favoured numbers with qualities.

Scientific Rationalism Prevails

While some individuals enjoyed joint membership of both the Academy of Sciences and the Academy of Inscriptions and Humanities (Académie des inscriptions et belles-lettres), a perceptible split was forming between the two academies in the 1780s as to what constituted an appropriately modern unit of measure. Ultimately, the deliberations of the Academy of Sciences were to prevail, not least because it was the one that had received government support and funding since 1790 for the very purpose of determining a new system of weights and measures. Certainly, Condorcet, in his capacity as secretary of the Academy of Sciences, vigorously opposed an archaeological and philological approach. His belief in the recent progress of society through science was such that comparison of modern French culture with the 'primitive' civilisations of the past was invidious. The eulogy he published in 1785 in memory of Jean Baptiste Bourguignon d'Anville (1697–1782), an academician with a foot in both camps, displays his reservations. D'Anville, a leading geographer and cartographer of his generation, had written on ancient geography, and ancient and modern measures (*Traité des mesures itinéraires anciennes et modernes*, 1769). Condorcet recorded his admiration for d'Anville's industry, while also pointing out that his deductions based on ancient writings and inscriptions had proved inconclusive – astronomers had also contradicted the findings set out in another of his books. He concluded that while classical scholarship could provide a context for the needs of modern society, it could never match the objectivity and precision of science. The final prototype for the new measure was not, however, based on pure scientific rationale, but on a compromise dictated as much by the human frailties of politics as objective science.[45]

A Summary of Recommendations

Borda's committee, with Condorcet as secretary, presented its recommendations to the National Assembly on 19 March 1791. They listed the pros and cons regarding the length of a seconds pendulum, a quadrant of the great circle of the Equator and a quadrant of the great circle of some meridian of the earth. They found that the length of the seconds pendulum was easiest to verify at 45° N latitude, halfway between the North Pole and the Equator. Against it, however, was the variable force of gravity and the arbitrary unit of time, a second of time being an awkward fraction – $\frac{1}{86,400}$ – of twenty-four hours. They therefore recommended a measure derived from one quarter of the terrestrial arc, which would be natural and without arbitrariness. Their preference had been for the quadrant of a meridian, of which 'one ten-millionth part of its length would be the ordinary unit'. Since it was impractical to measure one full quadrant of the earth, however, it was recommended that an accessible segment should be taken and the total quadrant length calculated from it. This segment ought not to be measured at the Equator, because this was inconvenient for Europeans and of little consequence to the nations located on or near it. The arc between the Channel port of Dunkirk in northern France and Barcelona in Spain was proposed because both cities were situated at sea level on approximately the same north–south meridian and equidistant from the 45th parallel (which runs through Bordeaux). Also, the total distance, of about 9° 39' (670 miles/1,070 kilometres) had been mostly surveyed before.[46] Of course, it would also be a largely French measure and compromise, a fact that was played down publicly.

The report was delivered to the National Assembly, accompanied by a letter from Condorcet. He was at pains to emphasise the universality and scientific impartiality of his committee's approach to this problem, and in making light of the unscientific assumptions the academicians had been forced to accept, such as the lack of sphericity of the earth, he was surely stretching the credibility of reason:

> [The] Academy had done its best to exclude any arbitrary considerations – indeed, all that might have aroused the suspicion of its having advanced the particular interests of France; in a word, it sought to prepare such a plan that, were its principles alone to come down to posterity, no one could guess the country of its origin.[47]

Talleyrand provided vital support. In reading out the academicians' report to the National Assembly on 26 March 1791, he echoed Condorcet:

> The only hope of extending the standardisation of measures to foreign nations and persuading them to accept it, lies in selecting a unit that is in no way arbitrary, nor particularly suited to the circumstances of any one nation.[48]

Further, he confirmed that a quarter of the earth's meridian – a distance from the terrestrial pole to the Equator – would be used to determine the length of the new unit. This dimension would be extrapolated from a new survey of a quarter of the earth's quadrant. The National Assembly duly accepted the academicians' advice, and the Academy was authorised to proceed to the next stage.

Five groups were appointed by the Academy to define the length of the earth's meridian. Jean-Dominique Cassini, Pierre-François-André Méchain (1744–1804), Jean-Baptiste-Joseph Delambre (1749–1822) and Adrien-Marie Legendre (1752–1833) were directed to determine the difference in the latitudes of Dunkirk and Barcelona and to triangulate between the two ends of the arc; Gaspard Monge and Jean-Baptiste-Marie-Charles Meusnier de la Place (1754–1793) were to measure the bases. Jean-Charles de Borda and Charles-Augustin de Coulomb were required to measure the length of the pendulum at the latitude of 45° N, and Lavoisier and René-Just Haüy (1743–1822) the weight of a given volume of distilled water, in a vacuum, at the temperature of melting ice. Tillet led a group who were to undertake a comparison of the old measures with the new, and construct scales and tables of equivalents.[49] By the end of spring 1791, the essential character of the proposed new system of weights and measures had been formulated and officially sanctioned. Still to be decided were the definitions of each measure and an appropriate nomenclature. Pierre-Simon, Marquis de Laplace, Lagrange, Monge and Borda were asked by the Committee on Education to prepare suitable names in advance of the survey of the meridian arc being undertaken.

The National Assembly supplied 100,000 *livres* to fund this complex operation on 7 August 1791. On 11 July 1792 the academicians reported their joint decision to call the fundamental unit for units of length and surface area the *mètre*,[50] a name derived from a French corruption of the ancient Greek *metron* and the Latin *metrum*, or 'measuring-rod'. This report also provides the systematic sequence of prefixes – 'deci', 'centi' and 'milli' – for divisions of the metre, and which would also be applied to units of weight. The doubts then set in. Over the next six months Borda, Lagrange and Monge had second thoughts about the suitability of their formulation: they worried that the names they had produced – *mètre*, *décamètre*, *hectomètre*, *kilomètre* and *myriamètre* – were too long for frequent use and would be confusing in ordinary usage, being easily mistaken for one another. Lagrange also harboured doubts about the length of the unit, believing that the *décamètre* would be a more convenient basic unit because ordinary people manage multiples more easily than subdivisions. They now thought it preferable to have a different name for each unit – as with customary measures – and they cited classical precedents as exemplars to follow. Borda' and Condorcet's committee submitted their revisions in a second report to the Committee on Education in May 1793, which were promptly rejected.[51]

The academicians already knew the approximate length of the metre. They had decided that for practical reasons it ought to correspond closely to the length of the seconds pendulum, as calculated by Huygens, on latitude 45° N and at sea level in a constant temperature. This was because at 36 *pouces* 8.428 *lignes* (Parisian inches and lines) it was close in length to the existing Parisian *toise* of 36 *pouces*. Scientific objectivity was being tempered by the need for practicality. Newton found Huygens's standard seconds pendulum to be equivalent to 39.14912 English inches, and therefore only fractionally more than 3 inches longer than the English yard of 36 inches. The seconds pendulum under these conditions is equivalent to 0.993 577 of the modern metre. The elaborate survey of France and northern Spain – itself the victim of inaccuracies – would only 'refine' the length of the metre by a fraction over 6 millimetres.[52] Closer still was the earlier geodesic survey of 1787 between Greenwich and Paris, which had determined the length to be chosen as the metre as 36 *pouces* 11 *lignes* 44 *centièmes*: just one third of a millimetre (0.33 mm) longer than the modern metre.[53] On 1 August 1793 the *mètre* was legally designated as the length equal to the ten-millionth part of the arc of the terrestrial meridian contained between the North Pole and the Equator: its multiples were designated in this legislation as *décamètre*, *hectomètre*, *kilomètre* and *myriamètre*.[54]

Surveying the Meridian

Two academicians were presented with the task of surveying the
arc of the decisive meridian between Dunkirk and Barcelona:
Delambre its northern half from Dunkirk to Rodez in southern
France, and Méchain from Rodez across the Pyrenees to
Barcelona. A large workforce was placed at their disposal to construct elevated viewing points, and the king issued a royal proclamation through the Legislative Assembly on 10 June 1792,
instructing the relevant *départements* to support the surveyors in
their work, by providing horses, carriages and scaffolding, safe-
guarding their work in progress and ensuring that their signals
were neither disturbed nor damaged. Méchain and Delambre
were provided with 300 copies of this proclamation to post along
their routes.[55]

Méchain was an accomplished astronomer and had been
actively involved in the joint Anglo-French exercise of 1787 to
triangulate the distance between the observatories at Greenwich
and Paris. He had become impressed during this project by a
new piece of surveying equipment, the repeating transit (*cercle
répétiteur*), designed by Borda, chairman of the Committee of
Weights and Measures. It took its name from the actions
involved in its use. Once the first set of readings had been sighted
and recorded, its telescopic sight was moved back to the original
line of sight by rotating the telescope on its circular base, without
having to disturb the tripod below. It included parabolic mirrors
for reflecting signals, and he judged it would be ideal for
the mountainous terrain he was about to survey. However,
Méchain's inexperience with the equipment caused him considerable anxiety towards the conclusion of the project, when he
became aware of a significant error in his survey.[56]

Problems plagued both expeditions. As the process of surveying advanced, the Revolution increased its grip on the nation,
and monarchists were placed under threat. A royal academician
leading an expedition of men accompanied by a suspicious array
of instruments, pinning up royal proclamations en route, was
greeted with suspicion in those troubled times. It did not help

that the timber pyramidal signals Méchain had erected were garbed in white cloth, which resembled the standard of the counter-revolution. Delambre began surveying near Clermont in the Beauvaisis, but was arrested in September 1792 for carrying outdated documentation: he was imprisoned as a counter-revolutionary and his release had to be expedited by Condorcet through his high-level contacts with the Minister of the Interior. The southern expedition began smoothly. Méchain encountered few difficulties and was greeted by sixty helpers at his first station: the white cloth of his signals (and Delambre's thereafter) being bordered with blue and red bands so as not to antagonise the revolutionaries. Méchain soon made good progress triangulating the arc south of Perpignan.[57] On his eventual arrival in Barcelona that winter, he used his astronomer's skills to establish the city's latitude, and – for additional accuracy – made plans to extend the meridian $2\frac{1}{2}°$ southward to the Balearic Islands.

Méchain was then struck by personal misfortune. In the spring of 1793 a friend invited him to examine a new hydraulic pump on the periphery of Barcelona. His friend and an assistant were caught in the mechanism while trying to start it up, and in his attempt to free them Méchain was thrown with great force by a lever, breaking a collar bone and several ribs. He was rendered unconscious for three days, and an immobile, three-month-long convalescence followed. By the time he was on his feet again, Louis XVI had been executed, France was at war with Spain, and Méchain was barred from leaving Barcelona. Nor could he make good use of his enforced sojourn in Spain. The extension of the survey to the Balearics proved unfeasible, since their distance from the mainland was greater than he had appreciated, and signals on the islands could not be seen from Barcelona.

While biding his time, Méchain established the latitude of Montjuic, a low hill that rises just south of the city centre. However, triangulating between the two latitudes he had made of Barcelona and Montjuic exposed a discrepancy in his initial survey of 3″, for which he could find no rational explanation. Méchain was terror-struck because it undermined the accuracy of his entire mission. He told no one, and managed to keep his secret intact during his lifetime. On his eventual return to France, his expedition was deemed a great success and Méchain was rewarded with the directorship of the Paris Observatory, the most prestigious post for a French astronomer. He could not fully enjoy these rewards, and endured a private torment – observed by his colleagues who commented on his sour demeanour – that gnawed away at his very being.

Delambre was also charged with establishing the base between Perpignan in the south and Melun just south-east of Paris, which would serve to measure the arc of the meridian, and he did not complete this task until 17 September 1798. Legendre and his team compiled the numerical data and concluded their calculations of the length of the arc, which were presented in manuscript form as the year reached its end, on 28 December 1798.[58] They defined the length of the quadrant of the meridian as 5,130,740 *toises*, and the metre was accordingly refined and set out as 3 *pieds* 11 *lignes* 296 *millièmes* (443.295936 *lignes*).[59] The definitive standards for the metre and kilogram were presented to the French legislature (Corps Législatif) by a delegation of the surviving commissioners of Weights and Measures, and their foreign deputies, on 22 June 1799.

Legendre resolved the triangles of Méchain' and Delambre's survey using the formulas of plane geometry. This involved the application of a theorem of his own devising, one that was intended to compensate for the earth's curvature. He later had his own misgivings about the accuracy of this method, which was based on the assumption that the curved survey triangles made by Méchain and Delambre followed the shape of a pure sphere, when of course it was well known that the earth's surface was an oblate spheroid. He was anxious enough to feel the need to justify his calculations in a paper presented in 1806,[60] perhaps because by then Méchain's own errors had surfaced posthumously.

Intent on finding a way of remedying his error without being exposed, Méchain had gained permission to return to Spain in 1803. But while still on board ship he became exhausted (some suggest by the anxiety that was consuming him) and fell victim to yellow fever. He was quarantined, and obtained permission to disembark with his notes only on the condition that they were sprinkled with an antiseptic of vinegar. He did not recover and he recorded his utter desolation just before he died: 'Hell and all the scourges it vomits upon the earth, tempests, war, the plague and black intrigues are therefore unchained against me!'[61] Delambre acquired Méchain's notes in order to publish their joint findings, and only on studying them was the secret revealed. He concluded that the equipment, not the operator, was to blame, that Méchain had simply put too much trust in the new surveying instruments.[62] The mission to establish a pure dimension derived from the earth and reason sought through science had been tainted by natural human fallibility.

Meanwhile, the entire French nation had suffered its own self-inflicted torment in the name of Liberty, Fraternity and Equality. In their quest for objectivity, rationality and modernity the revolutionaries finally rejected tradition and the institutions that had governed the nation. Louis XVI was put to death. The means of his execution provided a poignant climax for the destruction of the old standards and the introduction of the new.

4. The Decisive Separation

When, without the least embarrassment, people could
brazenly call into question the authority of God's
Church; when they could speak of the monarchy –
equally a creature of God's grace – and the sacred
person of the King himself as if they were both simply
interchangeable items in a catalogue of various forms
of government to be selected on a whim; when they
had the ultimate audacity and have it they did – to
describe God Himself, the Almighty, Very God of Very
God, as dispensable and to maintain in all earnestness
that order, morals and happiness on this earth could be
conceived of without Him, purely as matters of man's
inherent morality and reason [. . .] God, good God! –
then you needn't wonder that everything was turned
upside down, that morals had degenerated, and that
humankind had brought down upon itself the judgement of Him whom it denied. It would come to a bad
end.[1]

The National Convention was impatient for Méchain and
Delambre to produce the definitive length of the metre, and in
1793 the Minister of the Interior requested the introduction of
a provisional metre in order to eliminate the diversity of weights
and measures that was impeding free trade and the distribution
of grain. Borda, Lagrange and Monge duly wrote a report that
was presented to the Academy on 10 April 1793. It was for-
warded to the government and became law on 1 August of that
year, and the provisional standards were fabricated and distrib-

uted to the regions. The 'reason, justice and honesty' urged three years earlier was now moving a crucial step forward.[2]

Earlier that year, while the French were preparing to break their long-standing relationship with the traditional body-related measures, they were about to sever – all too literally – their relationship with the monarchy using a mechanism applauded for its rationality, egalitarianism and humanitarianism. At twenty-two minutes past ten on the morning of 21 January 1793, a machine new to France, and designed using the traditional measurements of the 'king's foot' (*pied du Roi*), was used to decapitate his person.

Guillotine: the Triumph of Rationality and the Severance of Ancient Standards

The guillotine, as this machine was commonly to be called, was derived from a law barely ten months old and was named after Dr Joseph-Ignace Guillotin (1739–1815). He did not invent the device, but set the scene for its creation. Guillotin had been an important participant in a debate on capital punishment that led to the new law being introduced on 20 March 1792 by the Legislative Assembly.[3] He had made his mark by submitting a proposition in six articles to the National Assembly, which included the recommendation that death by decapitation should become the sole and standard form of execution, 'whatever the rank and station of the guilty parties', and that this would be done 'by means of a simple mechanism'.[4] To what extent he specified any details about the 'simple mechanism' that has since borne his name is unknown. Certainly, there was considerable enthusiasm for his idea. One commentator remarked: 'the innovation of replacing the executioner with a mechanism which, like the law itself, separates the sentence from the judge, is worthy [. . .] of the new order into which we are about to enter'.[5]

Capital punishment by beheading dates back to the ancient Romans. Titus Manlius Torquatus had been decapitated for disobeying the Senate: his own father, a consul, had ordered the sentence.[6] The consul's 'selfless' act was later offered as a prime example of 'the triumph of civic virtue over sensibility', a principal theme of the Terror.[7] There were dissenters among the National Assembly, however, who aired alternative opinions over the succeeding months. Most notable among them were two abolitionists of the death penalty, Marguerite-Louis-François Duport-Dutertre – who, on becoming Minister of Justice, was later responsible for introducing the decapitating machine – and Robespierre, who chose to make Louis XVI an exception and, eventually, almost everyone else. They were all executed by the guillotine, as were many of the Legislative Assembly who ordered its construction. Except, that is, Dr Guillotin himself, who died of natural causes at the very reasonable old age of 76.[8]

No exact drawings survive of the machine in the form in which it was first brought into action.[9] It is therefore difficult to determine how precisely it differed from the many varied types of decapitating machine already in use elsewhere in Europe. Images of one used in Italy were widely circulated from 1530. The Revolution's guillotine was probably physically similar to the gibbet in Halifax, England, which was being operated during the reign of Edward III (1327–77), and the 'Maiden', which had been introduced to Scotland during the sixteenth century. The 'Maiden' certainly shared the scale of the guillotine – both were 10 feet tall (the Halifax Gibbet was taller at 15 feet). One French cleric who wrote of his European travels recorded that such a mechanism provided a swift and agreeable death for 'gentlemen and ecclesiastics', and that in England social eligibility was not the only criterion for execution by this means, 'so long as the sufferers are ready to pay for it'.[10] In Revolutionary France, in the prevailing spirit of enlightened humanity, of egalitarianism and humanitarianism, the right to die by guillotine was extended to all.

The first practical steps to create the guillotine had been submitted to the Legislative Assembly on 17 March 1792 by a surgeon, Dr Antoine Louis, who was secretary to the Academy of Surgeons (Académie Chirurgie) and was known for his ingenuity in perfecting surgical implements. It was his idea to angle the cutting blade of the guillotine so that the neck of the victim was simultaneously cut and sawn, guaranteeing the separation of head from body. His instructions to the state carpenter, Guidon, provide the only surviving written specification for the first guillotine. He instructed that it must consist of:

> Two parallel uprights in oak ten feet (*pieds*) high, joined at the top by a crosspiece and solidly mounted on a base with supporting braces at the sides and back. These two uprights will be a foot apart on the inside and will be six inches (*pouces*) thick; on the inner sides of these uprights will be longitudinal square grooves, one inch in depth, to take the side-pieces of a blade.[11]

In fact, the guillotine built for the execution of Louis XVI was not constructed by Guidon, because he demanded too much money, claiming that it was a disagreeable task that needed a compensatory reward. In his impatience to get the machine built quickly, Dr Louis approached a German harpsichord maker, Tobias Schmidt, 'who sometimes abandons this art to devote himself to discoveries of benefit to humanity', and who agreed to build it at a fraction of the cost quoted by Guidon. Schmidt completed the first prototype guillotine in mid-April 1792.[12] Then came the refinements. An architect, Pierre Giraud, wrote a report on 5 June 1792 that was critical of the contraption Schmidt had constructed. He argued that its specification ought to be improved so that it would operate more smoothly and be more durable. For example, brass ought to replace the wooden grooves the blade was to slide down. He also knew someone who could build it more cheaply than Guidon. With eighty-three French *départements* each in need of its own guillotine, Giraud's intervention was timely, and his associate promptly submitted an estimate for the improved machine that included its delivery already painted in Revolutionary scarlet.[13] Schmidt swiftly defended 'his' machine, and its very reasonable cost, and took out a patent in his name.[14] He was lucky not to lose his head.

The guillotining of Louis XVI was, of course, a remarkable event. Charles-Henri Sanson, hereditary Executioner of the

High Works and Criminal Sentences, an appointment first granted by Louis XIV to a Sanson in 1688,[15] presided over his former master's decapitation. Sanson recorded his account of the events that ensued in a popular measure of public opinion, *Le Thermomètre du jour*. The execution was stripped bare of regal ceremony:

> Descending from the vehicle for the execution, he [Louis XVI] was told that he must remove his coat. He made some objection, saying that he could be executed as he was. On being given to understand that this was impossible, he himself helped remove his coat. He made the same objection when it was a question of tying his hands, which he himself held out when the person with him told him that it was a final sacrifice. Then he asked if the drums were still beaten. He was told that this was not known, which was the truth. [. . .] He also suggested that he himself should cut his hair.
>
> And, to be quite truthful, he bore it all with a sang-froid and a firmness which astonished us. I am very sure that he derived this firmness from those religious principles with which no one could seem more endowed than he.[16]

Louis XVI was executed in the Place de la Révolution (the former Place Louis XV, which is now the Place de la Concorde) (fig. 8). It was a triumph of science and rationality over the divinity that kingship represented. Through the public destruction of the body of the king, royal authority and the religious principles that were channelled through him died. That this regicide was a public act, and was a ritual sacrifice rather than an assassination, was essential to the success of the new regime. In 1662 Bishop Bossuet had declared in a sermon before the king's grandfather: 'even if you [the king] die, your authority never dies [. . .] The man dies, it is true, but the king, we say, never dies.'[17] As Albert Camus observed more recently in *The Rebel*: 'The condemnation of the king is at the crux of our contemporary history. It symbolises the secularisation of our history and the disincarnation of the Christian God.'[18] It was a decisive break with the traditions of the old regime, and a memorable act of foundation for the new.

8 Execution of Louis xvi by guillotine, in the Place de la Révolution, Paris, 21 January 1793

Condorcet was opposed to the death penalty for the king. He argued that kings too were citizens – 'Long since kings have been mere men in the eyes of reason' – and as such they had rights that could not be violated by the will of the people. His close friend, the Englishman Thomas Paine (1737–1809), supported this viewpoint. Paine, outlawed from England for his political views, was admired in France for his support of American Independence. As an honorary Revolutionary in France, he had his views translated from English by Condorcet – for his French was limited – and read out to the National Convention. Paine proposed an alternative to execution. Let the

United States be the safeguard and asylum of Louis Capet [xvi]. There, hereafter, far removed from the miseries and crimes of royalty, he may learn, from the constant aspect of public prosperity, that the true system of government consists not in kings, but in fair, equal, and honourable representation.

Paine narrowly escaped the guillotine himself for expressing such views, and fled to America.[19] The Revolutionaries were determined to have the king executed publicly in order to appropriate and to redeploy his sovereignty for their own ends. As one historian of that era has argued:

> Royal publicists claimed that the king's body politic was immortal; the king with his crown could not die, even if an assassin struck down the man who wore the crown. But the public trial and execution of the king could and did destroy the king's body politic along with the man himself. It was precisely because he was 'twice-born', as body and embodiment, that the king had to die and to die in public.[20]

How the king's body might be reconstituted through the body politic for the benefit of all was hotly – and violently – debated during the political Terror that ensued. In an age of equality, when no one body was to be revered over any other, all were liable to the same physical fate as the king – whether of privileged birth or superior mind and body. An anti-intellectual and largely irrational hostility was generated against *savants* in particular. Following the death of the king, and into the summer of the next year, 14,080 death penalties were issued, and Robespierre and his supporters were among a group of 109 guillotined in just two days.[21]

The guillotine was a triumph of reason for the rationalists, yet the public were disappointed by its very efficiency. The frequency and relative passivity of the process – victims could make very few voluntary movements, since they were delivered bound and then tipped mechanically towards the yoke and blade – detracted from the spectacle. There was very little physical contact to attract crowds, none of the usual drama of vice being punished and no evidence of a priest providing consolation. In a macabre attempt to enliven the proceedings and to draw in more spectators, the authorities in Paris supplemented the executions with song and dance.[22]

The Revolutionaries placed the independently powerful royal academies under close scrutiny, doubting their loyalty to the new regime. The Academy of Sciences had two acknowledged masters – the monarchy and 'aristocratic' Newtonian science – and its regulations and internal hierarchy reflected for its detractors 'the notions of etiquette, status, rank, and propriety so prevalent in Old Regime society'.[23] Robespierre's Committee on Public Safety (Comité de salut public) disbanded it on 8 August 1793, and a Temporary Committee on Weights and Measures came into existence on 11 September 1793, purged of suspected moderates and lasted for two years. It had troubled beginnings during the ensuing Reign of Terror. Within four months of its formation, Laplace, Lavoisier, Delambre and Borda were accused of displaying neither 'republican virtues' nor 'hatred of kings', and were removed from office.[24] By then, Condorcet was already in hiding. Six academicians were guillotined – including Lavoisier – and twenty-five either imprisoned (two of them died during their incarceration) or had their research suspended. As secretary of the Academy, and as President of the Legislative Assembly since 1792, Condorcet was an indiscreet critic of the excesses perpetrated during the Terror. Once caught and imprisoned, Condorcet committed suicide to evade official execution. 'Citizen' Lagrange was one of the few former members who survived to continue work, on what was now to be referred to as the Committee on Republican Weights and Measures, and he was its president for a brief period of one month. This was just enough time for him to write to the Committee on Public Safety expressing his concern at the dismissal of Delambre. He asked the Committee to work with the municipal authorities to ensure that Delambre's work was not undone, and that his survey stations and markers were kept intact.[25]

With the old guard effectively vanquished, the Republican government – the Directory, which succeeded the National Convention – created the National Institute of Sciences and Arts in 1795. It formed an essential ingredient of the revolutionary vision. As a substitute for all the former Academies, the National Institute was intended to unify all knowledge: 'To maintain the renown (*gloire*) that the French people has acquired among all nations through the progress of knowledge and by discoveries useful to mankind'.[26] While condemned by some in government, the former academicians who survived execution were deemed too valuable to be excluded from the process of reform. Sur-

vivors of the Academy of Sciences were absorbed into the
National Institute's Mathematics and Physics *Première Classe*,
which was subdivided into ten sections: it was in the Mathematics section that the reform of weights and measures was continued (Moral and Political Science fell into the *Deuxième Classe*,
Literature and Fine Arts into the *Troisième*). Legislation was
passed on 24 October 1795 charging the National Institute 'with
all the operations related to establishing the unit of weights and
measures'.[27] It was required urgently, according to a spokesman
of the Directory, because it 'must be one of the greatest benefits of the Revolution': 'to interrupt this enterprise that has been
desired for so many centuries, begun under the kings who didn't
finish much of anything [. . . it] must be completed for the
republic'.[28]

In June 1795, after the Temporary Committee had become the
Temporary Agency for Weights and Measures, the Bureau of
Longitudes was created with Laplace and Lagrange as board
members. The Bureau of Longitudes controlled the Committee
on Weights and Measures and all the committees concerned with
navigation and astronomy, including the Paris Observatory.
Laplace was to become president of the Bureau.[29] Under his
leadership, the Temporary Agency for Weights and Measures
focused on the scientific aims with which the Revolution had
entrusted them. Efficient administrators who could push the
reforms through complemented them, since it was the responsi-
bility of the government, not the scientists, to regulate and
enforce the new standards. Legendre was retained as director of
the Temporary Agency. Even the politically rapacious recognised
that his experience was invaluable. He had earlier been involved
through the Academy of Sciences in the geodetic survey of 1787
made between the Greenwich and Paris observatories, and with
determining the standard length of the metre. Just before
becoming director of the Temporary Agency, he had been chief
of the Executive Committee on Public Instruction (Commission
exécutive de l'instruction publique), the bureau in the
Legislature that controlled the Committee on Weights and
Measures. Legendre derived his power and authority from polit-

ical and scientific circles, and he was an obvious replacement for Condorcet. As the only former academician to be engaged full-time on implementing and disseminating information publicly about the new system, he is usually credited with developing and overseeing its successful introduction.[30]

Other former members of the Temporary Committee – Lagrange, Laplace and Monge – were among the Twelve Commissioners who reported to the Temporary Agency. In this capacity Lagrange and Laplace lectured during 1795 to students at the École Normale to disseminate to the regions precise information about the formulation of the new system of weights and measures. Monge directed work on the platinum that would be used to manufacture the metre rod in advance of its distribution to the main centres of France. While well aware of their 'Temporary' status, and that 'Other men' would 'complete what has been prepared up to this time', its members were proud of their accomplishments, claiming that their successors would 'find active groups of workmen, [and] machines whose invention would be envied by England'.[31] England clearly remained the nation to beat.

Further rapid changes ensued. After only ten months the Temporary Agency came under the jurisdiction of the Ministry of the Interior and became the Office for Weights and Measures (1796–8), having been accused of being wasteful, extravagant and overly bureaucratised.[32] The Office had a Council governed by three directors including Legendre. 'Foreign' scholars augmented the Institute's Committee in 1798–9. They came mainly from French-dominated territories: the republics of Batavia (Netherlands), Helvetica (Switzerland) and Cisalpina (Milan), as well as the separate kingdoms of Denmark, Spain, the Piedmont (Turin) and Rome.[33] These foreign scholars provided objective criticism, and the Danish adviser, Thomas Bugge, expressed his concern about the accuracy of the surveying methods being used, and whether the resulting data would have to be superseded in the future.[34]

The social upheaval associated with revolution and war inevitably combined to affect the progress and introduction of the metric system. The seemingly perpetual changes to the new regime's public bodies did nothing to ease the general confusion surrounding the proposals. Debate had continued since 4 August 1789, when the seigneurial monopoly of weights and measures had been abolished, as to what precisely and practically the new standard should be; how it could be sustained; and how strengthened symbolically. On 31 July 1793, with Danton presiding, there was discussion in the National Convention of the fulfilment of the 'old dreams of the *philosophes*', of 'a new bond of Republican unity'. It was agreed that the new measures would provide 'a symbol of equality and a guarantee of fraternity that should unite the people', such that philosophers in centuries to come would 'admire the scientific wonder and humanity' of the new measures.[35] The new weights and measures would ensure liberty and equality for all citizens, and accordingly were to be named *Républicaines*. A report of mid-April 1795 to the Convention by the Committee on Public Instruction stated that the new measures would bear this name to distinguish them from the old measures, which preserved the 'vestiges of the shame of feudal serfdom' and tyranny, and that 'the interest and dignity of the Republic demand on every score that the reform of weights and measures be effected'.[36] The Republic – not the monarchy – had shown itself fit to implement the necessary reforms.

The political determination of the French Republic to impose this new system deterred British involvement. They would not endorse mensural reform led by France, a nation with which they had been at war since February 1793. Prime Minister William Pitt (1759–1806) fortified Britain against French force and radical ideology throughout his premiership (1783–1801, and 1804–06).[37] Talleyrand, who initially had been sympathetic to British involvement, by year VI of the Republic had taken a decidedly anti-British stance himself. He urged France's allies and neighbouring neutral countries to adopt this reform independently of commitment to it by either the British or the Americans.

At home, the French government needed to adopt a more pragmatic line. Since seigneurial control of measures had ceased in 1789 there had been no official national standard to replace the customary measures, only the provisional metric standard that had been introduced by the National Convention in 1793.[38] It was provisional because Delambre and Méchain had yet to finish their triangulation of the arc of the meridian.[39] The Academy of Sciences had been receiving the provincial measures controlled by the *seigneurs* since the summer of 1790, to establish 'a perfectly exact model of the different elementary weights and measures that are in use there'.[40] But many of these *seigneurs* were now in hiding and the old bronze standards they had maintained were no longer available locally, having been lost or destroyed, and there was nothing with which to verify their validity. While the new provisional standards had been distributed during the autumn of 1793, there is evidence that the old customary standards were still being fabricated in 1795, and that many municipalities were not abiding by the law: 1,000 posters were displayed in Paris to remind citizens of its provisions.[41]

The arrival of the provisional standards in the regions, accompanied by a pamphlet designed to instruct citizens on how to use the new weights and measures, and which explained arithmetical operations with decimal points, did little to ease confusion. The general public was largely illiterate and they required more practical help. It was for Legendre and his colleagues to ensure that they were instructed properly, and he saw to it that the metre standard was placed on public buildings: an example survives on the front façade of the Ministère de la Justice in Place Vendôme, Paris (fig. 9). Instead of numerical tables of comparison, graphic scales were used to estimate the old standards in relation to the new. Groups of citizens had the mysteries of its Greek prefixes and subdivisions – of *hecto*, *centi* and *kilo* – explained to them verbally. Lagrange and Laplace lectured to students at the École Normale about the workings and benefits of the system, so that they could spread the message with

9   Eighteenth-century metre standard on the front façade of the *Ministère de la Justice* in Place Vendôme, Paris. Photo by author

authority on returning to their *départements*. Eventually, a law was passed on 7 April 1795 that formally decreed the adoption of the *Républicaines* metric system in France, and officially at least the measures of the *ancien régime* were superseded. Even educated citizens, however, found the new system difficult to fathom. There was a complaint that while a tailor was familiar with 'half a quarter of the ell', trained accountants did not appreciate that 'half a quarter equals 0.125'.[42]

When Laplace presented the definitive length of the metre to the Directory on behalf of the surviving members of the Office of Weights and Measures on 22 June 1799, he spoke of the relevance of the French Revolution to the outcome:

> At all times men have been conscious of part of the advantages that the uniformity of weights and measures would have. But from one country to the next, and even in the interior of each country, custom and prejudices were in opposition to any agreement, to any reform in this matter [. . .]. A great event, a powerful political impetus, was needed to overcome popular reluctance.[43]

In October 1799 the Literature and Fine Arts Class of the National Institute was asked to compose an inscription suitable for a medal to commemorate the uniformity of weights and measures. Members contrived a motto on the republican theme 'À tous les temps, à tous les peuples' ('For all times, for all

10 Metric medal designed in 1799 and struck in 1837 to commemorate the uniformity of weights and measures: 'À tous les temps, à tous les peuples'

people'), a classical female figure grasping a metre rod in her right hand and a weight in her left, standing on a plinth calibrated by 5 centimetres. The obverse carries the motto 'Unité des mesures', and a winged male figure is seen measuring the dimensions of the globe with a pair if dividers. A ribbon draped around him bears the significance of the earth's diameter in relation to the metre, stating: 'Dix millioneme [sic] du quart du meridien' ('One ten-millionth part of a quarter meridian') (fig. 10).[44]

The following year the new measures became obligatory throughout the Republic.[45] By then Napoleon Bonaparte (1769–1821) was in the ascendancy. This charismatic leader, whose power was to be sanctioned by the overwhelming assent of the electorate, had initially risen to authority in a *coup d'état* of 18–19 Brumaire An VII (9–10 November 1799), establishing a new regime to replace the Directory called the Consulate. Under its constitution, Bonaparte, as first consul, had almost dictatorial powers. Within three years it was determined that he should be made consul for life, and two years later he became emperor.

Napoleonic Compromise

The Revolutionaries had attempted to replace the mystical and religious body of the king with enduring, rational and practical models representing the dignified public body of all people. Their ambition was thwarted with the installation of Napoleon as emperor.[46] His body effectively replaced the king's, and it came to symbolise the new public codes and institutions that were established during his reign, substitutes for the dismantled institutions of the *ancien régime*.

Reformed French civil law became known as the *Code Napoléon*. This official designation was applied to the reforms of 1807, though they had already been enacted in March 1804 as the *Code Civil des Français*. They date back to an initial draft for reform completed in 1793 at the outbreak of the Revolution, to resolve the extreme diversity in the laws then in force in different parts of France. But the National Convention had rejected them, and the task of preparing another draft was finally entrusted in July 1800 by the Consulate to a commission consisting of the most eminent jurists of France. Properly, the *Code Civil des Français* applies to the entire body of French law, and comprises five codes relating to civil, commercial and criminal law. These were to guarantee the rights and liberties won in the Revolution, and included equality before the law and freedom of religion.

The reform of weights and measures proved more difficult to install. Even after the legislation of 1799 that had empowered the metric system, there were still those who wished it would fail, and it is suggested that Napoleon was prominent among them. Nicholas François, Count Mollien (1758–1850) reported in his memoirs that the emperor was opposed to all metrological innovations, although there is only anecdotal support for his claim. During his military campaign in Russia in 1812, Napoleon famously described the bridge crossing the Berezina (just east of Minsk) as 40 *toises* wide and 300 *toises* long.[47] In testimony to a Select Committee of the British House of Commons in 1862, Michel Chevalier claimed that Napoleon had 'disliked the metrical system'.[48] He related that the son of Laplace had told him the story of how Napoleon's gifted 'Iron Marshal', Marshal Davout

> had the idea of setting up a bridge on the Elba [*sic*. The River Elbe west of Berlin], and the Emperor asked him what would be the length of the bridge. His answer was in metres. The Emperor said, 'What is that? What are metres?' [. . .] 'Speak' said the Emperor, 'in *toises*'.

Even today, anti-metric commentators frequently 'quote' Napoleon's opinion (without citing the source) that scientists went too far when standardising weights and measures:

> they adapted them to the decimal system, on the basis of the metre as a unit; they suppressed all complicated numbers. Nothing is more contrary to the organisation of the mind, of the memory, and of the imagination. [. . .] The new system of weights and measures will be a stumbling block and the source of difficulties for several generations [. . .] it's just tormenting the people with trivia![49]

Napoleon was certainly distant from France when legislation empowering the metric system was being enacted. His army had invaded Egypt in the spring of 1798 and within a few months had battled its way as far as Giza, where he established his headquarters in July. The great British naval victory over the French at the Battle of the Nile in August, orchestrated by Admiral Nelson, meant that Napoleon's Egyptian campaign was brief. Napoleon's more enduring triumph was the *Description de l'Égypte* (Paris, 1809–1828), a record crafted by a large team of 165 surveyor-engineers and artists that he had taken with him to provide an accurate inventory of the arts, sciences and culture of the Egypt he was intent on conquering. Gaspard Monge, the mathematician, surveyor and academician who had earlier advised on the metric system, was prominent among them. He was one of Napoleon's most senior civilian advisers in Egypt, and he was there at the personal request of Napoleon, who valued his experience and wisdom. Monge founded for

Napoleon the Institute of Egypt in Cairo in the palace of Qasim Bey, and the vast task of accumulating facts and figures began. Four groups concerned with Mathematics, Physics, Political Economy and Literature and the Arts led research, and Napoleon joined the mathematicians alongside Monge.

Monge was in his element. He combined his obvious administrative and political acumen with his passion for metrical reform and an energetic analysis of the Egyptian monuments. He impressed Napoleon with astounding facts: that the stones required to build the Great Pyramid at Giza could be used to construct a wall 1 metre thick and 3 metres high along the frontier of France.[50] Edmé Jomard, who wrote his account of surveying the pyramids for the *Description*, was particularly moved by the experience of surveying the Great Pyramid:

> When you almost touch the foot of the Great Pyramid, you are seized by a powerful and vivid emotion – tempered by a sort of fatiguing stupor. [. . .] The effect is in the grandeur and the simplicity of the forms, and in the contrast and disproportion that exists between the stature of man and the immensity of the work which is derived from his hand. The eye is not able to seize it [and] the mind has difficulty to encompass it.[51]

It took nineteen years to complete the publication of the *Description*. The published results were impressive even by the standards of the day: it comprised 13 volumes of text and 11 folio volumes of plates (fig. 11). As well as the pyramids, precise surveys were made of ancient Egyptian temple remains and were presented in the *Description* in engraved plans, sections, elevations and perspectives that represented the monuments to a consistent scale. Two linear scales were used in the architectural plates, which are set out in plan, section and elevation. Those at the bottom left were the traditional measures of *pouce*, *pied* and *toise*, and at the bottom right was the metric scale.[52]

Whatever his private misgivings, Napoleon supported metrical reform publicly. Soon after he became emperor, his Minister of the Interior announced to the Prefects on 7 February 1805:

11 View of the Second Pyramid, Giza. *Description de l'Égypte*, Antiquités: vol. v, plate 10, 'Pyramides de Memphis', Paris 1819

His Imperial Majesty has instructed me to inform you, gentlemen, that it is most definitely his unalterable wish to maintain the new system of weights and measures in its entirety, and to accelerate its extension through the empire.[53]

A similar statement was issued the following year, prompted by widespread resistance to the new system. The Republican calendar was abandoned in 1806, and the metric *Républicaines* might well have been abandoned with it. Laplace, however, was a canny operator. He wrote to Napoleon on 7 May 1811, setting out the advantages of the decimal system it embodied, while conceding that some modifications would be worthwhile. He also suggested – contrary to the central Republican principles of neutrality and universality that had marked the birth of the new measures – that the system should be renamed after the emperor, as *Mesures Napoléones*.[54]

The special pleading of Laplace, and other influential representations, convinced Napoleon to remain supportive of the fledgling metric system. But compromise was necessary, and on

12 February 1812 the emperor decreed that for everyday retail transactions the names in the old system could be retained to describe the quantities in the new (wholesalers had to use the new system). This was necessary because traders and their customers continued to refer to weights and measures using the nomenclature to which they were accustomed: the old *toise* was everywhere equivalent to 6 feet, the *pied* to 12 *pouces*, the *aune* divided into halves and thirds. Also, it was accepted that the old divisions of units into quarters, eighths and so on could be used instead of the decimal system, which remained poorly understood, despite the educational efforts of the Ministry of the Interior. With the Napoleonic compromise, one-third of a metre would be called a foot (*pied*); the bushel (*boisseau*) was accepted as equivalent to an eighth of the hectoliter; and similar equivalents were found for the other main quantities. This parity was possible because the customary Parisian measures closely approximated those of the metric – an eighth of the hectolitre being only $^4/_{100}$th smaller than the Parisian bushel – and because the measures of Paris were widely known throughout France.

The Republican metric system next faced the critical scrutiny of the Bourbon monarch Louis XVIII, who replaced Napoleon during his first fall from grace in 1814 and then for the decade between 1815 and 1824. Of course, the new king had a natural aversion to the metric system because it had been promoted by the Revolution. Yet, he was successfully persuaded by his ministers to state his support for the uniformity sought 'by your royal predecessors', as well as to maintain the Napoleonic compromise. Official support for the metric system was declared on 4 July 1837, and again on 1 January 1840 during the July Monarchy.[55]

Of all the major reforms instigated during the Revolution, only the new metric system and the reform of education survived. As president of the Legislative Assembly, Condorcet had been a prime mover of both. Regardless of the regime governing France, the desire to create a rational and uniform system outweighed opposition to it. It would, of course, have been easier to make the Parisian measures the national, Republican standard, but

Condorcet's and Talleyrand's insistence that there must be a universal system of weights and measures, divorced from the customs of the past and much of national chauvinism, meant that the metric system remained independent of the ideological changes of successive governments. It provided the French people with the uniformity and equality they demanded, but at the cost of relinquishing the familiar anthropomorphic vestiges of a system that most of the population understood.

Architecture and the Rejection of Body Measures

The reforms to education had a marked and lasting effect on the training of architects and engineers, and therefore on their conception of buildings and structures. Buildings had been designed using a range of body-related measures since antiquity. With the appointment of Jean-Nicolas-Louis Durand (1760–1834) as professor of architecture at the new École Polytechnique in 1795, architectural education became decidedly anti-body, and the young designers in his charge adopted metric measures without reservation. Durand's teaching epitomised the rationalised thinking of the late Enlightenment, and he absorbed and represented the innovative architectural thought of his teachers, of Blondel and Boullée in particular.[56]

In the pre-Revolutionary era, Jacques-François Blondel (1705–1774) had founded, in 1747, a school of architecture independent of the older Royal Academy of Architecture (Académie royale d'architecture), where architecture was taught somewhat haphazardly. The new school was to have an extensive and carefully organised curriculum, which had not been readily available to apprentice architects. Blondel's school also taught a broader range of architectural theory and technique, which gave its students the confidence to design buildings in their entirety. In tune with the science of the time, Blondel placed a new emphasis on rational analysis and the understanding of cultural context, which was intended to foster progressive and responsible change without promoting a particular style of architecture. His approach was favoured by engineers at the National School of

Bridges and Roads (École des Ponts et Chaussées), which sent
its students to Blondel to receive an architectural context for
their education. He proved to be so successful an educator that
the Royal Academy of Architecture was placed under his direction in 1762.

Among the reforms that Blondel instituted was the introduction in 1763 of a monthly *prix d'émulation*, a design competition
sponsored by the Academy and intended to strengthen students'
design and draughting skills. Each design was to be presented
through related plans, sections and elevations so that it could be
rationalised – like an industrial object for manufacture – in its
entirety.[57] One of his best-known students was the precociously
talented architect, teacher and theorist Étienne-Louis Boullée
(1728–1799). He had joined Blondel's classes at the insistence of
his father, who rejected Étienne's wish to become a full-time
painter, an art in which he would probably have been equally
successful. Boullée proved to be a visionary architect, and he
considered three of his theoretical designs to be his most important contribution to the architectural discourse of the time –
ideal projects for public buildings, a church, cemetery and
cenotaph. His approach is characterised by the quality of his
draughtsmanship and the vast scale of his conceptions, which
dwarf the activities of the mortals they enclose. It was not
function and practicality that interested Boullée, but exploration
and pursuit of the Sublime experience: the awesome effect of
vast scale and space on the diminutive human body and mind.

It was the British theorist Edmund Burke (1729–1797) who
wrote the definitive enquiry into the qualities of the Sublime as
an aesthetic experience, in *A Philosophical Enquiry into the Origins
of Our Ideas of the Sublime and Beautiful* (London, 1757; French
translation, 1765). Burke defined the source of the Sublime as
anything that excites 'ideas of pain and danger, that is [. . .] in
any sort terrible [. . .]; that is, it is productive of the strongest
emotion which the mind is capable of feeling'.[58] The Sublime is
concerned with self-transcendence, a state of mind that leaves
behind the body and its earthly bonds. The enormity of the
cosmos in relation to man was certainly a primary source of

inspiration for Boullée. He worked in his studio with the portraits of two scientific divinities looking down on his mortal labours, Copernicus and Newton, the principal authors of modern celestial order. He dedicated the cenotaph to Newton (1784) to honour and immortalise the great scientist's name and 'divine' intelligence, and to celebrate the immensity of nature and the cosmic order he had discovered. Inspired by Newton's unique blend of science and theology, Boullée designed the cenotaph as a simulacrum of earthly scale and power, and as a demonstration that the sublime immensity of space could be captured – by an architect with his vision – on earth. In an unpublished treatise on architecture (*Architecture, essai sur l'art*) Boullée addressed his hero:

> Sublime mind! Prodigious and profound genius! Divine being! Newton! Deign to accept the homage of my feeble talents! Ah! If I dare to make it public, it is because I am persuaded that I have surpassed myself in the project which I shall discuss [. . .] By using your divine system, Newton, to create the sepulchral lamp that lights thy tomb, it seems that I have made myself sublime.[59]

Boullée's cenotaph for Newton was designed to represent in microcosm the universe whose single underlying and unifying law, gravity, Newton had discovered. It was shaped as a vast spherical cavity, partly embedded in the ground (fig. 12). The upper masonry of its spherical skin was to be pierced by relatively small openings, which, when lit by the sun and viewed from within, would resemble the heavenly firmament. As Boullée wrote, 'I wanted to give Newton that immortal resting place, the Heavens.'[60] It was an extraordinarily idealised rendering of the heavens in an age seeking truth through scientific exactitude. Boullée's heaven celebrated perfect geometry and the static. Had it been built, Newton's cenotaph would have resembled the ancient classical perception of the earth before it had been deformed through rotation:[61] the earth as pure idea, rather than a simulacrum of astronomical and mathematical reality. The fact that the great scale of the sphere dwarfs humankind serves to

12   Section through Boullée's cenotaph for Newton at night

reinforce the power of nature, the emptiness of space and the
authority of the 'Supreme Being'. Newton had described this
incorporeal omnipresence in the *Principia* as lacking 'any body
and corporeal shape, and so he cannot be seen, or heard, or
touched',[62] a phenomenon that Burke relates back to the 'noble
effect' of 'rotund' buildings through his concept of the 'artificial
infinite'.[63]

The potential of Newtonian limitless space, a universe of
reasoned order permeated by the essence of the Supreme Being,
excited a community that embraced scientists and architects
alike. In 1785, the year after Boullée completed his design, the
Royal Academy of Architecture sponsored a *prix d'émulation* on
the same theme, a cenotaph to Newton that would be characterised by an 'ingenious and analogous allegory'. A cenotaph to
Newton was also the subject of a *prix d'émulation* held at the
Academy in 1800, when it was stipulated that the design should
include 'a hollow sphere in the middle of which will be a globe
representing the sun and the urn which would contain Newton's
ashes'.[64]

Newton also inspired a new kind of science-based religion, the Religion of Newton. Henri de Saint-Simon promoted this in 1802 based on Newton's science and broader speculations about religion: the Religion of Newton would be run by scientist-priests.[65] Had Boullée's design been built, the cenotaph may well have provided the centrepiece of this new worldwide religion, a community of humankind governed by reason in which the universal is higher than the particular. There was a determined ambition within the pan-European culture of the day to escape what was perceived as a body-centred selfishness, a focus that was seen to divide rather than reconcile societies.[66]

The poetic symbolism of Boullée's architectural approach contrasts starkly with his most influential architectural pupil, Jean-Nicolas-Louis Durand (1760–1834), who had also studied under Blondel at the Royal Academy of Architecture. Durand rose rapidly to prominence, and was appointed professor of the newly established École Polytechnique in Paris aged 35. This was a new kind of teaching institution, whose immediate forerunners – the School of Military Engineering (École du Génie) and the National School of Bridges and Roads – had been founded fifty years earlier. It was conceived to meet the technological demands of post-Revolutionary France. The future of humanity, it was argued, was in the hands of those who could apply science, and to this end the curriculum of the École Polytechnique was organised to produce scientists and technicians with specialised skills. Students were provided with a solid general mathematical and scientific foundation before specialising in a particular discipline and entering public service. The architects produced by this system were well versed in mathematical reasoning, but they were given little encouragement to study art and the humanities, since the arts cannot be reduced to the formulaic certainties of mathematics. In this regime, the technology of building was considered superior to the art of architecture, the main worth of which was ornament and decoration – or so it was reasoned – and architecture came to be regarded as a mere sub-discipline of civil engineering. This was the direct consequence of Napoleon's appreciation of the certitudes of mathematics and

his firm belief that architecture was a luxury of marginal worth
to an expanding empire: he put his trust in mathematicians and
engineers.[67]

Durand was completely in tune with the times. As professor
of architecture at the École Polytechnique he taught that efficiency and economy of operations were fundamental to successful architectural design and practice. By composing designs
on a grid of squares, or modules, each representing a scaled
dimension, the main architectural elements could be located in
an orderly fashion: columns at the intersections of the grid,
walls on its axes and openings at the centres of modules. For a
building's main spaces, simple, pure geometries were preferred,
and sections and elevations were derived directly from a well-
organised plan. Architectural design was more akin to organis-
ing an efficient military campaign than being a physical
representation of human aspirations and understanding – which
is how it had been regarded before the Enlightenment. Method
was everything.[68] Durand's approach was based on the miscon-
ception that man does not inhabit a qualitative place, but universal geometrical space.[69] The objectivity of infinite Cartesian
geometry was promoted over traditional, subjective notions as to
what constituted inhabitable space. Expanding the rational mind
took precedence over satisfying the sensual desires of the body.

Durand's approach proved influential internationally. His
Recueil et parallèle des édifices de tout genre (Paris, 1800/1) was the
first scientific survey of the principal architectural monuments
constructed since classical times (Egyptian and Roman) and
includes Italian and French examples up to the late eighteenth
century. The buildings are arranged systematically, drawn to a
common scale and grouped by building type. In so doing the
buildings were isolated from any cultural and physical context,
with building types – such as churches – arranged on the same
sheet of paper for ease of comparison. With the emphasis on scientific method, Durand's idea was that the *Recueil* would make
it possible to derive fixed architectural principles separately from
historical style and urban context. This would encourage architects to arrive at rational planimetric solutions for different types

of building form. It was of no interest to Durand that the differences in the forms of these buildings were a result of specific rituals or cultural traditions peculiar to a place, region or nation; or that the designs were responses to the constraints imposed by physical context, such as the proximity of adjacent buildings or street layouts. The examples he chose were represented as small-scale cartoons of buildings, simplified to elemental expressions (plans, section and elevation) to provide universal design lessons for architects everywhere. Of course, the measuring scale that Durand used for this physical comparison was the metric system.

Delambre, following the acclaim of his (and Méchain's) terrestrial survey, edited and published the first history of science in Paris in 1810, the *Rapport historique sur les progrès des sciences mathématiques depuis 1789*.[70] Its method resembles Durand's earlier *Recueil*: knowledge is divided linearly, and according to separate scientific disciplines, in order to demonstrate how scientific progress had benefited humankind. Much as Durand presented only the finest examples of historic architecture, Delambre excluded the failures of science. His rhetoric supported the notion that the application of science would determine the future of humanity, and that scientists were the new aristocrats. The École Polytechnique was the elite institution that educated the nation's new technical specialists in the direction in which these texts were pointing so positively.

Durand followed the success of the *Recueil* with a précis of a lecture series he had delivered on architecture at the École Polytechnique, the *Précis des leçons d'architecture données à l'école polytechnique* (1802–5) (fig. 13). This presented his far-reaching proposals for the teaching of architecture, which remained influential through several editions in France and abroad. Fundamentally, he questioned the rationale of the Vitruvian tradition, particularly the analogy of body to building, and he used reason to unpick several millennia of belief. In the introduction to volume 1 of the *Précis* Durand asks, rhetorically, whether Vitruvius's ideal proportions are true imitations of the human body. He begins with Vitruvius's description of the Doric order:

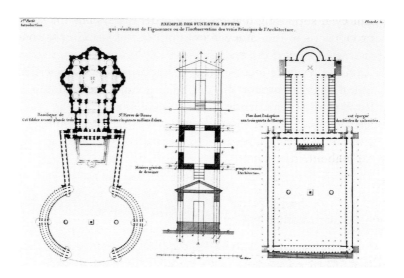

13   Jean-Nicholas-Louis Durand: *Précis*, vol. i, plate 2; 'Example of the baleful results of ignoring or of not observing the true principles of architecture'. His preference was for the economical plan on the right, compared to the extravagance of St Peter's Basilica, Rome, on the left. At the centre the format for drawing architecture readily and accurately is set out. The metric scale used to measure these buildings is located at the centre and bottom of the plate

the Greeks, it is said, defined [the Doric] by the proportion of six diameters, because a man's foot is one-sixth of his height. First of all, a man's foot is not one-sixth but one-eighth of his height. What is more, in all Greek buildings, the proportions of Doric columns are endlessly varied; and, within this infinite variety, the exact proportion of six to one is not found in a single case. [. . .] The same variety is observed in the proportions of the other orders, supposedly imitated from the body of a woman and from that of a girl. It is therefore untrue that the human body served as a model for the orders.[71]

The question having been posed, Durand then delivers the hammer blow against any notion that the human analogy is appropriate to architecture:

But even supposing that the same order always has the same proportions in the same circumstances; that the Greeks consistently followed the system attributed to them; and that the length of a man's foot is one-sixth of his height: does it then follow that the proportions of the orders are an imitation of those of the human body? What comparison is there between a man's body which varies in width at different heights, and [the column shaft] a kind of cylinder with a constant diameter throughout?[72]

By volume II of the *Précis*, Durand had clarified his rational response to these ancient myths. Analogy and imitation are appropriate to other arts but not architecture,

For, if any pleasure is to result from imitation, the object imitated must be an object of nature, beyond which we know nothing, and beyond which, in consequence, nothing can interest us. The imitation of the object must, furthermore, be perfect [. . .] the human body, bearing no formal analogy to any architectural body, cannot be imitated in its proportions.[73]

The separation of the human body from architectural discourse that Durand initiated was as decisive as the separation of the king's body from the authority of the State. Attempts were made to reconnect them, but, for the most part, architectural expression was now the servant of rationality and science. Architecture was to become global, even universal in outlook, and – in a profound sense – modern architecture was born.

Before the political and social torment of the Revolution, the Montgolfier brothers were making hesitant voyages into the limitless potential of space on aerial globes – balloons. The balloonists, or *aérostats*, would be the first to experience the earth separated from the ground, between the solidity of the expansive terrestrial globe and the immensity of the sky and universe beyond. This was the most sublime experience possible. Uncoupled from its earthly chains, the human body was free to detach itself from the earth, and to release mind and imagination into infinite space.[74] Two men, Pilâtre de Rozier and the Marquis d'Arlandes, famously made the first untethered flight in a Mont-

14 Pilâtre de
Rozier and the
Marquis d'Arlandes
making the first
flight in a
Montgolfier balloon
on 21 November
1783

golfier balloon on 21 November 1783 (fig. 14). Sébastien Mercier
reported on their ascent:

> On this day, before the eyes of an enormous gathering, two
> men rose in the air. So great was the crowd that the Tuileries
> Gardens were as full as they could hold; there were men
> climbing over the railings; the gates were forced. This swarm
> of people was in itself an incomparable sight, so varied was it,
> so vast and so changing. Two hundred thousand men, lifting
> their hands in wonder, admiring, glad, astonished; some in
> tears for fear the intrepid physicists should come to harm,
> some on their knees overcome with emotion, but all following
> the aeronauts in spirit, while these latter, unmoved, saluted,
> dipping their flags above our heads. What with the novelty, the
> dignity of the experiment, the unclouded sky, welcoming as it

were the travellers to his own element, the attitude of the two men sailing into the blue, while below their fellow-citizens prayed and feared for their safety, and lastly the balloon itself, superb in the sunlight, whirling aloft like a planet or the chariot of some weather-god – it was a moment which never can be repeated, the most astounding achievement the science of physics has yet given to the world.[75]

The geometry of the sphere and the enormity of that first balloon flight are symbolised equally in the great globe that Boullée designed as Newton's cenotaph. This balloon flight provided the most powerful demonstration yet of the prestige of science, and its ability to impress the general populace. The sky, the ancient seat of the gods, formerly a sacred place to which only the very privileged could ascend, was yielding to scientists, the new mediators between the mysteries of the universe and human experience on earth.[76] The balloon ascent was a promise that man would one day leave the earth behind, and reach for the moon. – to journey into the immeasurable vastness of outer space.

5. Anglo-Saxon Resistance

The French have [. . .] completely pulled down to the ground their monarchy, their church, their nobility, their law, their revenue, their army, their navy, their commerce, their arts and their manufactures. [. . .] The age of chivalry is gone, that of sophisters, economists and calculators has succeeded.[1]

Suspicion fuelled by separate trade interests, conflicting political ambition and war meant that Britain and America existed and conducted their national affairs independently of France. In London, the initial reaction of liberals to revolution in France had been positive. The Whig leader, Charles James Fox, acknowledged the storming of the Bastille as 'much the greatest event that has ever happened in the world'. His contemporary, the polymath Erasmus Darwin, proclaimed that it marked 'the dawn of universal liberty'.[2] Edmund Burke, who was also well known for his liberal views at the time, had publicly supported the cause of the American rebels during the 1770s, and in his *Reflections on the Revolution in France* (1790)[3] he observed that the French Revolution was 'the most astonishing that has hitherto happened in the world'.[4] Burke, however, had grave misgivings about the effects of reducing politics to a science (as his comments quoted above indicate), and he was appalled at the rapid destruction of France's long-established cultural institutions.

By 1792 the official British governmental line was hardening against the historic events in France. Thomas Paine was an important catalyst for this volte-face. There was evidence that his *Rights of Man* (1791–2) was having an impact on working people – there were some 200,000 copies of it in circulation by

1793 - and the prime minister, William Pitt, put a halt to all future 'seditious writings' in a proclamation issued in May 1792.[5] Paine fled England for France and eventually America, and in his absence the mob hanged an effigy of him. The British establishment was unsettled still further when Paine's *Age of Reason* (1794–6) was published. He advocated that the Church – all Churches and their creeds – should be abandoned by the masses, that the individual should be asserted. His dictum was: 'My mind is my own church.' Similarly, nationality would lose its relevance: 'My country is the world.'[6] With increasing anxiety about a popular uprising at home, official sympathy for the ideals of the French Revolution soon evaporated: attitudes and physical defences were readied to resist the spread of the 'contagion', and this proved to have been a sensible precaution when France finally declared war on Britain.

With defensive barriers in place, there were clear ideological and practical reasons why the British were unable to engage in the French-led discussions on the development of an international system of weights and measures. However, it may seem curious that the government of the United States also chose to resist the 'republican' metric system. Their reaction would have perplexed America's earlier revolutionary leaders. In his first message to the first Congress of 1789, President George Washington had recommended: 'Uniformity in the currency, weights and measures of the United States is an object of great importance, and will, I am persuaded, be duly attended to.'[7] The decree issued by the French National Assembly on 8 May 1790, that the Academy must devise a new system of weights and measures,[8] added further impetus to a review in America.

As newly appointed US Secretary of State, Thomas Jefferson (1743–1826) was formally requested by the House of Representatives to prepare a report on this matter. He was well suited to his task. He was both a lawyer and a politician, and was not afraid of reform. During the Second Continental Congress in Philadelphia (1775–81), Jefferson had chaired a five-man committee whose remit was to draft the united 'Declaration' that led to Independence from Britain.[9] In the form in which it was

enacted on 4 July 1776 it strongly reflected Jefferson's own thinking – his deeply felt belief in human equality, the natural rights
of man, the sovereignty of the people and the right to revolution. He was a hugely able polymath, and measure was of
primary interest to him, as a practical farmer, architect and engineer. He had also learnt surveying and mapping from his father,
Peter Jefferson, who had surveyed the southern colonies, producing the first accurate map of that region in 1751. In 1784
Thomas Jefferson, with Hugh Williamson, presented to Congress a proposal that the United States should be properly surveyed. They proposed that the newly mapped nation should be
subdivided into new townships, 6 miles square in plan, and the
federal lands divided into fourteen new states, each with a new
name.[10]

Jefferson on Measure

Jefferson's 'Plan for Establishing Uniformity in the Coinage,
Weights, and Measures of the United States' took him seven
months to write; it was submitted on Independence Day in 1790,
and was communicated to the House nine days later, on 13 July.
Its formulation was delayed by his travelling – between his home
in Monticello, Virginia, and the nation's capital of the time, New
York, where Congress was in session – and:

> A desire to lessen the number of its imperfections induced me
> to withhold it awhile, till, on the 15th of June, came to my
> hands, from Paris, a printed copy of a proposition made by
> the Bishop of Autun [Talleyrand], to the National Assembly
> of France, on the subject of weights and measures; and three
> days afterwards I received [. . .] the speech of Sir John Riggs
> Miller, of April 13th, 1790 in the British House of Commons,
> on the same subject.[11]

Thomas Jefferson had excellent contacts in Europe, and especially in France. Five years earlier, in 1785, he had relieved
Benjamin Franklin as America's Minister to the Court of France,
and he came to regard that nation as his second home.[12] He

admired France's cultured and glorious past, and in the wake of the Revolution Jefferson was among those who believed that the country had an equally promising future. As Jefferson opined: 'the American Revolution seems first to have awakened the thinking part of the French nation in general from the sleep of despotism in which they were sunk'.[13] Jefferson was talking with the benefit of his own direct experience of the French people, and as a witness of the immediate aftermath of the Revolution in France, and – not least – his own crucial role in the American Revolution. He was profoundly sympathetic towards the intellectual elite of France, and he invited the chief political figures in the new Constitution to his Parisian quarters, where he hosted debates, which he described as 'truly worthy of being placed in parallel with the finest dialogues of antiquity, as handed to us by Xenophon, by Plato and Cicero'.[14]

Jefferson was therefore in a strong position to judge the separate French and British proposals for the reform of weights and measures that were emerging during these years. His command of science enabled him to evaluate the principles underpinning the proposed system with a rational detachment, free of the complex commercial and political imperatives that weighed on French and British relations. Indeed, it was the lack of true rationality at the root of the metric system that troubled him from the outset of his enquiry, as his opening address to the American House of Representatives makes clear:

> To obtain uniformity in measures, weights, and coins, it is necessary to find some measure of invariable length, with which, as a standard, they may be compared.
>
> There exists not in nature, as far as has been hitherto observed, a single subject or species of subject, accessible to man, which presents one constant and uniform dimension.
>
> The globe of the earth itself, indeed, might be considered as invariable in all its dimensions, and that its circumference would furnish an invariable measure; but not one of its circles, great or small, is accessible to admeasurement through all its parts, and the various trials to measure definite portions of

them, have been of such various result as to show there is no
dependence on that operation for certainty.[15]

Jefferson considered the French system unworkable. If neither
nature nor the physicality of the earth could provide practical
constants, Jefferson favoured the alternative 'invariable length'
that the pendulum generated. What appealed to him was that its
length was derived from the motion of the earth, as well as the
calculation of a solar day, which, allowing for inequalities, has 'a
mean interval, or day' that divides 'into 86,400 equal parts' or
'seconds of mean time'. Since a pendulum can be adjusted to
oscillate every second, it becomes itself 'a measure of determi-
nate length, to which all others may be referred as to a standard'.[16] As he admitted, however, 'even a pendulum is not
without its uncertainties'. He was aware that the constancy of
the pendulum varied according to ambient temperature and its
position relative to the earth's poles and sea level. It also varied
according to its design, which he set out to refine. The
traditional pendulum had a rod and bob, the centre of the bob
being difficult to determine with precision. Jefferson preferred a
cylindrical pendulum made of a single iron rod, 'the least expan-
sible of the metals', and he had a prototype made by a 'Mr Leslie,
an ingenious artist of Philadelphia'.

Jefferson's initial preference was for the seconds pendulum to
be measured at the latitude of 38°N, the median latitude of the
United States. The 38th parallel also runs through southern
Spain, Sicily, Greece and Turkey, but not France and England.[17]
It was apparently Condorcet who succeeded in persuading
Jefferson that 45°N, which marks the more northern limits of the
United States would have greater international appeal: he refers
to his negotiations with Jefferson on this subject in a report dated
11 November 1790.[18] In agreement, Jefferson stated his hope that
the 45th parallel might 'become a line of union with the rest of
the world', and that the 'rest of the world' would agree with.
Neither the 38th nor the 45th parallel runs through England.

The value that Jefferson reported for the swing of a pendulum
in one second of mean time, at 45°N and at sea level and in a

constant temperature, 'according to Sir Isaac Newton's computation, must be of 39.14912 inches English measure', which is just short of the modern standard metre of 39.37 inches. Jefferson may have been relying on tables supplied by the French *Encyclopédie méthodique*, in which Newton's tables are recorded in Parisian feet,[19] which he converted back to English feet. It is possible that Newton's *Principia* was his starting point, although, as Voltaire once wrote, Newton was hardly read, even in his native country, 'because one must be very learned to understand him'.[20]

By comparison, Jefferson defined the length of the seconds rod (rather than with a bob) 'in latitude 45°, in the level of the ocean, and in a cellar, or other place, the temperature of which does not vary through the year, [where it] shall perform its vibrations in uniform and equal arcs, in one second of mean time', as 'exactly, 58.72368 inches' (1.4916 metres) – a seconds pendulum rod was therefore just under 5 foot long, while the bob version was just over 3 foot. He recommended that the seconds rod length should be adopted as standard in America, because it had 'an accidental but very precious advantage over the pendulum in this country [. . .] for the difference between the common foot, and those so to be deduced, would be three times greater in the case of the pendulum than in that of the rod' of almost 5 foot.[21] He made two alternative proposals. The first would be to render uniform the system already in practical use in America, so that the foot could be calibrated by this new scientific and universal standard. Alternatively, the entire system could be reformed, so that weights and measures as well as coinage could be decimalised. America had experimented successfully with decimal coinage since 1786, and in his report Jefferson advocated banishing 'the discordant pounds, shillings, pence, and farthings of the different States, and to establish in their stead the new denominations'.[22] He then suggested how measures and weights could be arranged in a decimal ratio using the oscillating seconds rod. The new American foot would be defined as one-fifth of the seconds rod and at 11.74474 inches (298 mm) would be only slightly shorter than the English foot; coincidentally, this is also

close to the length of the ancient Roman foot (*pes*), usually aver-
aged at about 296 millimetres. It would be subdivided by 10
inches, 100 lines, 1,000 lines; 10 feet would make a decad, 10
decads a rood, 10 roods a furlong, and 10 furlongs or 1,000 feet
a mile. According to Jefferson, this would be about $1^6/_7$th of an
English mile, yet close to the 'Scotch and Irish mile, and $^1/_2$ the
German mile'.[23]

If Jefferson's recommendations had been adopted wholesale,
America would have been left with a system independent of both
England and France. Jefferson therefore recommended cautious
steps towards reform: that a series of tables be established comparing his proposed system with the customary system of
America, which should then be compared with tables and measures provided by other leading nations. He urged diplomacy, and
that letters 'of a more special character' should be sent 'to the
Institute of France, and the Royal Society of England':

> The magnificent work which France has executed in the
> admeasurement of so large a portion of the meridian, has a
> claim to great respect in our reference to it. [. . .] With
> England, our explanations will be much more delicate. They
> are the older country, the mother country, more advanced in
> the arts and sciences, possessing more wealth and leisure for
> their improvement, and animated by a pride more than laud-
> able. [. . .] The subject should therefore be opened to them
> with infinite tenderness and respect, and in some way which
> might give them due place in its agency. The parallel of 45°
> being within our latitude and not within theirs, the actual
> experiments under that would of course be assignable to us.
> But as a corrective, I would propose that they should ascer-
> tain the length of the pendulum vibrating seconds in the City
> of London, or at the observatory of Greenwich, which we
> should do the same in an equi-distant parallel to the south of
> 45°, suppose in 38° 29'. [. . .] As this is really a work of
> common and equal interest to England and the United States,
> perhaps it would be still more respectful to make our propo-
> sition to her Royal Society in the outset, and to agree with
> them on a partition of the work.[24]

In conclusion, Jefferson recommended in this report that the United States should either adopt a simplification of the English system (not British, because Scotland and Ireland had their own) or determine its own decimal system.

A Senate committee studied Jefferson's report, and in 1791 recommended that America should adopt the standards and units of length he had proposed. But no legislative action followed immediately – there was no urgent demand for reform by the populace or any of the President's executive departments. A major consideration was that the English system of weights and measures and its authority worldwide were too well established and respected for reform to gain sufficient support in America. Nor did the metric system present itself as a viable proposition. Relations between France and the Anglo-Saxon nations were poor. At the time of the international conference on the metric system in Paris in 1798–9, England was at war with France and America in a state of undeclared war; consequently, neither England nor America would join that crucial conference of nations, nor did France invite them. Suspicion of France's motives for reform festered in England and America throughout the Napoleonic period.[25]

Jefferson did not revisit this issue again until after he had retired from the US Presidency. In a letter of 10 November 1811 to a Dr Robert Patterson, whose Philosophical Society of America was once again considering 'the subject of a fixed standard of measures, weights and coins' and was soliciting his views, Jefferson reasserted his preference that an American standard should be derived from the seconds rod, rather than the seconds pendulum or the measurement of the earth's surface. In addition, he proposed abandoning the names of the customary units so that coinage, weights and measures would interrelate decimally. Thus, the new measures would derive from the length of the seconds rod – called the 'unit': its tenth would be the 'dime', its hundredth the 'cent', its thousandth the 'mill', 1,000 units a 'kiliad'.[26] Such a change would have unified measure and coinage, and simplified everyday arithmetic and the transactions of commerce and exchange in general. But no official sanction was forthcoming.

President James Madison (1809–17) revived the inquiry into reform and in 1817 gave Secretary of State John Quincy Adams the task of preparing another report. Adams sensibly contacted Thomas Jefferson – by then an old man – who provided him with two reasons why he was fundamentally opposed to the metric system: it was based neither on sound natural principles nor, as a product of French nationalist ambition, could it be a universal system. Jefferson restated his preference for a truly natural, invariable standard derived from the seconds pendulum rod. His reasoning made additional sense because the Royal Society had been exploring ways of regulating the English units of measure since 1816.[27] Adams took a different, less rational line than Jefferson. He had already come out strongly in support of the metric system in 1812, extolling in writing its virtues 'with the admiration of a poet and the fervour of a prophet'.[28] He considered the metric system to be 'the greatest invention of human ingenuity since that of printing', and that 'its universal establishment would be a universal blessing'.[29] While Adams was passionate about the qualities of the metric system in principle, however, he did not push for reform in the US. The task of implementing a new system would be so enormous that it was essential to have confidence that what was being replaced was markedly inferior to what was replacing it. Now, Adams was in agreement with Jefferson on the shortcomings of the metric: 'it is believed that the French system has not yet attained that perfection which would justify so extraordinary an effort of legislative power at this time'.[30] The metric system had yet to be implemented effectively in France, and if Britain was not prepared to adopt it there was no compulsion for America to do so either. Britain and America were closely tied culturally and – perhaps more compellingly – commercially: in 1831 more than 40 per cent of US trade was with Britain and less than 10 per cent with France.[31] In any case, as Adams stated, there was no reason why America should abandon a system that worked:

Of all the nations of European origin, ours is that which least requires any change in the system of their weights and measures. With the exception of [formerly French] Louisiana, the established system is, and always has been, throughout the Union, the same.[32]

The political and practical ramifications for America and England accepting a French-inspired system of measures would long continue to be insurmountable. Meanwhile, Congress adopted Adams's recommendation 'that no innovation upon existing weights and measures be attempted'.[33]

Mensural Tradition and the Seconds Pendulum

If the English system was to be retained, it was necessary to be able to calculate the lengths and weights of its standards with scientific precision. Jefferson mentioned that in 1742 members of the Royal Society in London had used some 'very curious instruments, prepared by the ingenious Mr Graham', which enabled the English measures to be calculated 'at a distance' using the pendulum and measuring rod.[34] Jefferson also refers to two Select Committees of the House of Commons that had been appointed in 1757 and 1758 'to inquire into the original standards of their weights and measures'. Their conclusions regarding the efficacy of the pendulum as a regulator of measure provided Jefferson with the stimulus for his own report. Clearly, the British had been early advocates of a mensural system based on the seconds pendulum.

The George Graham to whom Jefferson referred had made a brass yard for the Royal Society in 1742, which was subsequently kept at Somerset House. As a point of fact, Graham had procured the equipment for his experiments from a Jonathan Sisson, another expert craftsman, and was not their devisor as Jefferson states.[35] Graham's achievement was to refine the length of the yard against the seconds pendulum, making comparisons with ancient British standards retained at the Tower of London and the Exchequer. The yard at the Exchequer, which comprised a brass bar, octagonal in section and about half an inch in diameter, dated back to the reign of Henry VII (1485–1509; Graham

estimated that the yard dated *circa* 1490), and there was an
Elizabethan yard (and ell) dating from 1588. Graham's brass
yard was a flat stretch of brass 42 inches long by $1\frac{1}{2}$ inches wide,
and he sent this to Paris in late 1742 so that the French Royal
Academy of Sciences could inscribe half of one *toise* alongside
it. On its return to London the *toise* was verified as equal to the
measure of 38.355 English inches.[36]

In 1780 Sir George Shuckburgh Evelyn, a Fellow of the Royal
Society, made further experiments with a vibrating rod in his
search for 'an invariable and imperishable standard of weight
and measure'. This was something he considered 'in a philosophical view, highly desirable, and likely to become extremely
beneficial to the public'.[37] He was not referring to a universal
standard in the French mould, however, but – continuing
George Graham's experiments – the need to define scientifically
the length of the English yard (and associated weights): 'I see no
possible good in changing the quantities, the divisions or the
names of things of such constant recurrence in common life.
[. . .] I would call a yard a yard and a pound a pound.' He published his findings in the Royal Society's *Philosophical Transactions*.[38] Although his essay was published in 1798, Shuckburgh
Evelyn makes no mention of the prototype metric system soon
to become the legal standard in France.

Shuckburgh Evelyn describes how he extended the experiments by 'a very ingenious' Mr John Whitehurst, published in
1787 in a pamphlet entitled *An Attempt to obtain Measures of
Length, &c. from the Mensuration of Time, or the true Length of
Pendulums.* Whitehurst stated here that the length of the seconds
pendulum in London was 39.2 inches,[39] which although close to
the statutory yard of 36 inches, was not close enough in his
opinion to be a future standard in England. It would mean
altering the 'customary measures of England and consequently
create general confusion and inconveniency to the public'. On
Whitehurst's death, Shuckburgh Evelyn bought his scientific
apparatus in order 'to verify and complete his experiments',
which he supplemented with some fine equipment made by a
Mr Troughton.[40] Shuckburgh Evelyn records that he measured

the length of two pendulums vibrating respectively at 42 and 84 times a minute, 'in the latitude of London, 113 feet above the level of the sea, under a density of the atmosphere corresponding to 30 inches of the barometer, and 60° of the thermometer'. He defined the length as very close to 60 inches or 5 foot,[41] which – like Graham – he then compared with the standards already in use in Britain 'that have been in use for 2 or 300 years past'.[42]

British scientists continued to focus their attentions on the pendulum, even though the French had settled on a terrestrially based measure for the metric system. In 1814 a committee of the House of Commons considered the pendulum to be 'the best invariable standard of measure' with which to define Imperial Standards.[43] In an Act of Parliament passed in 1824 the length of the Imperial Standard Yard was established as the ratio of 360,000 to 391,393, of a pendulum beating seconds in a vacuum, at the latitude of London and at sea level.[44] The physical standard itself was lost in the fire that burned down the Palace of Westminster on 16 October 1834, and another committee was established to determine how best to recreate the units. There was further discussion and experimentation concerning the feasibility of defining the yard in terms of the length of a pendulum of specified period, but it was decided that the pendulum would not provide a reliable basis and in 1845 a material standard was produced.[45] While officialdom maintained the status quo, there were advocates for more radical reform who called for the adoption of the metric system irrespective of whether it was truly universal or French.

Acknowledging the Metre in Britain

The first public acknowledgement in Britain of the advantages of the metric system by a scientist of eminence came from north of the border, from the Scottish mathematician and geologist John Playfair (1748–1819). He had reviewed Méchain's and Delambre's *Base du système métrique décimal* in the *Edinburgh Review* in 1807, concluding:

The system adopted by the French, if not absolutely the best, is so very near it, that the difference is of no account [. . .]. The wisest measure, therefore, for the other nations of Europe, is certainly to adopt the metrical system of the French.[46]

Fifty years later Chambers, the Edinburgh-based publishing house, took up the cause. The entry on 'British Weights and Measures' in its encyclopedia, *Chambers's Information for the People*, states:

The French system is established on a principle much more simple and unerring than that in use in Britain – the former is of universal application, the latter can never be anything but local.[47]

There was no official support for Playfair's viewpoint in England, and while it was acknowledged by the British government that weights and measures needed regulating, they made it plain that any future move towards uniformity, simplification and decimalisation would necessarily be refinements of the weights and measures already in use. During the nineteenth century the introduction of an entirely new system was never countenanced – officially at least.[48] The metric and British Imperial systems would simply have to coexist.

In anticipation of this pragmatic reality, during the autumn of 1801 French scientists (including Legendre and Méchain) had made precise comparisons between the official metre length and a calibrated English brass rod lent to the Committee by a certain Pictet of Geneva. Troughton, the London-based craftsman mentioned by Shuckburgh Evelyn, had constructed it.[49] At the temperature of ice they found that the official metre rod of platinum and iron was equivalent to 39.38272 English inches.[50] The first recognition by the British government that the metric system existed at all came with a request in 1816 for a copy of the metre standard, which would enable an official comparison of the yard and metre to be made.[51]

A comparison of English measures in relation to metric units was published in 1827. In recognition that the English and

Americans were unlikely to abandon their customary measures, Professor Francoeur vetted it and presented his findings to Legendre in Paris.[52] Legendre was clearly of fundamental importance to the success of the metric system. While Condorcet and Talleyrand were its progenitors, he has a legitimate claim – for his constancy and endurance – to be acknowledged as its midwife. Their offspring was born imperfect, however, and lacked the formidable commercial and cultural support of the English-speaking world. In order to survive, it demanded constant revalidation and redefinition over the next two centuries.

British and American Accommodations During the Nineteenth Century

While there was good sense in Jefferson's reasoning – that the two dominant English-speaking nations should maintain the standards they shared into the future – the British and American measures drifted apart in stages during the nineteenth century. For although each former British colony that now constitutes the United States enacted laws of weights and measure based on English standards, and in 1828 the United States adopted British Imperial Standards for the pound weight, and in 1831 obtained models of Britain's other standards, which were copied and distributed around the States by 1856, their national relevance was lost by 1893. The problem was that there was no uniformity of measures in Britain, and ten different systems of weights and measures were in use, most of which were legal, with separate Irish and Scottish miles. It was reported to a committee of the House of Lords in 1823 that approximately 200 attempts to enforce uniformity across the nation had resulted in some 500 different measures being introduced over the years.[53] Similarly in the United States, towards the end of the century, it was established that there were twenty-five units of length: three had the same length but different names, the remainder different names and values that were unrelated to one another.[54]

The Great Exhibition of 1851 provided Britain with a major catalyst for modernisation, with the Crystal Palace in Hyde Park,

London, its impressive technological focus. Of the nearly 14,000
exhibitors inside the Crystal Palace, about one half came from
non-British colonies. Their products generated public and commercial interest, and the metric measures were on display in the
form of a metre rod, a kilogram weight and a litre volume. They
had been sent for exhibition by the Conservatoire des Arts et
Métiers (Conservatory of Arts and Trades), which anticipated that:

> By viewing the objects themselves, by examining the very
> simple forms of the three units of the decimal metric system
> [. . .] the innumerable public who visited them [. . .] would
> agree to] the superiority of their usage over those of other
> more or less complex systems of different countries.[55]

The initiative taken by the Conservatoire was commendable.
International delegates – scientists, engineers, economists, merchants, manufacturers and government officials – came, saw and
were convinced of the value of the metric system. Many lobbied
their governments accordingly.

The Royal Society for Arts, Commerce and Manufactures
(RSA) and its hugely influential president, Prince Albert, were the
principal promoters of the Great Exhibition. The president and
his Society took an enthusiastic lead in promoting the benefits
of decimalisation throughout the empire, but even they were not
unequivocal advocates of the metric system. On 25 March 1853,
and in the context of the House of Commons Select Committee
on Decimal Coinage that was then in session, the RSA presented
to Her Majesty's Treasury a memorandum that acknowledged
'with great satisfaction' that the government was reconsidering
introducing the decimal system into the customary English
weights and measures.[56] The RSA realised that such a move would
'greatly facilitate scientific research', but they made it clear that
they were 'not desired to press any particular standard upon the
attention of the Government'.[57]

An equally influential exhibition was the *Exposition universelle
de 1855* held in Paris. The Conservatoire des Arts et Métiers also
exhibited metric weights and measures there to great effect, and
again, at its conclusion, the international commissioners and

jurors, some of whom were British and many of whom had taken part in the Great Exhibition of 1851, resolved to bring

to the attention of our respective governments, and of enlightened individuals friendly-disposed towards civilisation, and of advocates of peace and harmony throughout the world, the adoption of a universal system of weights and measures, based upon the decimal numeration for multiples and sub-multiples, and in the same way for the elements of all the different units.[58]

On the back of such strongly held opinions, the International Association for Obtaining a Uniform Decimal System of Measures, Weights and Coins – the first of its kind anywhere in the world – was formed in London in 1856. Its first president, the international banker Baron Jacques Rothschild, stated in his acceptance speech: 'Without wishing to prejudge the result of your inquiries, permit [me] to say that the rational system which has been adopted in France, after most serious deliberation, is worthy of the consideration of us all.'[59] The various international branches of the Association were instructed to consider a range of options. Their criteria when considering a viable unit of length were its utility in measuring the greatest variety of objects; that it was memorable and instantly recognisable; and that it was easy to carry and use. The British Branch found the English inch too short and the fathom too long, and the comparable length of the ell, yard and metre about right. They concluded that the most useful unit ought not to be based on a national standard, but – like the metre – should be derived from nature. The impartiality that this ponderous process implied led the British Branch to support (predictably enough) Baron Rothschild's subtle advocacy of the metre and metric system. They recommended to the International Association:

Its adoption is advisable, not only as the means of securing great political, social, and commercial advantages to the United Kingdom, but as a demonstration of a becoming desire to co-operate with other enlightened and powerful nations

[. . . and] by the strongest appeals of reason and science, of patriotism and of philanthropy.[60]

By the time of the fourth general meeting of the International Association in Bradford in 1859, its membership had grown to fifteen nations: Britain, France, the USA, the German Zollverein, Mexico, Portugal, Spain, Tuscany, Belgium, Greece, the Netherlands, Sardinia, Liberia, Russia and Switzerland. This international pro-metric group had as its president in 1859 an economist, senator and councillor of state for France, Michel Chevalier. Not surprisingly, Chevalier gave unequivocal support for 'the Metrical System now in use in France and many States in Europe and [South] America', and urged that the branches of the Association 'use their best efforts for the purpose of obtaining the concurrence of their respective governments in the adoption of one common system of weights, measures, and coins'.[61] The next great world exhibition in London in 1862 presented the British Branch of the Association with an excellent platform, and its members prepared a display independently of the French government that illustrated the benefits of the metric system and obtained copies of the standards themselves.[62]

In the same year, a House of Commons Select Committee on Weights and Measures was appointed to consider 'the Practicability of adopting a Simple and Uniform System of Weights and Measures, with a view not only to the Benefit of our Internal Trade, but to facilitate our Trade and Intercourse with Foreign Countries'. Hearings were held between May and July 1862. The first witness was Leone Levi, a statistician. He had also been one of the international jurors appointed to the Great Exhibition of 1851 'to examine the articles exhibited, and to ascertain which country stood highest with reference to the different classes of articles exhibited'.[63] The judges were aware of the need to find a common basis by which to assess the range of articles on display, and this had been no easy matter, as Levi explained to the Select Committee. The greatest difficulty came from the different weights and measures being used by the exhibitors of different countries, which crippled the jurors' task of arriving at an exact standard of comparison.[64] Levi was so perturbed by his experience at the Great Exhibition that he had become an advocate of the metric system.[65] He advised the Select Committee that Britain should adopt the metric system, but with modifications: English names should be substituted for the subdivision of units. Dr Van Eyck, Commissioner for the Netherlands for the Great Exhibition and an advocate of metrification, warned against substitution of this kind based on his own nation's experience (a view to which Levi also later subscribed).

The first witness to oppose the introduction of the metric system in Britain was the Astronomer Royal, Sir George Airy (1801–92). Airy wished for uniformity of weights and measures, but he considered that the customary system was 'not too inconvenient' and that reform in Britain was less necessary than it had been in France, where greater metrological diversity had existed.[66] As well as the Astronomer Royal, the witnesses presented to the Select Committee consisted of ten academics, professionals (including six architects and engineers), two industrialists and seven merchants, four actuaries and accountants, the Master of the Mint and the Secretary of the Post Office. Most of those called to give evidence were in favour of wholesale adoption of the metric system. There were also nine European witnesses in London attending the Great Exhibition who had experienced the positive switch to the metric system in their own countries. Their evidence was dismissed by one consulting auditor, who warned the Committee that 'the evidence taken from foreigners has been rather evidence of those known as advocates of change, than of [the opinions of] ordinary people'. Nonetheless, the prevailing view was that major reform was necessary, and the Committee appreciated that while they sought advocates of the existing Imperial system of feet and inches, pounds and gallons, 'they have found it difficult to discover them'.[67]

In its report to Parliament dated 15 July 1862, the Select Committee on Weights and Measures listed three alternative ways forward:

to retain the present system; to create a separate decimal system of our own, distinct from that of other nations; or simply to adopt, in common with other countries, the Metric decimal system.[68]

The unanimous recommendation of the Select Committee was that the metric system should be adopted wholesale. They concluded their report with great pomp:

> It has been the destiny of this country to lead the way in introducing the great principles of commercial freedom. Let us not reject the use of these implements which may facilitate their application. Most of all, let us rejoice, if, by adopting a system freely and rapidly extending itself, and becoming more and more an international one, we may assist in promoting the peace, and enlarging the commerce, of the world.[69]

By the end of 1862, the British Branch of the International Association prepared a Bill for introduction into the next session of the House of Commons that would allow 'the permissive use' of the metric system. This got no further than the Cabinet of the Government, which was opposed to the framing of the Bill, and its presentation was delayed. The replacement Bill was more direct, and instead of permitting the metric and Imperial systems to coexist, it provided for the metric system's immediate introduction and its compulsory national use within three years. The principal compromise was that English nomenclature should be substituted for the Graeco-Roman names the French had chosen. The Bill received its first reading on 12 May 1863 and its second reading on 1 July, when it was passed by 110 votes to 75. Gladstone, then Chancellor of the Exchequer, was one of those who voiced his opposition to the compulsory introduction of metrication. The summer recess prevented the Bill from being taken further in that session of Parliament.[70]

In anticipation of the final stage of the Bill, the International Association initiated a major propaganda campaign in its support, and they were joined by other British-metric advocates, including the RSA.[71] By then, however, governmental opposition to the compulsory introduction of the metric system had been effectively orchestrated, and to placate their authority the Bill of the previous session was remodelled, stripping it of any virility. A new Bill was introduced entitled 'An Act to render permissive the use of the Metric System of Weights and Measures'. This removed the objection of illegality to the metric system, but did nothing to promote its eventual wholesale adoption in Britain. The Bill was given its first reading on 18 February 1864 and amended in committee on 4 May to meet the government's insistence that the metric system should be legalised for contracts only, and not for everyday trading. At its second reading on 22 June, this compromise of a Bill was passed by 90 votes to 52. After completing the full circuit of the Commons and Lords it became an Act of Parliament on 28 July 1864, but the government – led by Viscount Palmerston – had made sure that it would have no immediate effect on everyday life in Britain.[72]

No matter, this was the beginning of the end for British Imperial standards. For although the Act did not impose the metric system on Britain, the wide support it had received was enough to convince the US government that there existed evidence of 'a deliberate intention to introduce the metric system into England, and as giving up any purpose of creating a separate system [. . .] and as paving the way for the ultimate exclusive adoption of the metric system'.[73] This tacit acknowledgement of the inevitability of a metric future led the US legislature to legalise the metric system fully from 28 July 1866. From that date onwards, the US Customary measures were redefined in relation to metric standards, and the two systems – Customary and metric – coexisted alongside one another.[74]

The US adoption of a metric, rather than British Imperial system, inevitably led to discrepancies. The US yard became fractionally longer than the British (by 0.00035 per cent). Weights and volumes were already markedly different, because Britain in 1824 had redefined the Imperial Standard gallon, and in the 1840s had abandoned the Troy-weight system. The Imperial pound was therefore lighter than the American (by 0.0000193 per cent), and the American gallon appreciably smaller than the Imperial gallon (by 16.732 per cent).[75] These disparities had a cumulative impact on industrial, commercial and scientific exchanges between the two nations, with inevitable consequences.

In response to this new legislation in the USA, a Bill was presented in Britain in 1868 that was intended to repeal the Act of 1864 and introduce the compulsory use of the metric system. The Bill was withdrawn on 1 July 1868, however, because a report on the subject of weights and measures requested from a Royal Commission, which had Airy, the Astronomer Royal, as its chairman, did not arrive in time.[76] It was presumably no coincidence that Airy, a voluble and influential critic of the metric system, was appointed by the government to chair the committee, and that their deliberations were extended beyond the time permitted for the Bill. There was also fierce and well-marshalled public opposition to the Bill, most notably from Beresford Hope MP, whose speech of 13 May 1868 was swiftly published in pamphlet form: 'In Moving the Rejection of the Metric Weights and Measures Bill'.[77] Hope enlisted the support of the internationally famous astronomer and Fellow of the Royal Society, Sir John Herschel (1792–1871), who had written a letter of support to Hope the month before (on 6 April 1868). In this Herschel argued against the presumed rationality of the length of the metre rod based on either the measure of the earth's surface or the seconds pendulum. Instead, he proposed a third basis for a rational natural measure, the axis on which the earth daily spins, which also happened to fit in well with the length of the English foot:

> The polar axis of the earth is a much better natural unit than the quadrant of the meridian through Paris, and, dividing this into 500 million inches, our actual foot comes within a 1000th part of 12 such inches, or a geometrical foot.[78]

Herschel then explains how this geometrical foot can be related to volume and weight to achieve a system as coherent as the metric, and which would not require the British to abandon their

historic Imperial weights and measures. His down-to-earth proposals for a modern measuring system were not received with
much enthusiasm. Mainly this was because he was promoting
a decidedly Anglocentric viewpoint, not one 'independent of
any nation'. In addition, the length of the polar axis would be
no easier to define precisely, since both poles terminated at
icecaps that were extremely hazardous to navigate. Undeterred,
Herschel developed his argument against the metric system, and
in 1872 defined a scientific 'universal inch', which was derived
from the English inch and was redefinable scientifically: he specified the polar axis as precisely 500,497,056 English inches, and
the universal inch as being $\frac{1}{500,000,000}$ of this distance.

Airy was the most prominent scientific supporter of Herschel's
proposal.[79] It is perhaps not surprising therefore, that the Royal
Commissioners under Airy's chairmanship missed not only
the deadline of June 1868, but that they also deliberated for
a further three years, during which time they produced a total
of five reports.[80] When the same Commissioners expressed a
majority view in 1871 that the metric system should be fully
embraced by the United Kingdom, Airy appended his own separate memorandum to the official report in fervent opposition
to its introduction: 'My opinion is, therefore, distinct, that
no step ought to be taken which can tend in any way to introduce material standards on the Metric or any other foreign
system'.[81] By then, as he and the government would no doubt
have appreciated, the primary impetus for metrical reform had
been lost. Although vigorous campaigns followed, they also
failed. It was fully 100 years before Britain subscribed fully to
the metric club – almost two centuries after the metric system
had been initiated.

The USA also lost its way. Anti-metric lobbies complained that
the metre length (unlike the foot) was unable to provide a convenient base unit; it was not well chosen (a discrepancy existed
between the actual and the theoretical metre, and it was based
on a curved rather than a straight line); and its decimal division
was impractical (decimalisation of the circle had failed in
Revolutionary France) and too difficult for ordinary use. It was

argued instead that the unit of length should be taken from a man's stride or some part of the human body.[82]

Mysticism, the Great Pyramid and Measure

More extreme were the views of an anti-metric organisation based in the United States, the International Institute for Preserving and Perfecting Weights and Measures, which in 1883 delivered the first issue of *The International Standard*, subtitled 'A Magazine devoted to the discussion and dissemination of the wisdom contained in the Great Pyramid of Jeezeh in Egypt'. Charles Latimer, an engineer and one of its leading luminaries, reminded his readers of the significance of thisform of structure: 'the reverse of the Great Seal of the United States is a pyramid unfinished', while, as he stated unequivocally in an earlier publication, the French metre was 'the Devil's work'.[83]

The dimensions of the Great Pyramid were sufficiently open to interpretation to serve the cause of the anti-metric societies of the nineteenth century in America. One group held that the English mensural system was directly descended from the ancient Egyptians, and Charles Piazzi Smyth, Astronomer Royal of Scotland, wrote two books on the Great Pyramid and was a prominent 'counsellor' to America's first anti-metric organisation, the International Institute.[84] Established in Boston in 1879, the International Institute was constituted to:

> promote the knowledge of and allegiance to our ancient standard of Weights and Measures, according to the Divine Command – 'Thou shalt have a Perfect and Just Weight, a Perfect and Just Measure shalt thou have: that thy days may be lengthened in the land which the Lord giveth thee'. – Deut. 25:15. [. . .] The membership will participate in all worthy efforts to arrest the progress of the French Metric system.[85]

Other leading lights in the International Institute argued that the ancient measures were God-given, and therefore sacred instruments, never to be abandoned. Latimer, an early president of the

Institute, went as far as to write that the source of weights, measures and astronomy was not Egypt, but Noah,

who was prudentially cast upon the shores of what we call the new world. The possession of these measures by our race[,] the British or Anglo-Saxon race[,] shows overwhelmingly that we are the custodians of the measures; and that they are found in the Pyramid of Egypt, only goes to prove conclusively that our race built the Great Pyramid and idolatrous Egypt.[86]

Several members of the Institute claimed that the English system of weights and measures was also God-given, and therefore perfect, and evidence of these same measures in the Great Pyramid was merely coincidental. More rational metrologists have, of course, shed doubt on all such claims.[87] Indeed, it is doubted that there was any conformity of measures across the ancient civilizations, and all that has survived are the dominant measures that mark particular watersheds in their historical development.[88] Instead of the metre, and following the notion of Sir John Herschel, the International Institute promoted 'The inch, being one five-hundred-millionth of the earth's polar diameter, and in use by the people of God from the remotest antiquity, is of Divine origin, and therefore not to be displaced by man's invention.'[89]

Herschel was well known in the USA, though mostly for the wrong reasons. Fifty years earlier he had been the victim of an elaborate hoax that had been promoted by the New York *Sun*, with the support of the proprietor, Benjamin H. Day, who was eager to promote the sales of his newspaper.[90] An English journalist in his employment called Richard Adams Locke concocted the story, which became known as the 'Great Lunar Hoax', and was picked up and developed by journalists around the globe.

It had innocent enough beginnings, Herschel having arrived in Cape Town in January 1834 to observe the constellations of the southern latitudes. Aware of Sir John's journey, and the public utterances of his famous astronomer father William Herschel, who had happened to speculate that the moon might be populated, Locke decided to give this quite unexceptional astronomical expedition a popular twist.[91] For his readers in the *Sun* he cited a 'special supplement' that he had recently read in the *Edinburgh Journal of Science*, a periodical that had in fact ceased publication six years earlier. This defunct scientific journal provided the 'facts' for Herschel's 'Great Astronomical Activities', which Locke serialised for his readers. As he was on the other side of the globe, Herschel was oblivious to the literary fabrications being conducted in his name. By January 1835 Locke was quoting Herschel's supposed findings through 'verbatim' reports made by the astronomer's assistant, a Dr Andrew Grant. Grant allegedly talked of the life forms he and his master had observed on the moon through their telescope. There were 'herds of brown quadrupeds' supported by luxuriant woods, and creatures walking in groups and erect 'like human beings':

> They averaged four feet in height, were covered, except on the face, with short and glossy copper-coloured hair, and had wings composed of a thin membrane, without hair, lying snugly upon their backs, from the top of the shoulders to the calves of the legs.[92]

As was intended, sales of the New York *Sun* soared, and, at a daily rate of 19,360 copies, even surpassed the circulation of the London *Times*. Throughout 1836, Locke's fiction was translated into every European language, and the story expanded to suit individual national interests in science and the promise of the future in each translation. Science had demonstrated that anything was possible, and the public at large was ready to receive whatever was presented in the name of science as valid and legitimate. A new popular pact was emerging; a fantastic act of faith would increasingly fill the void in the human imagination left by reason.

In the USA, fact was also turned into popular fiction by the International Institute, which became increasingly cranky, making all sorts of esoteric and bizarre claims for the mystical power and authority of the nation's symbol, the Great Pyramid. In fact, this had a negative effect on the cause. Such outpourings of fantasy only contributed to the general apathy in America about the metric system, which sane books and articles promoting the metric system were incapable of countering.[93] In the face of this national mood, and in the absence of an overwhelming support for change, no American government was willing to carry the high financial cost that introducing the metre would bring with it, or risk the potential political cost. Meanwhile, the metric system was becoming the mensural *lingua franca* of the rest of the world.

The New Empire of Science

The modern metric system was extended beyond the boundaries of France most effectively by traditional means – by the conquering armies of Napoleon's expanding empire and the institutions that were installed in their wake. But brute force alone rarely has an enduring effect on a conquered nation and, as Napoleon's fortunes waned, reinstated national leaders were quick to denounce French reforms. But the metric system survived Napoleon's retreat, the intellectual ground for its survival having been prepared long before by the Enlightenment *philosophes* whose influential writings did not halt at national boundaries. The firm intellectual foundations they had laid enabled the new metric weights and measures to exist through the turmoil of adoption and periodic rejection. Without the all-pervasive influence of international scientists, supported by their respective governments, universities and academies, as well as the bureaucratic support of governmental administrators to ensure that the system was properly implemented, the metre would not have survived or flourished.

Across Europe, the foreign *départements* still controlled by the central administration in Paris adopted the metric system. Each set up their own commission for weights and measures to compare local standards with the metre, and compiled conversion tables. Similarly, French-dominated republics were enthusiastic about the new system. The Helvetic Republic (Switzerland) accepted the metre as standard in 1801, and the Batavian Republic (Netherlands) in 1802. The *département* of

Dyle (Brussels) adopted the metre in 1799, and when Belgium became an independent nation in 1836 it remained the official measure.[94] On the Italian side of the Alps, the newly conquered Cisalpine Republic had Milan as its seat of government. The Austrians, the Revolutionaries' immediate predecessors in Lombardy, had already been rationalising weights and measures within the region during the eighteenth century, scientifically verifying the length of the Milanese *braccio* that had been the standard measure since 1781. Following French occupation, the Milanese authorities decided initially to decimalise its length, along with their standard weights, and a commission for weights and measures was established in 1794. They contributed positively to discussions regarding the definitive standard for the new metric system, sending representatives to Paris in October 1798 to meet the Committee of the National Institute and other foreign representatives.[95] The Cisalpine Republic expressed its determination to adopt the metric system in preference to the 'Gothic diversity' that existed, and which 'was the ineluctable outcome of the partition and fragmentation of Italy into small seigneuries, as well as a direct consequence of the feudal law'. It was adopted as standard in 1801, though – as elsewhere in the empire – the process of adoption had to be started again when the Italian republics became independent after Napoleon's fall from power.[96] The metric system, which many political leaders had initially accepted as a scientific advance and benefit for all humanity, was now tainted with the personal identity and specific nationality of a conquering emperor.[97]

Napoleonic compromise had enabled the metre to survive in France by temporarily merging its identity with the customary measures of Paris, and similar practical and symbolic compromises were sought elsewhere in Europe. The ancient kingdom of Piedmont, which incorporated Savoy and Sardinia, lay adjacent to the Cisalpine Republic with Turin as its capital. Although the *piemontesi* had been examining the potential of the metric system before Napoleon's invasion, the metric system did not become their official standard until 1809. In 1797, when Piedmont was still a kingdom independent of France, A. M. Vasalli-Eandi, professor of physics at the University of Turin, published a book on the metric system, and in October 1798 Count Cesare Balbo, Piedmont's ambassador in Paris and an eminent scientist, joined the General Committee of Weights and Measures. Again, practical adoption took longer than official acceptance, and with Napoleon's temporary demise, the newly restored king of Piedmont repealed all French laws in 1814, and initiated a return to the former measures.[98] The government and scientists of Piedmont, who still supported the metre, settled initially on an ingenious compromise. The Piedmont foot would be retained for everyday use, but it would be given scientific legitimacy by relating its length to one second of the meridian as it passed through Turin, at longitude 2° E.[99] This would enable the Piedmont foot to be regarded as a modern measure, since it was derived from the dimensions of the earth, like the French metre. The compromise was finally made legal twelve years later, in 1826.[100] A gradual reduction of the range of weights and measures available was effected over the following years, and by 1844 the main units of length, the Piedmontese *canna* and *palme*, were regularised as 3 and 0.25 metres, respectively.[101] A major impulse for unification in Italy came from Piedmont, and the metre was adopted as the standard of the new nation on 28 July 1861. These were the watershed years for the metric system, as major European nations progressively made it first legal and then obligatory in practice: Spain went metric in 1869; Germany and Portugal followed in 1872.

In the Western Hemisphere the spread of the metric system began in the 1850s, and it became obligatory first in the Republic of New Granada (later Colombia) in 1854, and in Ecuador in 1866. Mexico was still struggling to implement it in 1896, and along with Venezuela, which started implementation in 1857, did not complete the process until the early twentieth century.[102] A meeting of some forty nations at the Paris *Exposition Universelle* of 1867 laid the foundations of an international metrological organisation, and an International Commission of interested countries met in Paris in 1872. At their next meeting on 8 May 1875, the International Convention was formed along with the International Bureau of Weights and Measures. Here it was resolved that the metric system did not belong to a single nation, but to all nations, and that the prototypes should be retained for all on neutral territory. The French government donated the Pavillon de Breteuil to the international cause, which is located at the entrance of the Parc de Saint-Cloud in the Parisian suburb of Sèvres.[103]

The International Bureau moved into its new accommodation in 1878. The definitive prototypes were installed in underground vaults in the grounds on 28 September 1889. By then, the prototype metre was well on the way to becoming universally accepted, except in Britain and North America. The emasculated British Act of 1864 did eventually deliver the aims of its supporters, by default. Had Britain and the US been able to reach agreement and reunite their customary measures, they would have achieved a powerful transatlantic metrical conformity to be reckoned with. Once divided from the US by the Act of 1864, however, Britain made itself isolated and increasingly vulnerable. Two world wars during the twentieth century, and the commensurate downgrading of empire into commonwealth, weakened Britain's international status and authority. With the corresponding growth in stature of the European Union, Britain's most immediate overseas marketplace, a relatively coherent entity that traded exclusively in the metric system, the odds were stacked against Britain's continued independence. By the 1960s, 68 per cent of the world's population lived in nations where the metric system was official, and successive British governments saw the sense and joined the majority club.[104]

Britain began the process of abandoning its traditional weights and measures with the Weights and Measures Act of 1963, when an Imperial yard was defined against the metre as exactly 0.9144 metres. Surviving ancient weights and measures, including the rod, pole, perch, square rod, bushel, peck and pennyweight, were abolished on 31 January 1969. Members of Britain's former empire, now independent commonwealth nations – Canada, Australia, New Zealand and South Africa – followed Britain's lead. In Britain, as in France, customary practices were not so easy to change, and the Weights and Measures Acts of 1976 and 1985 were introduced to restate the government's resolve, and to abolish the linear measures of furlong and chain, as well as area, solid and weight measures. Omitted, however, were the yard, mile, square foot and gallon, and the process of governmental rationalisation has continued into the next millennium. Yet, it remains commonplace – in the twenty-first century – for Britons to gauge their height in feet and inches, and to think in miles rather than kilometres; traffic signs and car gauges still register speed and distance in miles.

The USA remains the only world power not to have adopted the metric system officially, and Liberia and Myanmar (Burma) are the only other nations operating their own systems. The USA started edging towards national recognition and implementation of the metric system during the 1970s,[105] and on 23 December 1975, President Gerald R. Ford signed the Metric Conversion Act, and the US Metric Board was established. The American people largely ignored its efforts, and President Regan disestablished it in 1982 in an attempt to reduce Federal spending. Consequently, most US citizens continue to measure their roads in miles, the height and weight of their bodies in feet, inches and pounds, fill the tanks of their cars with gallons of gas, and measure temperature in Fahrenheit.

When this most powerful and technically advanced of nations landed the first man on the moon on 20 July 1969, it achieved this feat without metric dimensioning. Can that independence be maintained? Is it necessary for most ordinary human beings, who live outside the scientific community, to adopt the measures prescribed by science for their everyday exchanges? Influential figures in twentieth-century art and architecture demonstrated their scepticism and attempted to provide alternatives – ironically and practically – to the empire of science.

6. Measures of Pure Conception

> Have you not heard of that madman who lit a lantern
> in the bright morning hours, ran to the marketplace,
> and cried incessantly, 'I seek God!' [. . .] 'Whither is
> God?' he cried. 'I shall tell you. *We have killed him* – you
> and I. All of us are his murderers. But how have we
> done this? [. . .] What did we do when we unchained
> this earth from its sun? Whither is it moving now? Away
> from all suns? Are we not plunging continually? [. . .]
> Are we not straying as through an infinite nothing? Do
> we not feel the breath of empty space? [. . .] Is it not
> night and more night coming on all the while? Must
> not lanterns be lit in the morning? [. . .] God is dead.
> God remains dead. And we have killed him. How shall
> we, the murderers of all murderers, comfort ourselves?
> [. . .] What festivals of atonement, what sacred games
> shall we have to invent?[1]

Delambre and Méchain's terrestrial survey lengthened the 'official' metre distributed by the French government in 1800: the quarter meridian was 10,002,288 multiples of the authorised metre, not the perfect 10,000,000 it was intended to be.[2] Moreover, the over-arching scientific rationale that the new measure was to serve was constantly critical of its offspring, undermining its very creation. After nearly a century of struggling with the irrationality of the measure created, and of imposing the new metric system on reluctant populations, the First General Conference of Weights and Measures agreed, on 1 September 1889, to revert to the pre-triangulated metre of 1795 as the official standard – the metre of pure conception – effectively, to ignore the 'facts' painstakingly accumulated by Delambre and

Méchain. After almost 100 years it was acknowledged that the dominant nations could not agree on a scientifically verifiable natural physical standard of measure.

The pre-triangulated metre, the irrational metre of pure conception, took on a new significance and it was accorded mythological, even sacred status. The installation of the definitive prototypes in the underground vault in the grounds of the International Bureau at Sèvres on 28 September 1889 took the form of a ceremony of deposition. This was to be re-enacted every six years, a procedure more familiar to a religious sect or secret society than a rational scientific organisation. It involved four keys of admission that were distributed among the foreign signatories of the International Committee. When they met sexennially at Sèvres, four designated delegates were required to bring the key they had retained, enter the underground vault, and inspect and confirm the safe condition of the prototype standards. The keys were then passed on to another representative of a designated member nation to retain until their next meeting. The member nations were also permitted to keep their own tangible copy of the prototypes, called the National Prototype Standards. The original prototypes, however, 'among science's most sacred relics', as *Time Magazine* later reported, were retained in the 'underground shrine at Sèvres'.[3] To ensure its longevity – for all people, for all times – its scientist-custodians, out of reach of common humanity at large, controlled the metric system independently of nations. The Religion of Newton had been realised at Sèvres, complete with its scientific priesthood and sacred ritual.

With the metric prototypes enshrined at Sèvres, protected and isolated from national, political, social and any normal human interference, scientists perfected the qualities and characteristics of the metric prototypes. Instead of referring to the visible, tangible natural qualities of the human body or the earth, both of which had proved difficult to define, it was argued that the metre length ought to be set in relation to the immaterial wavelengths of light. This would ensure that the standard was independent from that false ideal – the physical world in which humans dwell.

If the prototype were itself intangible, it would be able to resist any loss or destruction of molecules that might befall a physical prototype. It would be infallible, beyond criticism – beyond human experience.

The thinking in this direction had been stimulated by research in the 1870s by the Scottish physicist James Clerk Maxwell (1831–1879), who developed a system of absolute units of weights and measures based on a specified type of light emitted from a vaporised metal in a vacuum tube. Its wavelength would provide a definitive unit of length, its vibration the unit of time, and one molecule of the metal the unit of mass.[4] In 1891 the American physicist Albert A. Michelson (1852–1931) took Clerk Maxwell's ideas a stage further with the backing of the International Bureau. Michelson's experiments suggested that the light from the metal cadmium would provide a suitable alternative standard, such that the metre length could be defined as equivalent to a specific number of wavelengths of the primary coloured light of the cadmium spectrum, red, green and blue.[5]

This new level of precision gratified astronomers and physicists in particular, and in 1913 the metre was determined by the International Bureau to be equal to 1,553,164.13 cadmium red line wavelengths. This served as a supplementary definition of the metre, which was ratified by the Seventh General (International) Conference of Weights and Measures held in 1927. Following that agreement, other light sources have been the objects of experiments: the American physicist Luis W. Alvarez (1911–1988) proposed mercury as a superior medium to cadmium for this purpose, and in the 1950s German scientists favoured light derived from a krypton isotope.[6] In 1953 a ten-nation advisory committee meeting at Sèvres was ready to recommend the abandonment of the physical metric prototype, in favour of its definition solely through wavelengths of light. On 14 October 1960 it was agreed to return to a truly 'natural' and scientifically verifiable definition for the metre rod derived from the radiation of the orange-red light emitted by the radioactive krypton-86 atom, so that the metre would equal 1,650,763.73 wavelengths in vacuum of the radiation corresponding to the transition between the levels $2p^{10}$ and $5d^5$ of the krypton-86 atom.[7] Since 1983 it has been defined more simply (though it is no easier to comprehend) as the distance that light travels in a vacuum in the fraction of time of $^1/_{299,792,458}$ of a second.

The metre has undergone extraordinary transformations since 1795. Originally, it was a length of pure conception, a simple fraction of the earth's circumference. But once Newton's thesis was confirmed, that the earth is non-spherical and could not provide a natural unit of measure, the rationality of a terrestrially derived metre was placed in permanent doubt. In 1799 the assumed natural authority of the earth was abandoned in favour of a man-made measure, the 'definitive' platinum metre length. Delambre and Méchain based the length of this manufactured artefact on the premise that the sample of the meridian measured between Dunkirk and Barcelona was representative of the earth's curvature. Another falsehood, which Delambre had fretted over in the early nineteenth century, was that the earth's curvature had to be flattened notionally to define a constant universal measure. One ideal was exchanged for another: yet it turned out that the earth cannot be idealised any better – any more scientifically – than the human body.

The physical, natural and invariable standard proposed by Condorcet and Talleyrand was abandoned for something immaterial and unknowable – except to scientists using finely calibrated tools of their own creation. While a fundamental unit for all times had been settled on, it is one that can be comprehended only by scientists and verified in a laboratory under their control. Revealingly – or rather, quite the opposite, the Greek word *krypton* means 'hidden' – the metre is no longer a visible symbol of the earth on which we dwell. It has no relation to human form, the shape or extent of the earth, or to any form at all. Like Newton's *sensorium*, it is a measure of everything and nothing. It is culturally removed from the mainstream experience of society. It is a measure of total abstraction.

Marcel Duchamp and the Metre 'Diminished'

The cultural imbalance of a universal measure, ostensibly designed for all people for all times, that was the creation of scientists and politicians alone has perplexed artists, architects and writers – those who have traditionally defined society's cultural symbols. The French avant-garde artist Marcel Duchamp (1887–1968), one of the most influential artists of the twentieth century, demonstrated his concerns about the origins and expression of the metric system and the autonomy of science. Not that he was anti-science: scientists and their notions of rationality fascinated him. Yet he was somewhat sceptical of the reverence with which society accepted the authority of science and its 'laws':

> We have to accept those so-called laws of science because it makes life more convenient, but that doesn't mean anything so far as *validity* is concerned. Maybe it's all just an illusion. We are so fond of ourselves, we think we are little gods of the earth – I have my doubts about it, that's all. The word 'law' is against my principles. Science is so evidently a closed circuit, but every fifty years or so a new 'law' is discovered that changes everything.[8]

Duchamp's attitude was influenced by the writings of the celebrated mathematician and physicist Henri Poincaré (1854–1912), who succeeded in popularising science in France in the early part of the twentieth century. Poincaré's most famous books of that period include *La Science et l'hypothèse* (*Science and Hypothesis*, 1902), *La Valeur de la science* (*The Value of Science*, 1905) and *Science et méthode* (*Science and Method*, 1908). His books were popular across the breadth of French society, and *La Science et l'hypothèse* ran to twenty editions by 1912. It was translated into English in 1913. What Poincaré asked his readers to reconsider were the apparently inalienable facts that science projects: 'all these rules, all these definitions are only the fruit of an unconscious opportunism [. . .]. The scientific fact is only the crude fact translated into convenient language.'[9] He reasoned that the laws of nature defined by Newton were just some of an infinite number of possible hypotheses for helping us to master and make experience. Newton may offer a convenient insight into nature, but there may still remain other ways of defining nature, which – if we knew them – might be vastly more advantageous to humanity. Poincaré therefore proposed that the scientific laws of nature should in fact be understood as pure symbols – conventions that man creates for 'convenience' (*commodité*).[10]

In *Science and Hypothesis* Poincaré argued that

> The fundamental propositions of geometry, as for instance Euclid's postulate, are nothing more than conventions, and it is just as unreasonable to inquire whether they are true or false as to ask whether the metric system is true or false.

Ultimately, neither truth nor falsehood can be attached to a standard; it is simply the most convenient agreement available at that time for the particular task in hand.[11] Poincaré defines two types of truth – scientific, and moral or ethical – the former is demonstrable, the latter is felt truth. We need both simultaneously, since they combine to shape the totality of human experience.

Johann Kaspar Schmidt (1806–1856) was another important influence on Duchamp. Writing under the nom de plume of Max Stirner, his *Der Einzige und sein Eigentum* of 1845 (*The Individual and His Own*), first published in French in 1900 (entitled *L'Unique et sa propriété*), attacked every kind of social and political authority. He regarded the State as the enemy of the individual and of individualism. Instead of revolution, Stirner sought rebellion and the right of every individual to express him or herself as a unique being through philosophical egoism – the conscious projection of individual identity into the public realm. Duchamp united both lines of thought – demonstrated and felt truths – in order to express individuality. He questioned the reverence towards science and, as an artist, he looked for 'another sort of pseudo explanation', a complementary rationale for the phenomena that science has presented to humanity.[12]

Duchamp's own artistic identity was cast after his Cubist-inspired painting *Nude Descending a Staircase* (*Nu descendant un escalier*, 1912) was rejected from the Salon des Indépendants in Paris of 1912. Apparently, out of frustration and annoyance, Duchamp rejected painting completely, and became an assistant librarian at the Bibliothèque Sainte-Geneviève in Paris. He read widely and developed through mixed media a narrative context for his art that was highly personal and individualistic. He sought a new medium of self-expression, one that would refer to the irrationality of scientific method, and which would provide science with a cultural frame:

> All painting beginning with Impressionism, is antiscientific, even [that of] Seurat. I was interested in introducing the precise and exact aspect of science [. . .]. It wasn't for the love of science that I did this; on the contrary, it was rather in order to discredit it mildly, lightly, unimportantly. But irony was present.[13]

The *Three Standard Stoppages* (*Trois Stoppages-Étalon*, 1913–14) is the first of Duchamp's non-paintings, and his first challenge of scientific rationale: it was in part 'a joke about the metre'.[14] More seriously, the *Three Standard Stoppages* was intended to question the accepted authority of the metre rod as a pure, rational scientific object, and to expose it as a human construct, illusory and deluding. He argued (along similar lines to Poincaré) that the relationship between science and life is never entirely predictable, and he offered, alongside the metre rod, a unique system of measurement (after Stirner), of pure 'canned chance' ('du hasard en conserve'). 'Pure chance', he later explained, 'interests me as a means to combat logical reality'.[15]

As a creation by an individual artist-anarchist, the *Three Standard Stoppages* would be of no practical use to science.[16] Instead, it was intended to question what had become customary and a convenience, by contrasting the logical scientific certitudes of the metre rod with demonstrations of 'canned chance'. The subjective idealism of Duchamp is clearly expressed through his statement 'There is no solution because there is no problem [. . .]'

Problem is the invention of man – it is nonsensical.'[17] The *Three Standard Stoppages* is composed of three sinuous curves generated by a metre-long thread as templates for display in an exhibition. It was an important first step for Duchamp, a fundamental work in his artistic output, 'a first gesture liberating me from the past'.[18] He referred in later life to this particular manifestation of 'canned chance' as his favourite work.[19]

Instead of describing the metre length scientifically, as a precisely calibrated flat rigid metal rod that represents a unit derived from the earth's meridian, Duchamp defined it individualistically and through chance. He cut white thread to a length of one metre, which he held at either end horizontally and in tension. He dropped it from a height of one metre onto canvas painted Prussian blue (perhaps an ironic reference to the precision popularly associated with Prussian authority), and 'twisting as it pleases, he fixed the fallen thread to the canvas with varnish as it lay, so preserving the unique long sinuous curve that chance had created during its fall to ground. This process was repeated twice more, 'in more or less similar conditions'.[20] The canvas had the overall metric dimensions of 40 × 120 centimetres, a proportion – width to length – of 1 : 3. It was then cut into three strips, each framing a fallen thread – these were then glued onto strips of plate glass. Duchamp recorded his method on the back of each strip: 'Un mètre de fil droit, horizontal, tombé d'un mètre de haut'. The strips were placed in a wooden croquet box for presentation, alongside two standard metre rods (fig. 15).[21]

Croquet is, of course, played with mallets, swung like pendulums against spherical balls: an oblique reference perhaps to the origins of the terrestrial measure. Duchamp's idea for lengths of thread as a suitable medium may have come from Poincaré. In a chapter in *Science and Hypothesis* on 'The Classical Mechanics', Poincaré opens with a distinction between the 'English' (that is, British) and continental European approach to mechanics, between demonstrating science physically and abstractly through formulaic symbols: 'The English teach mechanics as an experimental science; on the continent it is always expounded as more

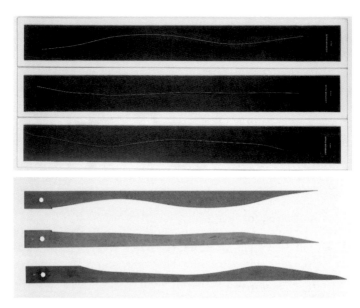

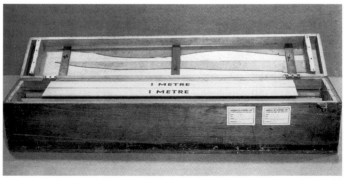

15 Marcel Duchamp, *Three Standard Stoppages* (*Trois Stop-pages-Étalon*, 1913–14). Assemblage: (a) 3 threads glued to 3 painted canvas strips, $5^{1}/_{4} \times 47^{1}/_{4}''$ (13.3 × 120 cm), each mounted on a glass panel, $7^{1}/_{4} \times 49^{3}/_{8} \times {}^{1}/_{4}''$ (18.4 × 125.4 × .6 cm); (b) three wood slats, $2^{1}/_{2} \times 43 \times {}^{1}/_{8}''$ (6.2 × 109.2 × .2 cm), $2^{1}/_{2} \times 47 \times {}^{1}/_{8}''$ (6.1 × 119.4 × .2 cm), $2^{1}/_{2} \times 43^{1}/_{4} \times {}^{1}/_{8}''$ (6.3 × 109.7 × .2 cm), shaped along one edge to match the curves of the threads; (c) the whole fitted into a wooden box, $11^{1}/_{8} \times 50^{7}/_{8} \times 9''$ (28.2 × 129.2 × 22.7 cm). The Museum of Modern Art, New York. Katherine S. Dreier Bequest. © Succession Marcel Duchamp/ADAGP Paris and DACS, London 2007

or less a deductive *a priori* science. The English are right, that goes without saying.'[22] Newton had demonstrated the truth of mechanics through experiment in the *Principia*, and Poincaré goes on to make reference to the German physicist Gustav Kirchhoff (1824–1887), who had reduced Newton's 'laws' to no more than definitions. Poincaré exposed the inadequacy of Kirchhoff's mechanics.[23] For example, Kirchhoff argues that the Newtonian notion of force does not need to be measured physically because it is intuitive and apparent to us from infancy. Poincaré considers this argument to be absurd:

> Whatever does not teach us to measure it is as useless to mechanics as is, for instance, the subjective notion of warmth and cold to the physicist who is studying heat. This subjective notion cannot be translated into numbers, therefore it is of no use [. . .]. But more than that: this notion of effort does not teach us the real nature of force.[24]

Kirchhoff's mechanics – his 'anthropomorphism', as Poincaré defines his approach – reduces experimental science to a symbol.

Poincaré concludes his account of 'Classical Mechanics' by referring to the symbol employed by 'The School of the Thread' ('L'École du Fil') – another form of anthropomorphic mechanics as J. F. C. Andrade had rejuvenated it in his *Leçons de mécanique physique* (1898).[25] This school of thought used evenly tensioned thread as a symbol of negligible mass in its experiments. As Poincaré relates:

> A thread which transmits any force is slightly elongated under the action of this force; the direction of the thread tells us the direction of the force, whose magnitude is measured by the elongation of the thread.[26]

Poincaré is highly critical of such naive anthropomorphism, and considers that science has progressed to a higher plane; having developed from a 'rather crude experiment', science can now demonstrate 'a law [. . .] the certainty of which we regard as absolute. This certainty we ourselves have bestowed upon it voluntarily, so to speak, by looking upon it as a convention'. They are conventions, because they have been justified through experiment and demonstration.[27]

The *Three Standard Stoppages* was not intended to provide an antidote to the authority of science, but Duchamp does pursue Poincaré's original enquiry, 'whether the metric system is true or false', by questioning its relevance as a convention. Through the demonstration of canvas strips as canned chance – and what else is the metre of pure conception but canned chance? – Duchamp made an ironic reconciliation of science and art. The title, *Three Standard Stoppages*, provides the key to a more complete understanding of that work as a statement of reconciliation. Duchamp considered the number three symbolic of 'a series': 'one is unity, two is double, duality, and three is the rest'.[28] And, although he does not spell this out himself, *étalon* means standard (as in an official standard such as weights and measures) and also 'stallion'. Through this double-entendre he may be referring (ironically, of course), through the stallion's role as stud, to the *Stoppages* as the generators of new form. The French word *stoppage* refers to the white thread used by seamstresses for invisible mending, and perhaps Duchamp chose this word to refer to Andrade's 'The School of the Thread', and to suggest that the chance fall of the thread could 'mend', or reconstitute the rift distancing art from science. As he stated: 'considered in their relation to one another they [the three *Stoppages*] are an approximate reconstitution of the unit of length'.[29] By producing three 'new' metres he was therefore not suggesting an alternative to what science had created, but a complete and independent system, one that promoted reconciliation over opposition: 'a new image of the unit of length [. . .] the meter diminished'.[30]

The *Three Standard Stoppages* were absorbed into two of Duchamp's later compositions: the *Network of Stoppages* (*Réseaux des stoppages étalon*, 1914) and *The Large Glass*, also known as *The Bride Stripped Bare by Her Bachelors, Even* (*La mariée mise à nu par ses célibataires, même*, 1915–23). The *Network of Stoppages* was one of his last pictorial works. Indeed, in creating it, he effectively destroyed a much larger but incomplete version of his

16   Marcel Duchamp, *Young Man and Young Girl in Spring* (*Jeune homme et jeune fille dans le printemps*, 1911). Oil on canvas, $25^7/_8'' \times 19^3/_4''$ (65.7 × 50.2 cm). Private collection. © Succession Marcel Duchamp/ADAGP, Paris and DACS, London 2007

earlier painting *Young Man and Young Girl in Spring* (*Jeune homme et jeune fille dans le printemps*, 1911). This depicts figures reminiscent of Adam and Eve in the Garden of Eden, their naked stretched bodies providing the edge boundaries of the composition (fig. 16). Placed in the distance between them is an impressionistic circle of naked dancing figures, which resembles a figural celebration of the joy of life represented in *The Dance*, a painting completed by Matisse one year before.[31] In amending his original painting for the *Network of Stoppages*, Duchamp par-

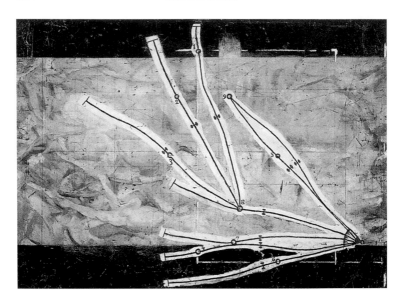

17 Marcel Duchamp, *Network of Stoppages (Réseaux des stoppages)* (1914). Oil and pencil on canvas, $58\frac{5}{8}'' \times 77\frac{5}{8}''$ (148.9 × 197.7 cm). The Museum of Modern Art, New York. Abby Aldrich Rockefeller Fund and gift of Mrs. William Sisler. © Succession Marcel Duchamp/ADAGP, Paris and DACS, London 2007

tially obscures the lower bodies of Adam and Eve with a complex network of rectilinear lines scored onto its surface like a grid: it looks almost as if a cartographer has mapped the painted surface of the canvas with coordinates (fig. 17). Duchamp then rotated the canvas by 90° and provided the long edges of the rectangular composition – now top and bottom – with thick dark border strips. Over the grid of lines and the figurative painting beneath, the stoppages have been superimposed as black lines that fan out from a starting point located near the bottom right corner of the new setting. The sinuous metre-long lines connect with numbered (perhaps calibrated?) red circles and pass beyond them. Short red bars are placed at right angles to and at the mid-point of each line. All three of the standard stoppages are used: two emanate from the starting point, the third branches out from a point placed on one stoppage, and they cross the two outer borders of the painting. These meandering lines are edged by a halo of white and are partially contained by a sketchily drawn rectangular frame, also in white.

This was a transitional work for Duchamp, and he had little to say about it. In any case, according to one commentator, it was usual for Duchamp to 'take every precaution to see that nothing of [his work] should be intelligible to an outsider':[32] nor has it been the subject of much critical interpretation. Evidently, it was the first application of Duchamp's new standards to an artistic composition, and he may once again have been questioning established scientific rationale. Indeed, it may contain an explicit reference to the triangulated survey of the arc of the meridian by Delambre and Méchain.[33] According to cartographic convention, maps are drawn with the north-point uppermost. As we know, the eighteenth-century surveyors traversed the length of the arc of the meridian as it ran through Paris, from Dunkirk in the north to Barcelona in the south. This took them beyond French territorial borders, and in the course of the survey they cut through red tape, custom and landscape, guided by scientific method and the overriding desire for precision. The *Network of Stoppages* may be interpreted as a reference to the grandeur and ultimate futility of their endeavour. Perhaps Duchamp concealed the display of human passion and frailty (symbolised by Adam and Eve), and turned the canvas from its original portrait format to emphasise – with irony, of course – the new importance of the landscape to the terrestrial surveyors. Thus, he rotated the canvas from its original orientation sideways, from top to bottom or north–south, to east–west, so that Adam and Eve are recumbent, stressing the earth's apparent infinite horizontality (from the human perspective) and asserting the secondary importance of human form in relation to the primacy of the earth. The lines of connection that Duchamp created with the three stoppages over the surface of the canvas appear to have no relation to the human landscape beneath, which is partially obscured by these new lines with their inflated aura. Perhaps Duchamp is referring here to the way that new methods and ways of thinking have been superimposed on the old, whereby old patterns always remain just beneath the surface. Read in this way it is a palimpsest of contradictions and opposites – of pseudo-purposeful superficial lines drawn over the deeper conventions of form, culture and meaning.

If Duchamp is vague regarding the *Network of Stoppages* – deliberately or otherwise – two sets of his notes provide useful insights into the connections between the *Three Standard Stoppages* and *The Large Glass*. The first of these notes was published in Paris and is known as *The Box of 1914*. It comprises a selection of sixteen preliminary notes and an early drawing he had made of this composition, three of which related to the *Three Standard Stoppages*. Exactly twenty years later he published *The Green Box*, which contained ninety-four documents, mostly directly connected with *The Large Glass*. According to Duchamp, these publications provided 'a wedding of mental and visual reactions', which give clues to, but do not fully explain, his creative process. Enough can be gleaned from his notes to provide an insight into his way of thinking. As a biographer of Duchamp, Calvin Tomkins, observed: 'Duchamp invented a new physics to explain its "laws", and a new mathematics to fix the units of its measurement.'[34] He formulated a condensed, poetic language to describe its ideas, which he jotted down on scraps of paper as they occurred to him and he stored these in a green cardboard box for future reference. *The Large Glass* draws attention to 'Laws, principles, phenomena'.[35] And Duchamp once explained to Schwarz, his biographer, that *The Large Glass* was organised according to the principles of 'playful physics', so that it could exist as 'a reality which would be possible by slightly distending the laws of physics and chemistry' (fig. 18).[36] According to Schwarz, it is both 'Cartesian in its rigor and Jarryesque in its humor'.[37] The French playwright Alfred Jarry (1873–1907) was famous for having lambasted traditional views of authority in his play *Ubu roi*, which describes the rise to power of a grotesque and pompous king. It was the first work of the Theatre of the Absurd, and enormously influenced Surrealism and Dada, art movements with which Duchamp was associated.

18 Marcel Duchamp, *The Large Glass*, also known as *The Bride Stripped Bare by Her Bachelors, Even* (*La mariée mise à nu par ses célibataires, même*) (1915–23). Oil, varnish, lead foil, lead wire and dust on two glass panels (cracked); overall 109¼″ × 69¼″ (277.5 × 175.8 cm). Philadelphia Museum of Art, Katherine S. Dreier Bequest, 1953. © Succession Marcel Duchamp/ ADAGP, Paris and DACS, London 2007

For *The Large Glass*, Duchamp had three wooden rulers cut from draughtsmen's straightedges, and the curves of the stoppages transferred to them as templates. Again he used multiples of the number 3, 'as a kind of architecture for the Glass', to lend it 'some sort of unitary organisation'.[38] The trinity appears to refer to the coordinates of width, height and depth of Euclidian space. Duchamp writes in his notes about the 'fourth-dimension', or time, and how it can be represented in *The Large Glass*. He refers to 'the shadow cast by a 4-dimensional figure on our space', as '3-dimensional'. He makes an analogy 'with the method by which architects depict the plan of each story of a house' using '3-dimensional sections', and – by a mental process – how these are linked as four dimensions: 'In other words: one can move around the 4-dim'l figure. [*sic*] according to the 4 directions of the continuum'.[39] His interest in the metre length in this composition is as a phenomenon – not as a law or principle: the phenomenon 'of stretching'.[40] Presumably, this is a reference to the act of stretching a flaccid thread as a starting point for generating and capturing the chance measure.

An artist as profound and entertaining as Marcel Duchamp may make memorable statements, delight the eye and provoke us to question accepted truths. An architect can do this and more, by offering meaning and enjoyment to the built environment we inhabit, and creating places that can support and delight us for generations. If Duchamp was one of the most influential and provocative artists of the twentieth century, his twin in architecture was the Swiss-French architect Charles Édouard Jeanneret-Gris, known as Le Corbusier (1887–1965). Indeed, a major international retrospective of his architecture held in London in the 1980s referred to him as *the* architect of the twentieth century. His was certainly a towering intellect, and like other great artist-architect-philosophers before him, he had a vision as to how humanity might best enjoy the advantages of the new challenges of his era.

Le Corbusier's primary ambition was to create architecture – houses, cities and urban landscapes – that would enable humankind to live in a new form of harmony with nature. His urban dwellers were to enjoy sun, light and air, with views of landscape and natural beauty. His designs are thought-provoking, demanding that their occupants rethink their daily routine of inhabitation: rooftops become gardens; the dark attic and basement are banished; and the lower levels of his dwellings float above a verdant landscape. In his *Vers une architecture* (*Towards a New Architecture*) of 1923 (translated 1927), Le Corbusier refers back to the Pompeian house of Roman antiquity, and – by referring to the great ocean-going liners of his day – even alludes to Noah's Ark for the Flood, which he recreated as a great dwelling complex, the Unité d'habitation. To the detriment of his popular reputation, he is most usually associated with the notion of a modern dwelling as 'a machine for living in'. But his approach to architecture was certainly not mechanistic, and he sought to mend the rift between metric and anthropomorphic measures – not by diminishing the value of the metre, as Duchamp had done, but by creating a new union using the laws of beauty found in nature. He was that extraordinary character, the architect as principled hero, the kind celebrated by Ayn Rand in *The Fountainhead* (1943). Except that her fictional architect – Howard Roark – was all-American, and perhaps a blend of the famous heroic Modernist architectural personae of Frank Lloyd Wright, Mies van der Rohe and Le Corbusier. Certainly, Le Corbusier was a man of considerable artistic principle, who upheld nature as the primary source of beauty, and did not bend to commercial pressure or accept the rationality of others without question. He criticised the abstraction of the metric system and devised a human-related measuring scale, which he called *Le Modulor* (the Modulor). The first application of the Modulor to a building occurs with his design for the first Unité d'habitation, in Marseilles in the 1950s.

Humanising the Earth: Le Corbusier's Modulor

Le Corbusier ridiculed the metre rod as 'nothing but a length of metal at the bottom of a well at the Pavillon du Breteuil', the headquarters of the International Bureau of Weights and Measures laboratory at Sèvres.[41] He designed his new measure, the Modulor, so that architects and engineers might humanise the metric system, by combining its scalar dimensions with traditional, classical geometry and modern anthropometrics. He began work on the Modulor during (and despite) the Nazi occupation of Paris during the Second World War in his studio in Paris at 35 rue de Sèvres: en route, that is, to the International Bureau of Weights and Measures laboratory at Sèvres. After the war, as his fame and opportunities increased, he applied the principles of the Modulor to the design of buildings that were to have a major impact on the development of modern architecture.

What Le Corbusier sought was a system of measurement for architecture that could be applied anywhere. The metre rod did not satisfy his objectives, for it was 'a mere number without concrete being: centimetre, decimetre, metre are only the designation of the decimal system', whereas he would design the Modulor with numbers that 'are *measures*', by which he was re-emphasising the need to relate human physicality and culture.[42] To this end, Le Corbusier assimilated recent and ancient aesthetic theories about natural beauty in art and architecture, and literally vivified the metric system through association: the Modulor is a measuring scale derived from traditional ideal notions about the measurements of the human body.

An early encounter with Édouard Schuré's *Les Grands Initiés* (Paris, 1908) is thought to have predisposed Le Corbusier to believe that Pythagoras, an 'initiate' of universal natural order, was uniquely relevant for his own ambitions for architecture in the twentieth century. Pythagoras he regarded as a pre-eminent philosopher-mathematician, whose observations of the natural world enabled him to reveal the universal truths underpinning harmony and proportion.[43] He was also familiar with the compositional studies of Renaissance art and architecture made by three distinguished nineteenth-century historians, Adolf Zeising, Heinrich Wölfflin and August Thiersch, who were pioneers of art history as an academic discipline, and who reached influential conclusions for modern designers on the fundamental rules of classical beauty.[44]

Zeising attempted to prove in his new theory on human proportions (*Neue Lehre von den Proportionen des menschlichen Körpers*, Leipzig, 1854) that the Golden Section resides in every beautiful form, both in nature and art. His starting point was the Fibonacci number series, named after an Italian mathematician, Leonardo of Pisa (*circa* 1170–1250), better known as Fibonacci. Influenced by the work of Arabic mathematicians, his series starts with two equal numbers, and the next in the sequence is always the sum of the preceding two numbers, thus the first Fibonacci numbers are 0, 1, 1, 2, 3, 5, 8, 13, 21, 34, etc. As the astronomer Johannes Kepler later observed, the sequence tends towards the 'perfect' ratio, which Luca Pacioli (1445–1517) called the 'Divine Proportion' (*De divina proportione*, 1509) and which subsequently became known as the Golden Section (among many other related names for this ratio incorporating 'Golden'), or *phi*.[45] It has the ratio of $1:1.618$, which approximates to $10:16$, and so incorporates the three perfect numbers that Vitruvius referred to as essential to architecture: 6 and 10, and the most perfect number, 16.

Wölfflin in his theory of proportion (*Zur Lehre von den Proportionen*, 1889) and Thiersch in the proportion of architecture (*Die Proportionen in der Architektur*, 1893) also proposed that successful works of art and architecture embody fundamental geometries that recur throughout their composition.[46] Wölfflin further argued that rectangles of similar proportions could be used to demonstrate the perfect compositional qualities of classically designed façades. The Englishman John Taylor had been influential in this thinking when he argued in *The Great Pyramid* (1859) that the ancient Egyptian numbers *pi* and *phi* may have been deliberately incorporated into the design of the Great Pyramid at Giza: its perimeter being close to 2 *pi* times its height, a notion taken up by Charles Piazzi Smyth.[47] A few years later, in 1864, Taylor wrote *The Battle of the Standards*, in which he campaigned against the adoption of the metric system in England, and referred to his book on *The Great Pyramid* to demonstrate a divine origin for the British units of measure.

Le Corbusier – like Duchamp – was influenced by Poincaré, and he incorporated symbolic geometry and number in his art, making paintings composed of equilateral triangles and the Golden Section during his Purist period from 1918 to 1929.[48] As an architect, he used *tracés régulateurs* (regulating lines) to study past buildings and to 'purify' the elevations of his own designs. Le Corbusier emphasised in his early designs 'the placing of the right angle' and the role of rectangles proportioned by the Golden Section, which he illustrated in a chapter on 'Regulating Lines' in *Towards a New Architecture*, perhaps the most influential architectural treatise of the twentieth century. His publication *Le Modulor* (1948–9) describes the Golden Section series – the *séries d'Or* (hence *Modul-Or* or Golden module[49]) – arranged as two related scales colour-coded red and blue, which

19   Le Corbusier,
'Modulor Man',
sketch dated
6 January 1946.
Le Modulor
(1948–9).
© FLC/ADAGP, Paris
and DACS, London
2007

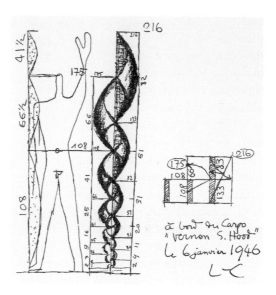

relate to the proportional heights of two parts of the body, the
head and the outstretched arm of a man (fig. 19). He proposed
that the measures or proportions of the Modulor man should be
taken from either coloured scale, separately or together, and used
by architects to ensure that their designs would be proportional
and naturally beautiful.

Initially, Le Corbusier determined the overall length of the
Modulor according to the idealised height of 'the Frenchman',
1.75 metres tall. He extended this to the height of the Frenchman's raised hand, an upper dimension of 2.164 metres, which
was also arrived at by doubling the height of the Frenchman's
solar plexus, or mid-point above the ground. Unfortunately, the
Frenchman's height of 1.75 metres did not relate well to British
Imperial feet and inches since it led to awkward subdivisions,
and it would therefore prove difficult to use the Modulor in the
dominant Anglo-Saxon nations of Britain, the Commonwealth
and the United States. Le Corbusier's assistant Marcel Py found
a way of resolving this dilemma. Unshackled by the national
chauvinism of his co-researchers, Py made a seemingly random

and somewhat audacious observation: 'Have you never noticed that in English detective novels, the good-looking men, such as the policemen, are always six feet tall?' Immediately, as Le Corbusier relates the story, the Modulor was adjusted in length to 6 feet, or 1.83 metres, and, almost miraculously, 'the gradations of a new Modulor [. . .] translated themselves before our eyes into round figures in feet and inches!'[50] Le Corbusier made the blue scale twice the size of the red. The red scale descends, according to the Fibonacci series, from 6 feet, or 72 inches, to 4 inches, the blue from 144 to 8 inches: 144, the multiple of 12 × 12 inches or 2 × 6 feet, also appears in the Fibonacci series.[51]

The primary colours – red, blue and yellow – like geometry and measure, are the building blocks of art and composition. It is probably no coincidence that Le Corbusier's decision to use two of the primary colours for the Modulor scales also relates to the scientific experiments of the American physicist A. A. Michelson, who had evaluated the primary colours of light as a means of precisely formulating the length of the metre rod during the late nineteenth century. Michelson suggested that the light from the metal cadmium would provide a suitable alternative standard to a physical measuring rod, such that the metre length could be defined as equivalent to a specific number of wavelengths of the primary coloured light of the cadmium spectrum – red and blue.[52] As already stated above, using light to define the metre found an increasing number of supporters in the global scientific community after the Second World War, and on 14 October 1960 international agreement was eventually reached to set the metre against the radiation of the orange-red light emitted by the radioactive krypton-86 atom. Scientists regarded this as a return to a natural and verifiable definition for the metric system – although, compared to Le Corbusier's Modulor, their notion of natural measure is hidden to all but the high priests of science.

Le Corbusier chose to imbue the Modulor with meaning, to humanise measure through myth, something else he enjoyed constructing: his assistant Py was certainly aptly named for research into number and proportion. In reality, the evolution of the Modulor may have been less magical than he would have us believe. Le Corbusier undoubtedly initiated the search for a more meaningful human measure, one that would reconcile French universal rationality with Anglo-Saxon commercial global dominance. Indeed, it was an Englishman, Gerald Hanning, who completed the groundwork that defined his revolutionary scale. From the outset, according to surviving evidence, Hanning worked up a set of dimensions based on the height of a man in Imperial (British) inches: the idealised French heights were superimposed onto these, not the other way around as Le Corbusier presents the story.[53]

No doubt, Le Corbusier remained the architect of the process throughout. On receipt of Hanning's number sequence in the spring of 1944, Le Corbusier recommended that Hanning should read a recently published book by Elisa Maillard on the Golden Number sequence, *Du nombre d'Or* (Paris, 1943). Hanning then subdivided the Imperial dimensions using the ratio of the Golden Section, and the Modulor was born. It would appear that Hanning began with subdivisions of the Modulor in inches. Meanwhile, Le Corbusier persisted with the dimensions of a metric 'standard' man, 1.75 metres tall. He apparently did so until 1950.[54] By the end of 1947 the Modulor was sufficiently resolved for Le Corbusier to send a manuscript version of it to Prince Matila Ghyka in London for comment. Ghyka was the author of *Esthétique des proportions dans la nature et dans les arts* (1927) and *Le Nombre d'Or* (1931), and was well placed to offer Le Corbusier and Hanning an authoritative opinion on a scalar measuring standard relative to the Golden Section. Ghyka was sufficiently enthusiastic about the Modulor to write an explanatory and supporting account of it in the *Architectural Review*, published in February 1948.[55]

Le Corbusier first applied the Modulor to an architectural project when developing his innovative and influential housing concept, the Unité d'habitation, in Marseilles between 1946 and 1952. As built, the Unité has an overall form 24.5 metres wide, 56 metres high and 137 metres long, and Le Corbusier claimed that the Modulor permeated every part of this complex build-

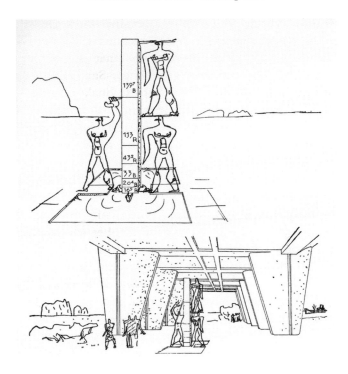

20   Le Corbusier, Modulor 'stele of measures' for the
Unité d'habitation, Marseilles, 1946–52. *Le Modulor*
(1948–9), © FLC/ADAGP, Paris and DACS, London 2007

ing.[56] He stated that only fifteen of its scalar measurements were
repeated throughout its massive form. The measures are related
to the figure of Modulor man, and he enshrined these in a symbolic concrete block, which he called a 'stele of measures', at the
building's base, like an ancient Egyptian hieroglyph (fig. 20).[57]
As Le Corbusier concluded about this innovative structure: 'We
may safely say that such exactitude, such rigour of mathematics
and harmony have never before been applied to the simplest
accessory of daily life: the dwelling.'[58]

While conceived as a new form of suburban housing, the
Unité d'habitation more obviously resembles a beached ocean-
going liner. Certainly, Le Corbusier was fond of the ship analogy

for communal living. In *Towards a New Architecture* he enthuses about the modern liner, for it can accommodate and sustain whole communities. He was particularly impressed by Cunard's *Aquitania*: 'the *Aquitania* carries 3,600 persons', and its design was functional, simple and lacked superfluous ornament. These are qualities that informed his architectural principles. Each Unité d'habitation was built to contain 1,600 people (there were intended to be a 'fleet' of these buildings around the world), and is raised above the landscape on a series of vast paired columns, like a vessel propped in dry dock. It has gangplank-like access points, with decks and rooftop funnels. Historians have pointed to the obvious parallels in scale between Le Corbusier's Unité d'habitation and French early nineteenth-century utopian set-tlements, or *phalanstères*, proposed by the French socialist philosopher Charles Fourier (1772–1837), where a single building was to house a carefully selected community of 1,600.[59] Fourier's own visual references for the building containing this community, however, were to the landlocked palaces and estates of the eighteenth century. A more obvious formal reference for Le Corbusier is biblical. He made reference in *Towards a New Architecture* to the Jewish Ark of the Covenant, describing (after the Bible) the use of simple geometry and ratios in its form and proportions.

When designing the Unité, it is possible that Le Corbusier was also thinking of a structure that would link the modern era with Noah's Ark, a man-made structure whose form was guided by God's instruction. Noah's Ark was, of course, built to contain the hand-picked community with which Noah (the appointee of God) and his wife sailed to save humankind and the earth's natural creatures from the Flood. It is surely no coincidence that the Unité d'habitation was initiated immediately after the human catastrophe of the Second World War, in which 50 million people had perished. Le Corbusier built it to offer a new life to the victims of war, as well as a new way of living in harmony with nature – where sunlight, clean air and distant landscape views provided a healthy environment for its inhabitants. Formally, Le Corbusier's Unité at Marseilles is ark-like: as built, its 'hull' is made of *béton brut*, rough board-marked concrete with the appearance of fossilised timber. In its overall form, the Unité is taller and almost double the length of the biblical archetype, which had a width, height and length equivalent to the ratios of 2 : 3 : 6, proportions also considered perfect in the Pythagoreo-Platonic tradition.[60] The Unité d'habitation was designed instead using the perfected modern relations of the Modulor.[61]

It is perhaps no coincidence that this was the first building to be designed with the Modulor – the metre modified. The Unité d'habitation was intended for communal living anywhere on the globe, and its name can also be read as a subtle inversion of the *Système international d'unités*, the united international system that regulated metric weights and measures. Le Corbusier intended that the inhabitants of his 'Unité' would dwell in harmony with nature in a vessel that celebrated the form, senses and intellects of humanity. It was a valiant attempt to reunite body and architecture – to put people before krypton atoms and the speed of light: to save mankind from an abstract measurement system, the product of pure science.

Le Corbusier's Modulor was created from the union of the world's two dominant measurement systems, the metric and the Imperial, utilising the practical and symbolic ideal of the human body. As a concept, the Modulor was intended to reunite tradition with modernity, and – for Le Corbusier and his followers – this resolution enabled measure to become useful and meaningful once again. The universal authority of the two dominant measures, however, combined with the misuse of the Modulor by architects – who applied it unthinkingly, as a short cut to design – caused Le Corbusier to abandon its promotion and usage. No matter, he had the qualities of a universal man in an era in which the tendency for specialisation and the separation of the arts and sciences undermined such a concept. He will long be remembered for his stand on this issue. It is ironic, then, that the ultimate sanctioning of the Modulor came from the most famous scientist of the twentieth century, Albert Einstein (1879–1955), who commented on the Modulor in 1946. As Le Corbusier proudly – almost breathlessly – boasts:

I had the pleasure of discussing the 'Modulor' at some length with Professor Albert Einstein at Princeton. [. . .] In a letter written to me the same evening [as our meeting], Einstein had the kindness to say this of the 'Modulor': 'It is a scale of proportions which makes the bad difficult and the good easy.' There are some who think this judgement is unscientific. For my part, I think it is extraordinarily clear-sighted. It is a gesture of friendship made by a great scientist towards us who are not scientists but soldiers on the field of battle.[62]

Building New Foundations

The nature of measure was of fundamental importance to Einstein. Natural philosophers since Newton had been trying to understand the nature of matter and radiation, and how they contributed to a unified world picture. Neither the mechanical nor the electromagnetic worldviews were capable of providing a consistent explanation for the way that matter and radiation interact when viewed simultaneously by an observer at rest and an observer moving at uniform speed. In the spring of 1905 Einstein realised that the problem was not the understanding of matter, but the absence of a theory of measurement. Three papers he wrote that year helped him to explain his thinking. The first, on Brownian motion, was concerned with the movement of particles in fluid; the second, on the photoelectric effect, re-evaluated the nature of light; and, finally, he wrote the most far-reaching of his papers, *Zur Elektrodynamik bewegter Körper* (*On the Electrodynamics of Moving Bodies*).

In what became known as his Special Theory of Relativity, Einstein stated that all measurements of time and space were relative; that is, the position of two separate events derived from judgements about the measured distance between them. He concluded that the speed of matter and radiation were universal constants when in a state of inertia; that the speed of light in a vacuum never changed. Three centuries previously, Newton had stated that gravitational forces determined the movement of bodies, or matter. Through *Die Grundlage der allgemeinen Rela-*

tivitätstheorie (*The Foundation of the General Theory of Relativity*) of 1916, Einstein could account for unexplained variations in the orbital motion of the planets, and he predicted the bending of starlight in the vicinity of a massive body such as the sun. He explained the interaction of bodies in four dimensions, through the geometry of space-time: that is, the three dimensions of Euclidean space with the addition of time, as the fourth dimension.

Between 1915 and 1930 the mainstream of physics was concerned with the development of a new conception of the fundamental character of matter, known as Quantum Theory. This theory contained the Uncertainty Principle, formulated by the German physicist Werner Heisenberg in 1927, which states that precision in measuring processes has its limitations, that it is impossible to specify precisely certain quantities simultaneously. Probability calculations are used in quantum mechanics to replace the precise predictions of classical mechanics. The Uncertainty Principle – also known as the indeterminacy principle – appeared to contradict the traditional conception of causality, which is essential to the method of modern science. Causality is the belief that the cause of any event is the event that preceded it back to the root cause, which contributes to an understanding of the fundamentals of the natural order.

There are those who deny the fundamental validity of the causal relation. The French philosopher Henri Bergson (1859–1941) maintained that ultimate reality is not bound by exact causal sequences. Life is a process of growth in which the unpredictable, and therefore the uncaused, constantly occurs. Instead of cause and effect, Bergson advanced a theory of evolution based on the spiritual dimension of human life. His thesis, published as *Essai sur les données immédiates de la conscience* (*Time and Free Will*, 1889; translated 1910), had widespread influence. He presents his theories on the freedom of the mind and on duration, which he regarded as the succession of conscious states, intermingling and unmeasured. His *L'Evolution créatrice* (*Creative Evolution*, 1907; translated 1911) probes the entire problem of human existence and defined the mind as pure energy, the *élan vital* – vital force – responsible for all organic evolution. Bergson emphasised the importance of intuition over intellect, and promoted the idea of two opposing currents: inert matter and organic life as the source of the vital urge that strives towards free creative action.

Much as Le Corbusier attempted to synthesise British and metric measuring systems, Einstein found a way of merging traditional ideas about causality with the uncertainties of the evolutionary process. He believed that scientific theory was arrived at creatively through intuition, and was not based on experiment alone. The goal of modern science is to be able to state a good theory simply, by reducing what is known about the natural world into a unified and minimal statement. This is evident in the very sparseness of the postulates in Einstein's work, such as his famous formula for the relationship between energy and mass, $E = mc^2$ – not that this makes it any more comprehensible for the uninitiated!

Art and science is fused, intuitively and rationally, in the creations of Duchamp. His presentations of 'canned chance' satisfy mind and eye, and the relationship of our body and senses to the physical and sensory world we have constructed. His concern with measure, and the search for precision, parallel that of scientists and philosophers, except that he elevated quality over quantity. Fundamentally, he did not seek a solution, 'because there is no problem'.[63] As an artist he was able to find a point of equilibrium that enabled him to question the abstract phenomena of the natural world, and to imbue them with human qualities. As the French poet Guillaume Apollinaire observed in *Méditations esthétiques: les peintres cubistes* (*The Cubist Painters*, 1913; translated 1949), 'It will perhaps be reserved for an artist as disengaged from aesthetic preoccupations, as occupied with energy as Marcel Duchamp, to reconcile Art to the People.'[64] With the benefit of hindsight, Apollinaire might have written, 'to reconcile Art *and* Science *for* the People'.

Heidegger and Weil: Providing New Roots for 'Being'

The influential German philosopher Martin Heidegger (1889–1976) was concerned – like Duchamp – not only with how things appear, but also what they mean for mankind, and how we sense their 'being' in the world. They were both ironists.[65] Heidegger, however, presented his findings not as Duchamp had done through conceptual images informed by ideas, but primarily through the careful construction of language.

Heidegger focused his intelligence on words – their meaning, weight and measure – through poetry, and he published *Sein und Zeit* (*Being and Time*) in 1927. By 'being', Heidegger meant our ability to locate ourselves – through the senses, mind and body – in the world. He articulated the concern that modern technology had separated thought from 'being', and that they needed to be reunited if humankind was to exist complete and authentically, to be 'rooted' on earth. In 'Wozu Dichter?' (translated as 'What are the Poets for?' by A. Hofstadter, in *Poetry, Language, Thought*, 1971) Heidegger uses fourteen lines of a poem written by Friedrich Hölderlin (1770–1843) to explain this 'rootedness', and emphasises that it will come about only when mankind can dwell poetically. His extract from Hölderlin runs as follows:

> May, if life is sheer toil, a man
> Lift his eyes and say: so
> I too wish to be? Yes. As long as Kindness,
> The Pure, still stays with his heart, man
> Not unhappily measures himself
> Against the godhead. Is God unknown?
> Is he manifest like the sky? I'd sooner
> Believe the latter. It's the measure of man.
> Full of merit, yet poetically, man
> Dwells on this earth. But no purer
> Is the shade of the starry night,
> If I might put it so, than

Man, who's called an image of the godhead.
Is there a measure on earth? There is
None.

Heidegger draws attention to three aspects of this extract: the
meaning of the poetic and its relationship to dwelling, for 'poetically man dwells'; the measuring of words through spiritual,
physical and metaphysical distance – he says that 'poetry is a
measuring' (as in poetic metre); and to God, the 'godhead', the
ultimate measure for humankind.

Heidegger's views on measure and measuring are helpful here.
In order to dwell, humankind needs to be able to measure the
distance between the sky and the earth, but this distance cannot
be measured quantitatively: 'the *nature* of measure is no more a
quantum than is the *nature* of number. True, we can reckon with
numbers – but not with the *nature* of number [his italics].'
Instead, the true nature of measure and number for Heidegger
is appreciated through all the senses – and it is the poet (and, of
course, the visual artist such as Duchamp) who can reveal its
qualities, by inducing thought, imagination and reflection.[66] It is
suggested in Hölderlin's poem that God is in and revealed
through the sky, and to measure God we must appreciate the
qualities and dimensions of the heavens in relation to earth. This,
he admits, is a 'strange measure' to understand and use ordinarily, and of little use for all 'merely scientific ideas'; nor is it
'a palpable stick or rod but in truth [it is] simpler to handle
than they'. According to Heidegger's way of thinking, the only
authentic measure on earth is the all-embracing perception of
humankind, through the relation of body and mind. This
measure is realised and best enjoyed through the heightened
awareness of time, memory and the natural qualities that exist
around us.

Hannah Arendt (1906–1975) had a brief love affair with Heidegger in the 1920s, and he provided inspiration for her writings. In her book *The Human Condition* (1958), Arendt focused
on action – 'doing' rather than 'being' – and referred to the distinction made by John Locke between labour and work: 'the

labour of our body and the work of our hands'. Labour relates to our being and is a constant of our active lives, while work is the product of our hands, by *homo faber*, by which the artificial world we inhabit is fabricated. Together they are the fundamental activities of human life. The counterpart of human activity is contemplation, which can be achieved only if we are at peace with the world. Arendt referred back to ancient Greece and the early United States – of Washington and Jefferson – to a time when citizens successfully balanced the active and the contemplative life, and their public and private realms were clearly defined. A central theme of Arendt's writings is the need for us to separate political life (the public realm) from social and economic life (the private realm), and so be able to devote time – our activity – to the community. She laments the fact that our public and private worlds have been absorbed into the social and economic sphere of modern life.

A remarkable, but less well-known social philosopher, was Simone Weil (1909–1943). Weil was writing at a time when Heidegger was *persona non grata*, having declared his political allegiance to the German Nazi Party, which was then occupying her native France: his membership caused much debate in America at the time, not least because Arendt gained fame in America as a German-Jewish refugee scholar. Weil writes of her opposition to the totalitarianism of Hitler – and any such regime (as, indeed, Arendt also did in *The Origins of Totalitarianism* of 1951) – while retaining Heidegger's mistrust of modern science and its obsession with quantity over quality. General de Gaulle, as head of the Free French forces, was looking forward to a brighter future, and he commissioned Weil to write a report on the duties and privileges that France would confront when at peace once more. Her response, *L'Enracinement*, was written in 1942 and published posthumously in 1949 in English as *The Need for Roots: Prelude to a Declaration of Duties towards Mankind*, since Weil died in England of tuberculosis, aged 33, attempting in vain to subsist on the same rations as her compatriots in occupied France. Weil's text is arranged in three parts: 'The Needs of the Soul', 'Uprootedness' and 'The Growing of Roots'. In this work she is

addressing humankind in general, but in particular those who
share the spiritual heritage of the West, in which she was intellectually and spiritually immersed.

In his Preface to the first English edition of *The Need for Roots*
of 1952, the American-British poet T. S. Eliot (1888–1965)
relates how Weil sought to warn us against the 'evils of an over-
centralised society', and how she expressed 'a profound horror
of what she called the *collectivity* – the monster created by
modern totalitarianism. What she cared about was human souls.'
Eliot continues:

> Not the least striking example of her shrewdness, balance and
> good sense is her examination of the principle of monarchy;
> and her short review of the political history of France is at
> once a condemnation of the French Revolution and a power-
> ful argument against the possibility of a restoration of the king-
> ship. She cannot be classified either as a reactionary or as a
> socialist.[67]

However, if kingship and collectivity are incapable of sustaining
modern man, science is no substitute. Weil argues:

> The modern conception of science is responsible, as is that
> of history and that of art, for the monstrous conditions
> under which we live, and will, in its turn, have to be trans-
> formed, before we can hope to see the dawn of a better civi-
> lization.[68]

Weil was concerned with over-centralisation in government and
the loss of the individual, who had never before 'been so completely delivered up to a blind collectivity' – especially as it was
threatening Europe during the dark years of the Second World
War. She had observed at first-hand how ruthless dictators –
which the vacuum left by the French Revolution had made
possible – had rendered men 'less capable, not only of subordi-
nating their actions to their thoughts, but even of thinking'. Weil
characterised this collectivity as a 'social machine', one that had
been exploited 'for manufacturing irresponsibility, stupidity,
corruption, slackness and, above all, dizziness'. Collectivity exists
because

We are living in a world in which nothing is made to man's measure; there exists a monstrous discrepancy between man's body, man's mind and the things which at the present time constitute the elements of human existence; everything is in disequilibrium.[69]

Not only did she blame over-centralisation, but she also condemned the 'prestige which science and savants have acquired over people's minds' in democratically advanced societies.

As for the spirit and soul of humankind, post-Enlightenment science sits uncomfortably with such qualities: reason and faith are commonly regarded as incompatible extremes.[70] Yet Newton – the father of modern science – balanced his scientific discoveries with a continued fundamental belief in, and fascination for, the spiritual in life. It was his so-called followers – disciples even – who focused primarily on his mathematics and physics to the exclusion of his spiritual concerns. Indeed, it came to be believed that 'the new science could create a world view that would substitute for the religious order of the soul'.[71] Boullée's cenotaph to Newton, and the appeal of French intellectuals for a new religion in his name, provides clear evidence of this impetus in the late eighteenth century.

Weil concludes (as did Arendt in *The Human Condition*) that materialism fills the void left by the loss of faith: we measure our well-being instead through the gadgetry that technology – the most tangible product of the scientific revolution – provides. Technology, in this way, is consequently a symbol of the intellectual potency and virility of the first-world nations: 'our only claim to be proud of ourselves as Westerners, men of the white race, modern men'.[72]

The response of the United States to the initial lead taken by the Soviet Union's successful launch of the first man in space may furnish evidence, although, of course, this race had as much to do with politics as the hoped-for advancement of scientific frontiers, the US wishing to provide proof of the superiority of democracy and capitalism over the collectivism of the USSR. Interestingly, the astronauts – the most sophisticated high priests of advanced technology – did not allow their essential humanity to be displaced entirely by the political and scientific ideology that propelled their mission. The lasting images, words and deeds from that era have a complex significance: at once earthly and spiritual, as well as science-bound and mythical.

Humanising the Universe – Man in Outer Space

While scientists since Newton have argued that the body is not an appropriate medium by which to interpret the natural mysteries of the universe, this is exactly how the first astronauts experienced and described their relation to outer space – through their bodies and minds – and, perhaps more surprisingly, in spiritual terms. Neil Armstrong famously declared to the world, when first setting foot on the moon: 'That's one small step for a man, one giant leap for mankind.'[73] He left behind him a plaque that read: 'Here men from the planet Earth first set foot upon the Moon, July 1969, AD. We came in peace for all Mankind.' Body and mind – humanity – was united extraterrestrially on the moon.

Less known, but equally remarkable, are the actions of Armstrong's fellow astronaut Edwin 'Buzz' Aldrin, the second man to step onto the moon (fig. 21). On the day of the lunar landing, Aldrin celebrated Communion alone in the command module in orbit around the moon. He had with him a chalice of wine provided by the minister of his Presbyterian church, the Reverend Dean Woodruff,[74] and while Aldrin was traversing the heavens, Woodruff ministered a parallel Communion to his church congregation on earth. Very aware that this was no ordinary Communion, Woodruff modified the ancient Christian ceremony with symbolic intent, as Armstrong relates:

> As Mr Woodruff broke the loaf of bread and held it up for view, he pointed out that the loaf was not whole; he did not say what had happened to the missing piece, but the congregation understood that, symbolically, it had gone with Buzz.[75]

21 Edwin 'Buzz' Aldrin, the second man to step onto the moon on the lunar surface, NASA (AS11–40–5903), 20 July 1969

Addressing his congregation, Woodruff's final prayer ran:

> Even as the door to the universe is being opened by this flight, this crew, this man, deliver us all from pride and arrogance and all unrighteousness [. . .]. We dedicate unto Thee, Thy servant and our brother, Edwin Aldrin, to represent the Body of Christ, our nation, and all mankind on the first expedition to another planet.[76]

Buzz Aldrin – a blond-haired, blue-eyed, 5 feet 10 inches tall, 165-pound astronaut of Anglo-Saxon stock, whose deceased mother bore the maiden name Marian Moon – had asked Woodruff about a month before the moon flight 'to come up with some symbol [. . .] that transcended modern times'.[77] In preparation for that task, Woodruff wrote a paper entitled *The Myth of Apollo 11: The Effects of the Lunar Landing on the Mythic Dimension of Man*. He referred in this paper to the intellectual shifts caused by the ideas of Copernicus and Darwin, and the need for a symbol of the modern age – since 'myth and symbols are so pervasive in the psyche of man'.[78] He had been influenced by an essay written a decade earlier by the French literary critic, sociologist and philosopher Roland Barthes (1915–1980), who had observed that it was the nature of myth to turn historical event into natural object.[79] What transcended all ages for Woodruff was the 'magic flight' as described by the Romanian-born philosopher and poet Mircea Eliade (1907–1986) in *Mythes, rêves et mystères* (1957) (Woodruff refers to the English translation of 1961, *Myths, Dreams and Mysteries: The Encounter between Contemporary Faiths and Archaic Realities*). Eliade's writings are concerned with the symbolic ways through which communication is established between the sacred and the profane. By the 'magic flight' he is referring to one of the most ancient motifs found in mythology: 'the longing to break the ties that hold him [humankind] in bondage to the earth [. . .] a desire to free himself from his limitation, which he feels to be a kind of degradation [. . .] must be ranked among the specific marks of man'.[80] It led Woodruff to state unequivocally that 'Science, as the achievement of man, has created a worldwide technical civilization and, as yet, has not given birth to any cultural symbols by which man can live.'[81]

Certainly, the metric system has limited symbolic status, even though it is undoubtedly a standard by which most of the world has lived in recent generations: except, of course, in the United States. In the spirit of eighteenth-century rationality, however, Woodruff does grant the earth a symbolic role by relating it to the 'mythic dimension' of man:

> The Apollo event comes at a time when we need a symbol, and need to tap a myth that will graphically express the unending journey outward. Perhaps when those pioneers step on another planet and view the earth from a physically transcendent stance, we can sense its symbolism and feel a new breadth of freedom for our current cultural claustrophobia and be awakened once again to the mythic dimension of man.[82]

The moon landing on 20 July 1969 was a shared global experience through the medium of television. It represented the most extraordinary culmination of science, technology, human spirit and endeavour. The experience had a profound effect – even spiritual, as we have seen – on those who took part in and witnessed the lunar missions. Still, there were those who remained sceptical about their value, and whether the huge financial cost was warranted.

Once the race to place man on the moon was won, NASA set a new objective: to explore beyond the solar system that immediately defines our place in the universe. Intriguingly, the first man-made object to escape our solar system took with it, in the absence of humans, a plaque displaying a pictogram of the dimensions of an idealised man and woman. This was dispatched into outer space on the exterior of the NASA spacecraft *Pioneer 10* in 1972.

The plaque was conceived by Carl Sagan (1934–1996) and Frank Drake, and has artwork on it drawn by Linda Salzman Sagan, Carl Sagan's artist wife. An eminent astronomer, Frank Drake had conducted the first radio search for extraterrestrial intelligence from the National Radio Astronomy Observatory at Green Bank in West Virginia in 1960. Carl Sagan was also a pioneering exobiologist and a gifted teacher: he made the search for extraterrestrial life a respectable scientific discipline. The plaque, an engraved gold-anodised aluminium plate, was displayed on the exterior of *Pioneer 10*, in case intelligent extraterrestrial life forms stumbled across the spacecraft and questioned its origins fig. 22). It has human figures juxtaposed with a schematic diagram of our solar system, but it lacks an obvious reference to the metric system.

The plaque was given the dimensions, using the customary measure of the US, of 6 × 9 inches (152 × 229 mm), and it was bolted to the antenna support struts of *Pioneer 10*. A duplicate was attached to its sister ship *Pioneer 11*, which was launched the following year. Each spacecraft is composed of a large dish antenna 9 feet in diameter (2.7 m), from which other antennae booms extend, and this profile is shown in outline on the plaque, positioned behind the idealised depictions of a man and a woman. Around their bodies – to the left and at the base of the plaque – are circles and binary codes, and lines that emanate

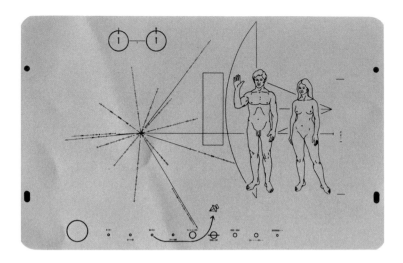

22   *Pioneer 10* Plaque, NASA: actual dimensions 6 by 9 inches (152 × 229 mm), 1972

radially from a single point. Together these are intended to identify our solar system, *Pioneer*'s trajectory from earth, the distance of the planets (then listed as numbering nine) from the sun in binary form, and the distance within our galaxy of fourteen pulsars from the sun.[83]

According to NASA's description of the plaque, the 'human figures represent the type of creature that created Pioneer', and the man's hand is raised 'in a gesture of good will'. NASA states that the proportions of their perfect nakedness were determined scientifically, 'from results of a computerised analysis of the average person in our civilisation', which is, most probably, a claim without foundation.[84] The figures stand in perspective, so that the top of their feet is visible, and the male is about 6 foot tall from head to instep, scaled from the 9-foot diameter of the spacecraft in silhouette behind him. The woman scales at about 5 feet 5 inches tall. The key to translating the plaque

Lies in understanding the breakdown of the most common element in the universe – hydrogen. This element is illustrated

in the [upper] left-hand corner of the plaque in schematic
form showing the hyperfine transition of neutral atomic hydrogen. Anyone from a scientifically educated civilization having
enough knowledge of hydrogen would be able to translate the
message.[85]

The hydrogen transition puts out a characteristic radio wavelength of 21 centimetres, and this is the base length for the
images on the plaque. To the side of the woman are small horizontal and vertical ticks that represent the number 8 in binary
form: 'Therefore', NASA's commentary concludes, 'the woman is
8 × 21 cm = 168 cm'.

The plaque is clearly conceived as a combination of measures:
the height of the man to the diameter of the spacecraft is as
6:9 feet; the dimensions of the plaque are 6 × 9 inches. The
hydrogen element, galaxy and solar-system diagrams and the
woman are all dimensionally related through scientific measures,
including the metre. It is as if the designers have combined two
orders, the ancient anthropomorphic tradition represented by
the body of man, and a new universal scientific order represented
by woman: the spacecraft – which is the product, perhaps even
the seed of man – unites humankind in its journey through the
universe. An eminent scientist, Sagan dwelt poetically. He could
make sense of the universe only through life forms. He sought
beings to make sense of mathematical abstraction. Intriguingly,
Sagan later, in the years 1990–92, commissioned Guillermo
Jullian de la Fuente, a protégé of Le Corbusier, to design a house
(for him and his subsequent wife, Ann Druyan, in Ithaca, New
York) using the proportions of the Modulor.[86]

Sagan's interest in extraterrestrial life forms has another
dimension to it. Consciously or otherwise he wished to imbue
the abstract quantity of outer space with qualities that ordinary
mortals can value. This is the driver for science fiction writers,
the hope and anticipation of discovering life – preferably
humanoid in appearance – beyond our solar system. In more
mainstream modern literature, too, Italo Calvino (1923–1985),
the celebrated Italian writer, derided the efforts of humans to

use science and technology to escape the physical world for outer space. He believed that what has to be confronted by humans resides with us already on earth. In his final book, *Six Memos for the Next Millennium* (1988), Calvino attempted to describe an anthropomorphic universe in which 'man has never existed', and concluded: 'it seems extremely unlikely that man could ever exist in such a universe'. He was convinced 'that our imagination cannot be anything *but* anthropomorphic'.[87] I am sure Calvino is correct. The manned moon landings are part of a similar thinking: they made outer space comprehensible in human terms, a marriage of scientific endeavour and technology with individual human bravery. There is a very necessary alchemy of science and art.

Of course, humanity has benefited from the considerable scientific advances of modern times, and the apparent freedom that was heralded by the political and social revolutions in France and America in the late eighteenth century. But, among the gains there have been some catastrophic losses – not least of balance: whether this is expressed as demonstrated or felt, or quantitative or qualitative. Ultimately, it would appear self-evident that rational knowledge (science) cannot exist without imagination (art), and the human mind cannot comprehend a universe of which it does not consider itself an essential and integral part.

I have described the search for universal measures appropriate to each age: from classical antiquity to modern times. Artists and scientists vied with one another to portray nature as fully as their different techniques permitted. The simulation of beauty through regulated and perfected bodily form was gradually displaced – by the anatomist's knife and the astronomer's gaze – into and beyond the body. Since the late eighteenth century science has dominated and shaped measure. Measure – through the metric system – has come to be regarded as a set of truths. This brings Richard Rorty's elegantly profound insight to mind:

> Truths are the skeletons which remain after the capacity to arouse the senses – to cause tingles – has been rubbed off by familiarity and long usage. After the scales are rubbed off a

butterfly's wing, you have transparency, but not beauty –
formal structure without sensuous content.[88]

Metric truths are measures – human conceptions – stripped
bare by reason. Evident in the ironic responses to the empire of
science during the twentieth century is an expression of the need
to connect directly with the mysteries that surround us, to reveal
and associate with the anthropomorphic that is manifest in
nature. This need will not be eradicated by science: balance
demands that it will become more pronounced. Our bodies
require a positive relation with the natural world, and measuring the world with and through our bodies is essential to civilised
– human – existence. It is doubtful that the balance will be
redressed quickly, though the obstinacy of the United States, and
its regard for human liberty, may yet supply an antidote.

Epilogue

The Statue of Liberty is perhaps the most famous gift made by the French nation to the American people, the most memorable symbol of the most potent of Revolutionary ideals. And more. The Statue might be regarded as equivalent to the Trojan Horse of antiquity: its surface both beguiles and conceals. Beneath her outwardly seductive, well-proportioned classical lines, the Statue embodies the metric values to which the United States has yet to subscribe.

The Statue of Liberty was the brain child of a Franco-American union and received encouragement from a prominent and influential French politician, Édouard Laboulaye (1811– 1883), who proposed in 1865 that the French should demonstrate tangibly their allegiance to the US at the centenary in 1876 of the American Revolution, when liberty – Independence – was gained from British rule. Originally known as *La liberté éclairant le monde* (*Liberty Enlightening the World*), Liberty symbolises the Revolutionary ideals shared by both nations, of *égalité*, or equality.[1] The copper figure of Liberty, designed by the architect-sculptor Frédéric Auguste Bartholdi (1834–1904), has an internal wrought-iron frame engineered by Alexandre Gustave Eiffel (1832–1923), who designed France's own great iconic structure in Paris, the Eiffel Tower.

The Eiffel Tower was built to mark the entrance of the *Exposition Universelle* (1889), an international exhibition commemorating the centenary of the Storming of the Bastille on 14 July 1789. The Eiffel Tower is a prominent demonstration of French Enlightenment rationality, a structure without body. Its frame rises to a fraction over 300 metres to the base of the antenna at its summit: it was conceived metrically. Its counterpart, the Statue of Liberty, the tallest figural sculpture in the world, would

23   Computer generated montage of the masterplan for the
World Trade Center and the Freedom Tower, New York City, with
the Statue of Liberty in the foreground as envisioned by Daniel
Libeskind in 2003. © Studio Daniel Libeskind

appear to be more traditional in conception. But she conceals
the same rationality beneath her metal folds, 2.5 mm thick,[2]
rising to a fraction over 46 metres (just over 151 feet). The granite
pedestal on which Liberty is located was designed by the first
Paris-trained Beaux-Arts American-born architect, Richard
Morris Hunt (1827–1895), and is close to 27 metres high (89
feet tall). Without information to the contrary, we must assume
that – designed and constructed in France (in the workshop of
Gaget, Gauthier et Cie on the rue de Chazelles, Paris) and then
dismantled and shipped to America in more than 300 crates –
Liberty is an embodiment of the metric system.[3]

After the terrorist outrage of 9/11 in 2001, and the tragic col-
lapse of the twin towers of the World Trade Center, entry to the
interior of the Statue of Liberty was denied to the public. That
remains the situation in December 2006 as I write the final sentences of this book. Meanwhile, architect Daniel Libeskind has
conceived a new symbol, the Freedom Tower, to replace the
destroyed building. His competition-winning design of 2002 was

for a slender, tapering tower rising to an asymmetrically placed spire, which evoked the outstretched arm and raised torch of the Statue of Liberty. The whole edifice would have been 1776 feet tall: the year of the American Declaration of Independence translated by a fundamental unit of human measurement into a new challenge to the world. Regrettably, in order to meet the commercial demands of the developer, Libeskind was required to rationalise its design in 2003, in collaboration with architects Skidmore, Owings and Merrill (SOM). The redesigned tower accommodated more commercial space at its upper levels, while retaining the same overall height, its twisting top and spire (fig. 23).[4] But a final redesign in 2005, led by SOM, will see the Freedom Tower stripped of its provocative figural characterisation: the sculptural and symbolic unity of Libeskind's earlier designs has been lost. Only the height of 1776 feet will survive in the building now under construction: a much-reduced standard with which to measure Liberty in the twenty-first century.

Notes

Preface: Smoot's Ear

1   I have been unable to find a definitive conventionally published source, and my account of the creation of the Smoot is derived from a collection of weblinks, some carried by MIT, others by Wikipedia and related links, all of which were accessible in September 2006. There is a corroborating interview with Mr Smoot on US National Public Radio on 7 December 2005 listed on Wikipedia (en.wikipedia.org/wiki/Oliver_R._Smoot), which can be heard at www.npr.org/templates/story/story.php?storyId= 5043041. See also Wikipedia: en.wikipedia.org/wiki/Smoot. MIT weblinks include: www-tech.mit.edu/V119/N49/this_week-_49_c.49f.html; web.mit.edu/newsoffice/1997/smoot-1105.html. See also www.iso.ch/iso/en/commcentre/news/archives/2003/ smoot.html and aether.lbl.gov/www/personnel/smoot/smoot-measure.html. Mr Smoot kindly read this Preface in October 2006, and it appears here as he corrected it.

2   See www.lambdachi.org/fraternity/creed.asp (accessed September 2006).

3   See Wikipedia: en.wikipedia.org/wiki/Harvard_Bridge (accessed September 2006).

Introduction: Measure and Meaning

1   An earlier version of this chapter was published in *Architectural Research Quarterly* and *Nexus*, following a conference paper presented at *Nexus IV: Architecture and Mathematics* in Portugal, 2002. See Tavernor 2002b.

2   See, for example, Cotterell 1986.

3   Chisholm 1997.

4   Alberti 1988; Palladio 1997; and see Rykwert 1976, Vitruvius 1960 and Le Corbusier 1987.

5   Alberti 1988; Palladio 1997.
6   Chisholm 1877: 27.
7   Cox 1957: 23–4.
8   Beal 1884: 1, 70–71; also quoted in Cox 1957: 23–4.
9   Plato, *Timaeus* 35b. See, for example, Cornford 1937: 67.
10   See, for example, Stewart 1978; Rykwert 1996: 104–12.
11   Plato, *Phaedrus*, 264c. See also Aristotle, *Poetics*, 1459a 17ff.
12   Cicero, *Orator*, 44.149, 49.164 and 65.220; and *Brutus*, 83.287 and 95.325.
13   Vitruvius, 1960: 72–5.
14   Tavernor 2002a.
15   Newton 1999: 59–60, 941–3; and see Voegelin 1948: 471.
16   Outram 1989.
17   For the origins of the metric system, see, in particular, Bigourdan 1901 and La Condamine 1747.
18   This was widely appreciated in France and abroad even while the metric system was being defined. See, for example, the report by the United States Secretary of State Thomas Jefferson to the US Congress in 1790, in Peterson 1984: 393–6.
19   Danloux-Dumesnils 1969: 36–42.
20   Le Corbusier 1951: 60.
21   See, for example, Chisholm 1877 and Klein 1988. Problems associated with the assumption that mensuration is a science are discussed in Fernie 1978.

1.   Body and Measure

1   Le Corbusier 1987: 70.
2   Vitruvius 1960: 27.
3   By extrapolation the ancient Egyptian *stadion* is equivalent to 157.5 metres. Working back from Eratosthenes' calculation of the distance between Aswan and Alexandria as 5,000 *stades*, 5,000 × 157.5 metres equals 787.5 kilometres. The official modern scientific dimension for the earth of 40,074 kilometres, rather than 40,000 kilometres.
4   Kidson 1990: 83.
5   Respectively, 5 × 0.3552 metres = 1.776 metres; and 6 × 0.296 metres = 1.776 metres.
6   Kidson 1990: 83.
7   Waele 1997: 30–32.

8   For example, one Roman foot (*pes* of 296 millimetres) equals
    11.654 English inches.
9   Vitruvius 1960: 253.
10 Kidson 1990: 77. Theon of Smyrna described the method of dif-
    ferential addition in the second century AD, which results in prac-
    tical approximations of $\sqrt{2}$ as the ratios of 5:7 and 12:17, which
    were still being used for this purpose in the Middle Ages.
11 Kidson 1990: 91. For similar reasons of compatibility and ease of
    calculation, a cubit of 24 digits was widely used by architects in
    antiquity.
12 Kidson 1990: 84.
13 See Panofsky 1970, especially p.128; and Dekoulakou-Sideris
    1990 for a less intact relief, fig. 2; and Wilson Jones 2000, fig. 3.
14 It has been suggested that the imprint of a fist or palm would have
    been placed above the missing forearm. Other commentators
    have identified an indent in the surface of the surviving forearm
    as the imprint of a fist: see Rykwert 1996: 99.
15 Fernie 1981; Hecht 1985; Berger, Müller-Huber and Thommen
    1992; Rykwert 1996: 99 and 426, n. 7.
16 Kidson 1990: 84.
17 Plato, *Statesman*: 283b–285b
18 Kreikenbom 1990; Rykwert 1996: 104.
19 Rykwert 1996: 100–10.
20 Philipp 1990; Rykwert 1996: 426, n. 8.
21 Vitruvius 1960: 72.
22 Vitruvius 1960: 72.
23 Vitruvius 1960: 73 and 134.
24 Vitruvius 1960: 74; Hultsch 1866: 113, 2: 57f; Kidson 1990: 81–2.
    The Roman system of measures appears to echo these idealised
    Greek human proportions, a Roman foot equalled 16 digits, 12
    inches (*unciae*) and 4 palms, and a cubit equalled one-and-a-half
    feet.
25 Vitruvius 1960: 134–5.
26 Vitruvius 1960: 73.
27 This is explored in Tavernor 2002a.
28 1 Timothy 2, 5: Augustine 1972: 643.
29 Augustine 1955: 26; Augustine 1972: 643.
30 Augustine 1955: 493; Augustine 1972: 643.
31 Augustine 1972: 1073–4.
32 Tavernor 1998.

33 Alberti 1988: IX.7.
34 Winfield and Winfield 1982: 3.
35 Vitruvius 1960: 72.
36 Winfield and Winfield 1982: 44–5.
37 The overall height of Panselinos' canonic figure is $7^1/_4$ heads and is consequently shorter than the overall height of Vitruvius's by $^3/_4$ of a head.
38 Winfield and Winfield 1982: 51–101.
39 Winfield and Winfield 1982: 103.
40 Vasari 1965: 50.
41 Manetti 1976: 48, fol. 295v.
42 Alberti 1988: 155.
43 Alberti 1972: 133.
44 Alberti 1972: 133–5.
45 Alberti 1972: 141, n. 12.
46 Although he switched from Vitruvius's description of the ideal man whose navel is the centre point of a square and circle, to one where the centre is more properly described by the base of the pelvis – something realised in the Florentine artistic community in the early fifteenth century: Aiken 1980: 81, n. 47. The navel, or *punto di vita*, although having lost its status as the centre of equilibrium, was accorded a perfect proportional position by Alberti, the height of the navel to the height of the whole body being governed by perfect numbers.
47 Stinger 1985: 65.
48 Coffin 1979: 12; and Delorme 1648: V, 1, fol. 131r–v.
49 Morsolin 1894: 501.
50 Walzer 1974: 17.
51 Kantorowicz 1955: 78–9.
52 Walzer 1974: 14–20.
53 Walzer 1974: 21–3.
54 The equivalent of 12.79 inches or 325 millimetres compared to 11.654 inches or 296 millimetres.
55 76.734 inches or 1.949 metres.
56 Paucton 1780: 48–9. The *aune* was equivalent to 46.77 inches or 1.188 metres.
57 Thorpe 1840: I, 269; Cox 1957: 30, n. 26.
58 *Great Britain* (1225–1806) 17 Edward II: I, 400.
59 Equivalent to 13.22 inches in length.
60 Baxandall 1972.

2. Science and Measure

1   Sagan 1974: 19.
2   Westfall 1980: 2–39. Harries 2001 has proved to be a valuable source for this chapter.
3   Snellius 1617; Cox 1957: 66. 55,100 *toises* equals 117,449 yards and 107,396 metres.
4   Mersenne 1644.
5   Voegelin 1948: 470–71.
6   Newton 1999: 59–60, 941–3; Cassirer 1922: 447; Voegelin 1948: 471.
7   Newton 1999: 942; Voegelin 1948: 471.
8   Newton 1717, Quaestio XVIII; Voegelin 1948: 462 94.
9   Hellman 1998: 59.
10 Newton 1999: 942; Voegelin 1948: 471.
11 Locke 1988 [1690]: I, ch. I, sect. I, p. 141.
12 Newton 1726: *scholium* to Definition VIII; Voegelin 1948: 468–9.
13 Locke 1988 [1690], II, XIII.4.
14 Locke 1988 [1690], II, XIV.1.
15 Middleton 1999: 31.
16 Locke 1988 [1690], II, XVII.3.
17 Westfall 1980: 732.
18 Hahn 1971: 12. Although its first official meeting was not until 22 December 1666.
19 Wren had been Professor of Astronomy at Gresham College in London since 1657, and became Savilian Professor of Astronomy at Oxford in 1660, the year of the king's restoration. See Jardine 2002: 109–14.
20 Sprat 1667: 8.
21 Keene, Burns and Saint 2004: 194; Jardine 2002: 86.
22 Wiener 1907: 103–4.
23 Whinney 1958; Jardine 2002.
24 Sprat 1667: 246.
25 Wilkins 1668; Wiener 1907.
26 Paucton 1780: 11–13.
27 Bigourdan 1901: 5.
28 Kula 1986: 180.
29 Crosland 1972: 278.
30 Bigourdan 1901: 3; Cox 1957: 32; Kula 1986: 161–84.
31 Clémenceau 1909: 104; Kula 1986: 169.

32   Clémenceau 1909: 89–92; Kula 1986: 168.

33   Clémenceau 1909: 94–8; Kula 1986: 168–9.

34   Kula 1986: 181–3.

35   La Hire 1714: 511–18; La Condamine 1747: 489–514, 721–58; La Condamine 1757: 566–8; La Condamine 1772: II, Part 2, 269–306; Danloux-Dumesnils 1969: 2; Cox 1957: 37.

36   Cox 1957: 58–9.

37   Young 1794: II, 43–6; Cox 1957: 54–5 and 58.

38   Young 1794: II, 43–6; Cox 1957: 54–5 and 58.

39   Mavidal and Laurent 1879–1913, XI; 104; Crosland 1972: 284; Cox 1957: 55.

40   Champagne 1979: 124.

41   Crosland 1972: 277.

42   Cox 1957: 10, n. 20.

43   Hellman 1936: 314–15; Crosland 1972: 280; Klein 1988: 108.

44   Riccioli 1704; Cox 1957: 73, n. 21.

45   One *virgula* had the equivalent length of 1.8553 metres.

46   Snell's name is Latinised to Snellius for his publications: Snellius 1731; Picard 1666: VII, 9; Cox 1957: 66–7; Crosland 1972: 280; Klein 1988: 108–10; Newton 1999: 822.

47   Picard 1666: VII, 133–42; Cox 1957: 74.

48   Wiener 1907: 103–4; Picard 1666: VII, 133–42; Cox 1957: 68–9.

49   Huygens 1673: *prop.* XXV; Huygens 1888–1950, XVIII: 348–50; Crosland 1972: 280.

50   Richer 1674; Cox 1957: 69.

51   Wilford 2000: 132–51.

52   Cassini 1720: 158–9; Cox 1957: 75; Wilford 2000: 120–21.

53   From the 1694 edition; Hahn 1971: 37.

54   Crosland 1972: 289–94.

55   Voltaire 1962 [1764]: 9.

56   Voltaire 1733: 41–2. See also Porter 2000: 6–7.

57   Diderot 1969: III, 416; Cru 1966: ch. 3; Porter 2000: 8.

58   Porter 2000: 7.

59   Lough 1982: 134 and 136–7.

60   Diderot and d'Alembert 1751–65, X, 'Mesure': 423; XII, 'Poids': 855.

61   Clarke 1979: 24–5.

62   Wilford 2000: 121–31; Cox 1957: 67, n. 8.

63   Wilford 2000: 125.

64   La Hire 1714: 511–18; La Condamine 1772: II, Part 2, 269–306; La Condamine 1747: 489–514, 721–58; La Condamine 1757: 566;

Danloux-Dumesnils 1969: 2; Cox 1957: 37, 76–7, 283 and 293; Wilford 2000: 121–31.

65   Crosland 1972: 278–9; Champagne 1979: 132. Cf. Téron 1801: 4; Kula 1986: 177.

66   Cox 1957: 59, 77–8 and n. 30. See also Crosland 1972: 279; Champagne 1979: 62, 146–8, 208–10, 451–2; Lough 1982: 135.

67   Cox 1957: 60–61; Kula 1986: table, 224–5.

68   Kula 1986: 210–11.

69   Cox 1957: 61; Kula 1986: 203–4.

70   Hahn 1971: 163; Kula 1986: 228.

71   Crosland 1972: 279; Champagne 1979: 322–5.

3.   Defining the Revolutionary Metric System

1   Condorcet here is reminiscing about his time in Turgot's inspectorate in *Mémoires sur les Monnaies* (1790–2). It is evident that Condorcet believed the reforms being demanded by the National Assembly meshed well with his own already well-developed theory of economics. Condorcet 1790–2: 3–4; Champagne 1979: 60–61.

2   Hahn 1971: 162–3; Mavidal and Laurent 1879–1913: XII, 104; Cox 1957: 55.

3   Champagne 1979: 125–7.

4   Prier 1790; Cox 1957: 84, n. 42, and 85, n. 44.

5   Duvergier 1824–1949: VI, 68; Cox 1957: 89; Hahn 1971: 164

6   Hahn 1971: 164.

7   Hahn 1971: 164.

8   Mémoires 1788; Devic 1851: 7–16, pp. 9 and 16; Crosland 1972: 287, 304–9.

9   Champagne 1979: 132–4; Schelle 1913–23: I, 31–3; Kula 1986: 177 and 228.

10   Translation after Cox 1957: 89.

11   See the list of pamphlets published on this issue in Cox 1957: 79–80, n. 33.

12   Cox 1957: 80; Crosland 1972: 282, 294.

13   Crosland 1972: 294.

14   Riggs Miller 1790, which includes Miller's correspondence with Talleyrand; Crosland 1972: 282.

15   Champagne 1979: 230, 336, 352.

16   Bigourdan 1901: II, 370; Kula 1986: 228.

17   Hahn 1971: 162.

18 At the International Meridian Conference held in Washington, DC, in 1884, the Greenwich Meridian was adopted as the prime meridian of the world, and the 0° line of longitude passes through it. France abstained from the vote and the French continued to maintain the Paris Meridian as a rival to Greenwich, until 1911 for timekeeping purposes and 1914 for navigation.

19 Mavidal and Laurent, 1879–1913: XVI, 200; translation in Champagne 1979: 238.

20 Mavidal and Laurent 1879–1913: XVI, 200; Cox 1957: 55; Crosland 1972: 284.

21 Lagrange, for example, had prepared a report on 5 August 1782 entitled 'A Method for Determining if the Earth is Flattened at the Poles and Expanded at the Equator', as quoted in Champagne 1979: 267.

22 Roy 1787; Maskelyne 1787; Dalby and Blagden 1787–8; Pictet 1791.

23 Napier adopted his principles when inventing logarithms during the following decade: Sarton 1934 and Sarton 1935.

24 Diderot and d'Alembert 1751–65, IV, 1754; Champagne 1979: 143–5.

25 Champagne 1979: 146.

26 Champagne 1979: 147.

27 Champagne 1979: 148.

28 Published posthumously in Paris in 1799, and now available in reprint, Paris 1988.

29 Champagne 1979: 152.

30 Champagne 1979: 153.

31 Champagne 1979: 154–5.

32 He was Naval Minister from August 1792 to April 1793, and he was absented from the latter stages of the committee from May 1796 to October 1799, when he spent time in Italy and then Egypt assisting the military campaigns of Napoleon Bonaparte.

33 Champagne 1979: 33–4, 145–6, 253–6, 284–5. Cf. Hellman 1936: 315.

34 Champagne 1979: 60.

35 Furet and Ozouf 1989: 538–9; Kula 1986: 237–8.

36 Furet and Ozouf 1989: 540–41.

37 Champagne 1979: 155, n. 5.

38 Gillispie 1970–80: 'Laplace', VIII, 335.

39 Champagne 1979: 165–9.

40 Cassini 1810; Devic 1851: 8off.; Crosland 1972: 300.

41 Greaves 1737. Derived from the original publication by Sir Isaac Newton, *A Discourse of the Romane Foot and Denarius, from whence the Measures and Weights used by the Ancients may be Deduced*, London, 1647.

42 Shalev 1967.

43 Paucton 1780: 102, 109.

44 Bailly 1779–82: I, 156; Lavoisier 1862–93: VI, 699; Romé de l'Isle 1789; Jomard 1817; Taylor 1859; and Nicholson 1912: 2–4, 14–121. On the Babylonians, see Lehmann 1890 (abstract in *Nature*, XLI, 1889: 167–8). See also Cox 1957: 24–6; Crosland 1972, 300–01.

45 Crosland 1972: 302–5.

46 Cox 1957: 91–4; Crosland 1972: 284; Champagne 1979: 33–4.

47 English translation after Mémoires 1788: 723; and see Crosland 1972: 286–9.

48 English translation after Mémoires 1788: 723; and see Crosland 1972: 286–9.

49 Cox 1957: 93–6.

50 Champagne 1979: 367–8.

51 Cox 1957: 96–9; Crosland 1972. 303; Champagne 1979: 174–5, 271.

52 Diderot and d'Alembert 1751–65, where the English foot is defined under 'Mesures' as 11 *pouces* 3 *lignes*. Crosland 1972: 304–5; Klein 1988: 109.

53 Cox 1957: 96; Champagne 1979: 125–7, 267, and cf. Hellman 1936: 323.

54 Cox 1957: 96–9; Crosland 1972: 303; Champagne 1979: 174–5, 271.

55 Champagne 1979: 366; and see Alder 2002 for a thorough account of Méchain's and Delambre's survey.

56 Duvergier 1824–1949: II, 271; Cox 1957: 100–01, n. 64; Kula 1986: 228–9, 241–3; Klein 1988: 110–11.

57 Champagne 1979: 368–9; Poincaré 1946: 539.

58 Legendre in Delambre 1799: 1–16; Cox 1957: 100–01; Champagne 1979: 397.

59 Delambre 1806–10: III, 402–14; Cox 1957: 102–4.

60 Given to the National Institute and published subsequently in Delambre 1806–10: 8–9; Champagne 1979: 172–3.

61 Poincaré 1946: 540.

62 Delambre 1806–10.

4. The Decisive Separation

1 Süskind 1986: 60–61, punctuation follows translation.
2 Champagne 1979: 125–7, 267.
3 Kershaw 1958: 12–18; Outram 1989: 109.
4 Kershaw 1958: 14.
5 Kershaw 1958: 14.
6 Edgerton 1972: 93–5.
7 Outram 1989: 107.
8 Kershaw 1958: 16–17; Walzer 1974: 80–82.
9 Outram 1989: 120, fig. XII.
10 Kershaw 1958: 19–28.
11 Kershaw 1958: 38–9, and pl. iv.
12 Kershaw 1958: 33–43.
13 Kershaw 1958: 56–60.
14 Kershaw 1958: 57.
15 Kershaw 1958: 134–6.
16 Kershaw 1958: 68–9, after *Le Thermomètre du jour*, 18 February 1793.
17 Kantorowicz 1957: 409, n. 319; Sennett 1994: 301.
18 Camus 1991 (first French edition 1951); Walzer 1974: 86.
19 Walzer 1974: 58–9, 127, 157 and 212.
20 Walzer 1974: 13; cf. Kantorowicz 1957: 23.
21 Outram 1989: 110.
22 Outram 1989: 110–18.
23 Hahn 1971: 76.
24 On 23 December 1793. See Champagne 1979: 250–51.
25 Champagne 1979: 50–53, 268–9.
26 Hahn 1971: 298–9.
27 Champagne 1979: 231.
28 *Le Moniteur Universel*, 17: 641; after Champagne 1979: 180.
29 Champagne 1979: 255–6.
30 Hellman 1936: 320; Scott and Rothaus 1985: 581–2; Champagne 1979: 107.
31 Champagne 1979: 190.
32 Champagne 1979: 279.
33 Ten foreign delegates are listed by Champagne 1979: 398–9. Hellman 1936: 335–6 lists twelve, including those from Liguria and Tuscany. This complex sequence of events has been unravelled by Champagne 1979: 24, 32, 50–54, 178–206, 279, 398–401; and cf. Hellman 1936: 324–7; Kula 1986: 253.

34 Crosland 1969: 205–11.

35 Kula 1986: 238–9.

36 Kula 1986: 240–43; Hellman 1936: 325.

37 Emsley 1979: 161.

38 Champagne 1979: 125–7, 267.

39 Kula 1986: 243.

40 Duvergier 1824–1949: I, 377; Champagne 1979: 201; Kula 1986: 245. The academicians thought this to be an excessive demand and requested later in the year that each *département* send only the principal standards of their region.

41 Champagne 1979: 204–5.

42 Hellman 1936: 327; Champagne 1979: 203–14; Kula 1986: 243–51.

43 Delambre 1806–10, III: 592–648; and see Champagne 1979: 245.

44 On 7 October 1799, though the medal was not struck until 1837. Moreau 1975: 45; Champagne 1979: 412.

45 Hellman 1936: 335–6.

46 Outram 1989: *passim*.

47 Bigourdan 1901: I, 194–5; Cox 1957: 121–2; Champagne 1979: 216; Kula 1986: 256–62.

48 Mollien 1845: I, 807; House of Commons 1862: 60; Cox 1957: 121, n. 10.

49 As quoted, for example, in *The Oxford Dictionary of Quotations*, 3rd ed, Oxford, 1980.

50 Russell 2001: I, 11–13.

51 Russell 2001: II, 377.

52 Russell 2001: I, 27–8.

53 Kula 1986: 255.

54 Morin 1870 IX, 607–8; Bigourdan 1901: I, 192–3; as cited in Cox 1957: 121, n. 11.

55 Lough 1982: 136; Scott and Rothaus 1985: 876–8; Kula 1986: 255–63.

56 See a summary of his lectures in Durand 2000; and also see Middleton 1982: 60–65; Rykwert 1982: 60–65

57 Blondel 1771–9; and see Pérez-Gómez 1983: 39, 42–5.

58 Etlin 1984: 103.

59 Rousenau 1976: 107. For the original French, see Boullée 1953: 83.

60 Rousenau 1976: 107.

61 Etlin 1984: 130.

62 Newton 1999: 942.

63   Burke 1766: Part II, Section IX, 'Succession and Uniformity', 108–11.
64   Etlin 1984: 138.
65   Manuel 1974: 53.
66   Harries 2002: 157.
67   Pérez-Gómez 1983: 277–9.
68   Pérez-Gómez 1983: 304.
69   Pérez-Gómez 1983: 308.
70   Delambre 1810.
71   Durand 2000: 81.
72   Durand 2000: 81.
73   Durand 2000: 133.
74   Etlin 1984: 130–34.
75   Mercier 1933: 314; Clarke 1979: 30.
76   Clarke 1979: 29–30.

5.   Anglo-Saxon Resistance

1   Burke 1982 [1790]: 113; after Porter 2000: 448.
2   Porter 2000: 447 and 604–5, n. 4 and 5.
3   Burke 1982 [1790].
4   Porter 2000: 448.
5   Porter 2000: 449 and 552.
6   Paine 1945: I, 274 and 464; Porter 2000: 454.
7   US Congress 1904–34: 266–72; Cox 1957: 80–83.
8   See epigraph in chapter 3, above.
9   Jefferson 1984: 19–24.
10   Wilford 2000: 217.
11   Jefferson 1984: 393.
12   Jefferson 1984: 55–7, 98.
13   Jefferson 1984: 62–3.
14   Jefferson 1984: 94–6, 98.
15   Jefferson 1984: 394.
16   Jefferson 1984: 395.
17   Jefferson 1984: 394–6.
18   Kula 1986: 242.
19   Jefferson 1984: 1258.
20   Westfall 1980: 750.
21   Jefferson 1984: 396–7.
22   Jefferson 1984: 398.

23 Jefferson 1984: 412, and 414 for his postscript of 10 January 1791.
24 Jefferson 1984: 1256–7.
25 Cox 1957: 83–4; 413–16.
26 Jefferson 1984: 1250–58.
27 Jefferson 1904–5: VII, 87–90; Cox 1957: 94, n. 55; 418–20.
28 US House of Representatives 1866: 7; Cox 1957: 422.
29 Adams 1821: 90–92; Cox 1957: 115–16.
30 US House of Representatives 1866: 117; Cox 1957: 424.
31 Cox 1957: 429.
32 US House of Representatives 1866: 93–4; Cox 1957: 423.
33 US Congress 1922: 288; Cox 1957: 426.
34 Jefferson 1984: 399–400.
35 Shuckburgh Evelyn 1798: 300–04. See editor's footnote, p. 304.
36 Shuckburgh Evelyn 1798: 310.
37 Shuckburgh Evelyn 1798: 300.
38 Shuckburgh Evelyn 1798: 300–04.
39 Slightly longer than Newton's measure, which is close to 39.15 inches.
40 Shuckburgh Evelyn 1798: 301.
41 Precisely, 59.89358 inches: Shuckburgh Evelyn 1798: 303–4, 307.
42 Shuckburgh Evelyn 1798: 303–4, 307.
43 Baily 1836: 51; Cox 1957: 91–2, n. 54.
44 Baily 1836: 50–54; Cox 1957: 92, n. 54.
45 Favre 1931: 127–8.
46 Jeffrey 1822: IV, 223–58; Cox 1957: 240.
47 Chambers 1857; Cox 1957: 248.
48 Cox 1957: 241–2.
49 Shuckburgh Evelyn 1798: 301.
50 Champagne 1979: 435–7.
51 House of Commons 1819; Cox 1957: 241.
52 Champagne 1979: 487.
53 Baily 1836: 35–184, especially 26–9; Cox 1957: 51–2.
54 Upton 1879; Cox 1957: 52–3.
55 Morin 1870: IX, 619; Cox 1957: 165.
56 Cox 1957: 252, n. 20.
57 *Journal of the Society of Arts*, 1852–3: 205; Cox 1957: 166–7.
58 House of Commons 1862: 10; Cox 1957: 169.
59 Yates 1856.
60 International Association 1858: 6–11; Cox 1957: 172.
61 International Association 1860: 18–19; Cox 1957: 174.

62 International Association 1862; Cox 1957: 178–9.
63 House of Commons 1862: 9.
64 House of Commons 1862: 9.
65 Levi 1871; Cox 1957: 164.
66 Cox 1957: 271–2.
67 Cox 1957: 122–3, 260–78.
68 House of Commons, 1862: iii–x.
69 House of Commons 1862: viii–x; Cox 1957: 279–80.
70 Cox 1957: 284–5.
71 Cox 1957: 286–7.
72 Cox 1957: 291–4.
73 US House of Representatives 1866: 13; Cox 1957: 294; 452.
74 Cox 1957: 42–3, 452–60.
75 Cox 1957: 49, 430.
76 Cox 1957: 304–7.
77 Wednesday, 13 May 1868, London 1868: Royal Society library, *Tracts 552/11*; Hope 1868: 9–10.
78 Hope 1868: 9–10.
79 Herschel 1872: 427–9, 440–48; Cox 1957: 87–8, and n. 48.
80 House of Commons 1868–9; Cox 1957: 307–12.
81 Cox 1957: 314.
82 Cox 1957: 466, 523.
83 Philadelphia *Record*, 14 November 1882, cited in Cox 1957: 536–7. Latimer 1880a; Cox 1957: 533.
84 Piazzi Smyth 1867; see also Totten 1884; and Cox 1957: 522–3.
85 Quoted in Cox 1957: 522.
86 Latimer 1880b: 70–91; Cox 1957: 529.
87 See, for example, Warren 1899: 222; Barnard 1883.
88 Flinders Petrie 1910–11.
89 Cox 1957: 537.
90 Clarke 1979: 62–8.
91 Knox 1999: 427–58.
92 Clarke 1979: 64.
93 Cox 1957: 455, n. 50.
94 Kula 1986: 278.
95 Crosland 1969: 226–31.
96 Champagne 1979: 398; Kula 1986: 269–72.
97 Kula 1986: 269–70.
98 Champagne 1979: 398; Kula 1986: 269–72.
99 Kula 1986: 273.

100 Turin 1816: 15; Kula 1986: 273.
101 Kula 1986: 274.
102 Cox 1957: 141–51.
103 Cox 1957: 185–202.
104 Cox 1957: 158–9.
105 De Simone 1971.

6. Measures of Pure Conception

1   Nietzsche 1882, III, par. 125, KSA 3: 480–81; Nietzsche 1959: 95–6.
2   Danloux-Dumesnils 1969: 39–40, n. 1.
3   Cox 1957: 201–3; *Time Magazine*, 'End of the Meter Bars?' (28 September 1953): 42.
4   Clerk Maxwell 1873.
5   Michelson 1894.
6   Cox 1957: 219–20.
7   Danloux-Dumesnils 1969: 36–42.
8   Molderings 1991: 264–5, n. 42.
9   Molderings 1991: 244; after Poincaré 1946: 234, 330.
10 Molderings 1991. 244; after Poincaré 1946: 255.
11 Molderings 1991: 246; after Poincaré 1946: 124.
12 Molderings 1991: 264–5, n. 42.
13 Cabanne 1987: 39.
14 Naumann 1991: 53.
15 Molderings 1991: 248.
16 Naumann 1991: 47–55.
17 Molderings 1991: 257.
18 Schwarz 1969: 131.
19 Cabanne 1987: 114.
20 Duchamp 1969: 150.
21 Schwarz 1969: 443–4; Duchamp 1969: 150; Judovitz 1995: 47–9.
22 Poincaré 1946: 92.
23 Poincaré 1946: 96–104.
24 Poincaré 1946: 103–4.
25 Jules Frédéric Charles Andrade (1857–1933).
26 Poincaré 1946: 104.
27 Poincaré 1946: 106.
28 Cabanne 1987: 47, cf. Naumann 1991: 55.
29 Schwarz 1969: 133; Duchamp 1969: 150 and 152; Molderings 1991: 246.

30   Schwarz 1969: 133; Duchamp 1969: 150 and 152; Molderings
     1991: 246.
31   Mink 1995: 18–25, 44–8; Judovitz 1995: 51–29.
32   Duchamp 1969: 6–7.
33   See the discussion of this above, pp. 94–8.
34   Tomkins 1996: 3; Judovitz 1995: 52.
35   Duchamp 1969: 202.
36   Schwarz 1969: 443–4.
37   Duchamp 1969: 2–4.
38   Schwarz 1969: 443–4.
39   Duchamp 1969: 36.
40   Duchamp 1969: 202.
41   Le Corbusier 1951: 57.
42   Le Corbusier 1951: 60.
43   Turner 1977; Benton 1987: 241.
44   Zeising 1854; Wölfflin 1889; Thiersch 1893.
45   Herz-Fischler 1987.
46   Wölfflin 1889; Thiersch 1893.
47   See above, pp. 140–1.
48   Eliel et al., 2001.
49   See the comments of a correspondent in Le Corbusier 1955: 91–2.
50   Le Corbusier 1951: 56. For a more complete account of Le Cor-
     busier's development of the Modulor and the contribution of
     Hanning, among others, see: Matteoni 1980.
51   Le Corbusier 1951: 82.
52   Michelson 1894.
53   Matteoni 1980: 14–15.
54   Benton 1987, n. 29: 245; See also Loach 1998.
55   Ghyka 1948.
56   Le Corbusier 1951: 132–53.
57   Le Corbusier 1951: 140.
58   Le Corbusier 1951: 136.
59   Beecher 1986.
60   See Tavernor 1998: 159–87, especially 173, where this proportion
     is described in relation to the biblical Temple of Solomon (after
     1 Kings 6) and Alberti's design of the influential Italian Renais-
     sance church of Sant'Andrea in Mantua.
61   Its overall proportions are approximately $2:4.57:11$.
62   Le Corbusier 1951: 58.
63   Schwarz 1969: 131.

64 As translated in Cabanne 1987: 37–8.

65 Rorty 1989: especially chapters 4 and 5. On page 73 he offers his definition of an ironist. Rorty argues that humans carry with them a set of words with which to justify themselves, which he calls a person's 'final vocabulary' – words that entwine with beliefs, such as (his examples) 'Christ', 'England', 'professional standards', 'the Revolution', 'the Church', 'progressive', 'rigorous', 'creative'. These words and beliefs underpin the account of human measures in this book. Rorty defines an ironist as someone who fulfils three conditions in relation to the final vocabulary: (1) radical doubts about the particular final vocabulary defining his or her life, which (2) their final vocabulary is incapable of either underwriting or dissolving; and (3) so they play the new off against the old. Rorty is dismissive of ironists.

66 Conversely, Rorty considers that 'Heidegger's definition of "man" as "Being's poem" was a magnificent, but hopeless, attempt to save theory by poetising it'. Rorty 1989: 119.

67 T.S. Eliot, in Weil 1987: x–xi.

68 Weil 1987: 227.

69 Weil 1958: 108.

70 Weil 1987: 233–5.

71 Voegelin 1948: 462.

72 Weil 1987: 227.

73 Armstrong et al. 1970: 268.

74 Armstrong et al. 1970: 251.

75 Armstrong et al. 1970: 228.

76 Armstrong et al. 1970: 229.

77 Armstrong et al. 1970: 21 and 224; *Daily Telegraph* (11 February 2002).

78 Armstrong et al. 1970: 224.

79 Barthes 1957; Barthes 1972: 129.

80 Eliade 1961: 103–6.

81 Armstrong et al. 1970: 224.

82 Armstrong et al. 1970: 224.

83 Pulsars are known to be slowing down and if the rate of slowing is constant, an otherworld scientist should be able to deduce roughly the time *Pioneer* was launched. Thus, we have placed ourselves approximately in both time and space. (NASA *Pioneer 10* and *Pioneer 11* website: spaceprojects.arc.nasa.gov/Space_Projects/ pioneer/PN10&11.html).

84 My enquiries at NASA have not led to any evidence of this research, and according to Sagan himself, 'there were a total of only three weeks from the presentation of the idea, the design of the message, its approval by NASA, and the engraving of the final plaque.' (Sagan 1973: 18)

85 NASA *Pioneer 10* and *Pioneer 11* website: spaceprojects.arc.nasa. gov/Space_Projects/pioneer/PN10&11.html

86 Though according to de la Fuente's partner in its design, Ann Pendleton-Jullian, there was no discussion between architect and client about the Modulor: Sagan took the need for such proportions 'on trust'. Email communication between Ann Pendleton-Jullian and the author of 27 January 2006.

87 Calvino 1968: 90

88 Rorty 1989: 152.

Epilogue

1 See Trachtenberg 1986.

2 Baboian, Bellante and Cliver 1990: 16.

3 Baboian, Bellante and Cliver 1990: 19.

4 See the Memory Foundation website of Daniel Libeskind (accessed in December 2006): http://www.daniel-libeskind.com/projects/pro.html?ID=68.

Bibliography

Adams 1821

Adams, J. Q., *Report of the Secretary of State, upon Weights and Measures (Prepared in Obedience to a Resolution of the House of Representatives of December 1819), read February 22 1821*, Washington, 1821.

Aiken 1980

Aiken, J. A., 'Leon Battista Alberti's System of Human Proportions', *Journal of the Warburg and Courtauld Institutes*, XLIII (1980): 68–96.

Alberti 1972

Alberti, L. B., *On Painting and On Sculpture: The Latin Texts of 'De pictura' and 'De statua'*, ed. and trans. C. Grayson, London, 1972.

Alberti 1988

—, *On the Art of Building in Ten Books*, ed. and trans. (from the Latin) J. Rykwert, N. Leach and R. Tavernor, Cambridge, MA, and London, 1988.

Alder 2002

Alder, K., *The Measure of All Things: The Seven-Year Odyssey that Transformed the World*, London, 2002.

Armstrong et al. 1970

Armstrong, N., et al., *First on the Moon: A Voyage with Neil Armstrong, Michael Collins, Edwin E. Aldrin*, with G. Farmer and D. J. Hamblin, Boston, MA, and Toronto, 1970.

Augustine 1955

Augustine, *Corpus christianorum: De civitate dei*, Series Latina, XLVIII, Turnhout, 1955.

Augustine 1972

—, *The City of God*, trans. H. Bettenson, Harmondsworth, 1972.

Baboian, Bellante and Cliver 1990

Baboian, R., E. L. Bellante and E. B. Cliver (eds), *The Statue of Liberty Restoration*, Houston, TX, 1990.

Bailly 1779–82
    Bailly, J.-S., *Histoire de l'astronomie moderne depuis la fondation de
    l'école d'Alexandrie jusqu'à l'époque de* MDCCXXX, Paris, 3 vols,
    1779–82.
Baily 1836
    Baily, F., 'Report on the New Standard Scale of this Society',
    Royal Astronomical Society: Memoirs, IX (1836).
Barnard 1883
    Barnard, F. A. P., 'The Metrology of the Great Pyramid',
    American Metrological Society: Proceedings, IV (1883): 117–225.
Barnes 1989
    Barnes, J., *A History of the World in $10^1/_2$ Chapters*, London, 1989.
Barthes 1957
    Barthes, R., *Mythologies*, Paris, 1957.
Barthes 1972
    —, *Mythologies*, trans. A. Lavers, London, 1972.
Baxandall 1972
    Baxandall, M., *Painting and Experience in Fifteenth Century Italy:
    A Primer in the Social History of Pictorial Style*, Oxford, 1972.
Beal 1884
    *Si-yu-ki: Buddhist Records of the Western World: Translated from the
    Chinese of Hiven-Tsiang (AD 629)*, trans. S. Beal, Boston, MA, 2
    vols, 1884.
Beecher 1986
    Beecher, J., *Charles Fourier: The Visionary and his World*, Berkeley,
    CA, 1986.
Benjamin 1933
    Benjamin, A. C., 'The Logic of Measurement', *Journal of Philo-
    sophy*, XXX/26 (21 December 1933): 701–10.
Benton 1987
    Benton, T., 'The Sacred and the Search for Myths', in *Le Cor-
    busier: Architect of the Century*, ed. M. Raeburn and V. Wilson (exhi-
    bition catalogue), Arts Council of Great Britain, 1987.
Berger, Müller-Huber and Thommen 1992
    Berger, E., B. Müller-Huber and L. Thommen, *Der Entwurf des
    Künstlers Bildhauerkanon in der Antike und Neuzeit*, Basel, 1992.
Bigourdan 1901
    Bigourdan, G., *Le Système métrique des poids et mesures: son éstab-
    lissement et sa propogation graduelle, avec l'histoire des opérations qui*

ont servi a determiner le mètre et le kilogramme, par G. Bigourdan, Paris, 1901.

Blondel 1771–9

Blondel, J.-F., *Cours d'Architecture,* ed. P. Patte, 9 vols, Paris, 1771–9.

Borg and Martindale 1981

Borg, A., and A. Martindale, *The Vanishing Past: Studies of Medieval Art, Liturgy and Metrology Presented to Christopher Hohler,* British Archaeological Reports, Oxford 1981.

Boullée 1953

Boullée, E.-L., *Boullée's Treatise on Architecture,* ed. H. Rosenau, London, 1953.

Brooks 1991

Brooks, P., 'The Revolutionary Body', in *Fictions of the French Revolution,* ed. B. Fort, Evanston, IL, 1991: 35–53.

Burke 1766

Burke, E., *A Philosophical Enquiry into the Origins of Our Ideas of the Sublime and Beautiful,* 4th edition, Dublin, 1766.

Burke 1982 [1790]

Reflections on the Revolution in France [and on the Proceedings in Certain Societies in London Relative to that Event. In a Letter Intended to have been Sent to a Gentleman in Paris] (1790), ed. C. C. O'Brien, Harmondsworth, 1982.

Cabanne 1987

Cabanne, P., *Dialogues with Marcel Duchamp,* trans. R. Padgett, New York, 1987.

Calvino 1968

Calvino, I., *Cosmicomics* (1965); trans. W. Weaver, New York and London, 1968.

Calvino 1988

—, *Six Memos for the Next Millennium,* New York, 1988.

Camus 1991

Camus, A., *The Rebel: An Essay on Man and Revolt,* New York, 1991.

Canali 1994

Canali, F., 'Measure of Length Corresponding to a Mantuan Braccio', in *The Renaissance from Brunelleschi to Michelangelo: The Representation of Architecture,* ed. H. A. Millon and V. M. Lampugnani, London, 1994, item 109: 491.

Cassini 1720
 Cassini, J., *De la grandeur et de la figure de la terre*, Paris, 1720.
Cassini 1810
 Cassini, J.-D., *Mémoires pour servir à l'histoire des sciences et à celle de l'Observatoire Royale de Paris*, Paris, 1810.
Cassirer 1922
 Cassirer, E., *Die Begriffstorm in mysthischen Denken*, Leipzig, Berlin, 1922.
Chambers 1857
 'British Weights and Measures', *Chambers' Information for the People*, Edinburgh, 1857.
Chambers 1959
 Chambers' Encyclopaedia, new edition, IX, London, 1959.
Champagne 1979
 Champagne, R. J., 'The Role of Five Eighteenth-Century French Mathematicians in the Development of the Metric System', unpublished PhD thesis, Columbia University, New York, 1979.
Chapman 1995
 Chapman, C. R., *How Heavy, How Much and How Long? Weights, Money and Other Measures Used by Our Ancestors*, Dursley, UK, 1995.
Chisholm 1877
 Chisholm, H. W., *On the Science of Weighing and Measuring and Standards of Measure and Weight*, London, 1877.
Chisholm 1997
 Chisholm, L. J., ed., 'Measurement Systems', *The New Encyclopaedia Britannica*, vol. XXIII, Chicago, IL, 1997: 693–7.
Clarke 1979
 Clarke, I. F., *The Pattern of Expectation, 1644–2001*, London, 1979.
Clémenceau 1909
 Clémenceau, E., *Le Service des poids et mesures en France à travers les siècles*, Saint-Marcellin, Isère, 1909.
Clerk Maxwell 1873
 Clerk Maxwell, J., *A Treatise on Electricity and Magnetism*, 2 vols, Oxford, 1873.
Coffin 1979
 Coffin, D., 'Pope Marcellus II and Architecture', *Architectura*, IX (1979): 11–29.

Condorcet 1788
'Rapport fait à l'Académie des sciences sur le choix d'une unité de mesures par mm. Borda, Lagrange, Laplace & Condorcet', *Mémoires de l'Académie Royale des Sciences*, 1788 [1791].

Condorcet 1790–2
Mémoires et discours sur les Monnaies et les Finances (1790–92), Paris, 1994.

Connor 1987
Connor, R. D., *The Weights and Measures of England*, London, 1987.

Cooper 1949
Cooper, D., *Talleyrand*, London, 1949.

Cornford 1937
Cornford, F. M., *Plato's Cosmology*, London, 1937.

Cotterell 1986
Cotterell, A., *A Dictionary of World Mythology*, Oxford, 1986.

Cox 1957
Cox, E. F., 'A History of the Metric System of Weights and Measures, with Emphasis on Campaigns for its Adoption in Great Britain, and in the United States prior to 1914', unpublished PhD thesis, Indiana University, 1957 (University Microfilms, Ann Arbor, MI, no. 22,681).

Crosby 1997
Crosby, A. W., *The Measure of Reality: Quantification and Western Society, 1250–1600*, Cambridge, 1997.

Crosland 1969
Crosland, M., ed., *Science in France in the Revolutionary Era Described by Thomas Bugge*, Cambridge, MA, 1969.

Crosland 1972
—, ' "Nature" and Measurement in Eighteenth-Century France', *Studies on Voltaire and the Eighteenth Century*, LXXXVII (1972): 277–309.

Cru 1966
Cru, R. L., *Diderot as a Disciple of English Thought*, New York, 1913 (reprinted 1966).

Dalby and Blagden 1787–8
Dalby, I. and C. Blagden, 'The Longitudes of Dunkirk and Paris from Greenwich', *Philosophical Transactions of the Royal Society* (1787–8): 236–45.

Danloux-Dumesnils 1969
Danloux-Dumesnils, M., *The Metric System: A Critical Study of its Principles and Practice*, trans. A. P. Garrett and J. S. Rowlinson, London, 1969.

De Duve 1991
De Duve, T., ed., *The Definitely Unfinished Marcel Duchamp*, Cambridge, MA, and London, 1991.

De Simone 1971
De Simone, D. V., 'A Metric America. A Decision whose Time has Come.' *Report to the Congress*. US Department of Commerce, National Bureau of Standards Special Publication 345, 1971.

Dekoulakou-Sideris 1990
Dekoulakou-Sideris, I., 'A Metrological Relief from Salamis', *American Journal of Archaeology*, XCIV (1990): 445–51.

Delambre 1799
Delambre, J. B. J., *Méthodes analytiques pour la détermination d'un arc du méridien par J. B. J. Delambre*, Paris, 1799.

Delambre 1806–10
—, *Base du Système Métrique Décimal; ou, Mesure de l'arc du méridien compris entre les parallèles de Dunquerque et Barcelone, exécutée en 1792 et années suivantes, par MM. Méchain et Delambre*, 3 vols, Paris, 1806–10.

Delambre 1810
—, ed., *Rapport historique sur les progrès des sciences mathématiques depuis 1789 et sur leur état actuel*, Paris, 1810 (reprinted Amsterdam, 1966).

Delorme 1648
Delorme, P., *L'Architecture*, Rouen, 1648.

Devic 1851
Devic, J.-F. S., *Histoire de la Vie et des Travaux Scientifiques et Littéraires de J. D. Cassini IV*, Clermont, 1851.

Diderot 1969
Diderot, D., *Oeuvres complètes*, ed. R. Lewinter, Paris, 1969.

Diderot and d'Alembert 1751–65
Diderot, D., and J. de Rond d'Alembert, eds, *Encyclopédie; ou, Dictionnaire raisonné des sciences, des arts et des métiers*, 17 vols, Paris, 1751–65.

Dilke 1987
Dilke, O. A. W., *Reading the Past: Mathematics and Measurement*, London, 1987.

Dodds and Tavernor 2002
Dodds, G., and R. Tavernor, eds, *Body and Building: Essays on the Changing Relation of Body and Architecture*, Cambridge, MA, and London, 2002.

Doursther 1976 [1840]
Doursther, H., *Dictionnaire universel des Poids et Mesures anciens et modernes contenant des tables des monnaies de tous les pays*, Brussels, 1840 (reprinted Amsterdam, 1976).

Duchamp 1969
Duchamp, M., *Notes and Projects for the Large Glass*, ed. A. Schwarz, trans. G. H. Hamilton, C. Gray and A. Schwarz, London, 1969.

Dufton 1953
Dufton, A. F., 'In Quest of a Module', *Journal of the Royal Institute of British Architects*, IX (July 1953): 382.

Durand 2000
Durand, J.-N.-L., *Précis of the Lectures on Architecture*, trans. D. Pritt, Los Angeles, 2000.

Dürer 1525
Dürer, A., *Underweyssung der Messung mit dem Zirckel und Richtscheyt*, Nuremberg, 1525.

Duvergier 1824–1949
Duvergier, J. B., ed., *Collection complète des lois, décrets, ordonnances, règlemens, avis du Conseil d'État depuis 1788*, 148 vols, Paris, 1824–1949.

Edgerton 1972
Edgerton, S. Y., '*Maniera* and *Mannaia*: Decorum and Decapitation in the Sixteenth Century', in *The Meaning of Mannerism*, ed. F. W. Robinson and S. G. Nichols, Jr., Hanover, NH, 1972: 67–103.

Eliade 1961
Eliade, M., *Myths, Dreams and Mysteries*, New York, 1961.

Eliel et al. 2001
Eliel, C. S., F. Ducros, T. Gronberg, eds, *L'Esprit Nouveau: Purism in Paris*, New York, 2001.

Emsley 1979
Emsley, C., *British Society and the French Wars 1793–1815*, London, 1979.

Etlin 1984
Etlin, R., *The Architecture of Death*, Cambridge, MA, and London, 1984.

Evans 1995
Evans, R., *The Projective Cast: Architecture and Its Three Geometries*, Cambridge, MA, and London, 1995.

Favre 1931
Favre, A., *Les Origines du systeme métrique*, Paris, 1931.

Fernie 1978
Fernie, E., 'Historical Metrology and Architectural History', *Art History*, I/4 (1978): 383–99.

Fernie 1981
—, 'The Greek Metrological Relief in Oxford', *Antiquaries Journal*, LXI (1981): 255–63.

Flinders Petrie 1877
Flinders Petrie, W. M., *Inductive Metrology; or, The Recovery of Ancient Measures from the Monuments*, London, 1877.

Flinders Petrie 1910–11
—, 'Weights and Measures: Ancient and Historical', *The Encyclopaedia Britannica*, 11th ed., 1910–11: 81–2.

Foat 1915
Foat, F. W. G., 'Anthropometry of Greek Statues', *Journal of Hellenic Studies*, XXXV (1915): 225–59.

Furet and Ozouf 1989
Furet, F., and M. Ozouf, eds, *A Critical Dictionary of the French Revolution*, trans. A. Goldhammer, Cambridge, MA, and London, 1989.

Ghyka 1948
Ghyka, M., 'Le Corbusier's Modulor and the Concept of the Golden Mean', *Architectural Review*, CIII/614 (February 1948): 39–42.

Gillispie 1970–80
Gillispie, C. C., ed., *Dictionary of Scientific Biography*, 16 vols, New York, 1970–80.

Gould 1981
Gould, S. J., *The Mismeasure of Man*, New York and London, 1981.

Great Britain (1225–1806)
Great Britain, *Statutes at Large, Magna Charta (1225 to 1806)*, London.

Greaves 1737
'A Discourse of the Roman Foot and Denarius and Origin and Antiquity of Our English Weights and Measures', in *Miscellaneous Works of John Greaves, Professor of Astronomy at the University of Oxford*, 2 vols, London, 1736–7.

Grierson 1972
Grierson, P., *English Linear Measures: An Essay in Origins*, The Stenton Lecture (1971), Reading, 1972.

Guilhiermoz 1913
Guilhiermoz, P., 'De l'équivalence des anciennes measures, à propos d'une publication récente', *Bibliothèque de l'École des Chartes*, LXXIV (1913): 267–328.

Hahn 1971
Hahn, R. *The Anatomy of a Scientific Institution: The Paris Academy of Sciences, 1666–1803*, Berkeley, CA, 1971.

Haldane 1985
Haldane, J. B. S., *On Being the Right Size, and Other Essays*, Oxford and New York, 1985.

Harries 2001
Harries, K., *Infinity and Perspective*, Cambridge, MA, and London, 2001.

Harries 2002
—, 'Sphere and Cross: Vitruvian Reflections on the Pantheon Type', in *Body and Building: On the Changing Relation of Body and Architecture*, ed., G. Dodds and R. Tavernor, Cambridge, MA, and London, 2002.

Hecht 1985
Hecht, N. S., 'A Modest Addendum to the Greek Metrological Relief in Oxford', *Antiquaries Journal*, 1985, LXV, 139–40 and 142.

Heggie 1981
Heggie, D. C., *Megalithic Science: Ancient Mathematics and Astronomy in Northwest Europe*, London and New York, 1981.

Heidegger 1971
Heidegger, M., *Poetry, Language, Thought*, trans. A. Hofstadter, London, 1971.

Hellman 1931
    Hellman, C. D., 'Jefferson's Efforts Towards the Decimalization of United States Weights and Measures', *Isis*, XVI (1931): 266–72.

Hellman 1936
    —, 'Legendre and the French Reform of Weights and Measures', *Osiris*, I (1936): 314–39.

Hellman 1998
    Hellman, H., *Great Feuds in Science: Ten of the Liveliest Disputes Ever*, New York and Chichester, 1998.

Herschel 1872
    Herschel, J. F. W., *Familiar Lectures on Scientific Subjects*, New York, 1872.

Herz-Fischler 1987
    Herz-Fischler, R., *A Mathematical History of Division in Extreme and Mean Ratio*, Waterloo, Canada, 1987.

Himmelmann 1998
    Himmelmann, N., 'The Stance of the Polykleitan Diadoumenos', in *Reading Greek Art: Essays by Nikolaus Himmelmann*, ed. W. Childs, Princeton, NJ, 1998: 156–86.

Hope 1868
    Hope, B., *In Moving the Rejection of the Metric Weights and Measures Bill, Wednesday May 13, 1868*, London, 1868.

House of Commons 1819
    House of Commons, *Report from the Commissioners Appointed to Consider the Need for Establishing Uniform Weights and Measures, 24 June, 1819*, in *Sessional Papers*, London, 1819.

House of Commons 1862
    House of Commons, *Report from the Select Committee on Weights and Measures: Together with the Proceedings [. . .]*, in *Sessional Papers*, VII, London, 1862.

House of Commons 1868–9
    House of Commons, *First Report of the Commissioners Appointed to Inquire into the Condition of the Exchequer Standards*, in *Sessional Papers*, London, 1868–9.

Hughes and Larkin 1969
    Hughes, L., and J. F. Larkin, eds, *Tudor Royal Proclamations: Volume XI, The Later Tudors (1553–1587)*, New Haven, CT, and London, 1969.

Hultsch 1866
Hultsch, F., ed., *Metrologici scriptores Romani*, Leipzig, 1866.
Hurry 1928
Hurry, J. B., *Imhotep*, London, 1928.
Huygens 1673
Huygens, C., *Horologium oscillatorium sive de motu pendulorum ad horologia aptato demonstrationes geometricale*, Paris, 1673.
Huygens 1888–1950
—, *Oeuvres Complètes*, D. Bierens de Haan, J. Bosscha, D. J. Korteweg and J. A. Vollgraff, ed., 22 vols, The Hague, 1888–1950.
International Association 1858
International Association for Obtaining a Uniform Decimal System of Measures, Weights, and Coins (British Branch): Second Report of the Council (February 25, 1858), London, 1858.
International Association 1860
International Association for Obtaining a Uniform Decimal System of Measures, Weights, and Coins (British Branch): Report of the Fourth General Meeting (Bradford, October 10–12, 1859), London, 1860.
International Association 1862
International Association for Obtaining a Uniform Decimal System of Measures, Weights, and Coins (British Branch): Fifth Report of the Council (June 26, 1861), and *Sixth Report of the Council (July 30, 1862)*, London, 1862.
Isidore of Seville 1911
Isidori Hispalensis Episcopi Etymologiarum sive originum libri XX, ed. W. M. Lindsay, Oxford, 1911.
Jardine 2002
Jardine, L., *On a Grander Scale: The Outstanding Career of Sir Christopher Wren*, London, 2002.
Jefferson 1904–5
The Works of Thomas Jefferson, ed. Paul L. Ford, 12 vols, New York and London, 1904–5.
Jefferson 1984
Thomas Jefferson: Writings, ed. M. D. Peterson, New York, 1984.
Jeffrey 1822
'Review of Méchain and Delambre', *Edinburgh Review*, IX (1807); reprinted in F. Jeffrey, *The Works of John Playfair*, Edinburgh, 1822.

Johnstone 1998
Johnstone, W. D., *For Good Measure: The Most Complete Guide to Weights and Measures and Their Metric Equivalents*, Chicago, 1998.

Jomard 1817
Jomard, E., *Mémoire sur le système métrique des anciens Égyptiens*, Paris, 1817.

Journal of the Society of Arts 1852–3
Journal of the Society of Arts and of the Institutions in Union, Washington, DC, I, 1852–3.

Judovitz 1995
Judovitz, D., *Unpacking Duchamp: Art in Transit*, Berkeley, CA, and London, 1995.

Kantorowicz 1955
Kantorowicz, E., 'Mysteries of State: An Absolutist Concept and its Late Medieval Origins', *Harvard Theological Review*, XLVIII (1955): 65–91.

Kantorowicz 1957
—, *The King's Two Bodies: A Study in Medieval Political Theology*, Princeton, NJ, 1957.

Keene, Burns and Saint 2004
Keene, D., A. Burns and A. Saint, eds, *St Paul's Cathedral Church of London, 604–2004*, New Haven, CT, and London, 2004.

Kelley 1990
Kelley, D. R., *The Human Measure: Social Thought in the Western Legal Tradition*, Cambridge, MA, and London, 1990.

Kershaw 1958
Kershaw, A., *A History of the Guillotine*, London, 1958.

Kidson 1990
Kidson, P., 'A Metrological Investigation', *Journal of the Warburg and Courtauld Institutes*, LIII (1990): 71–97.

Klein 1988
Klein, H. A., *The Science of Measurement: A Historical Survey*, New York, 1988.

Knaster 1974
Knaster, B., 'Méchain, Pierre-François-André', in *Dictionary of Scientific Biography*, ed. A. T. Macrobius and K. F. Naumann, vol. IX, New York, 1974: 250–51.

Knox 1999
   Knox, K. C., 'Lunatick Visions: Prophecy, Scientific Public and
   the Signs of the Times in 1790s London', *History of Science*, XXXVII
   (1999).
Koestler 1959
   Koestler, A., *The Sleepwalkers: A History of Man's Changing Vision
   of the Universe*, Basingstoke, 1959 (reprinted Harmondsworth,
   1990).
Kreikenbom 1990
   Kreikenbom, D., *Bildwerke nach Polyklet*, Berlin, 1990.
Kula 1986
   Kula, W., *Measures and Men*, trans. R. Szreter, Princeton, NJ, 1986.
La Condamine 1747
   La Condamine, C.-M., 'Nouveau projet d'une mesure invariable
   propre à servir de mesure commune à toutes des Nations',
   Mémoires de l'Académie Royale des Sciences, Paris, 1747.
La Condamine 1757
   —, 'Extrait d'un Journal de Voyage en Italie', *Mémoires de
   l'Académie Royale des Sciences*, Paris, 1757.
La Condamine 1772
   —, 'Sur la Toise-Étalon du Châtelet, & sur les diverses Toises
   employées aux mesures des Degrés terrestres & à celle du Pendule
   à secondes', *Mémoires de l'Académie Royale des Sciences*, Paris,
   1772.
La Hire 1714
   La Hire, P. de, 'Comparaison du pied antique romain à celui du
   Châtelet de Paris, avec quelques remarques sur d'autres
   Mesures', *Mémoires de l'Académie Royale des Sciences*, Paris, 1714.
Laan 1983
   Laan, H. van der, *Architectonic Space*, trans. R. Padovan, Leiden,
   1983.
Latimer 1880a
   Latimer, C., *The French Metric System; or, The Battle of the Stan-
   dards: A Discussion of the Comparative Merits of the Metric System
   and the Standards of the Great Pyramid*, Chicago, 1880.
Latimer 1880b
   —, 'The Origin of the Sacred Cubit', *International Institute, Pro-
   ceedings* (March 1880).

Lauer 1976
Lauer, J.-P., *Saqqara*, London, 1976.

Lavoisier 1862–93
Lavoisier, A.-L., *Oeuvres*, ed. J.-B. Dumas and E. Grimaux, 6 vols, Paris, 1862–93.

Le Corbusier 1951
Le Corbusier, *The Modulor: A Harmonious Measure to the Human Scale Universally Applicable to Architecture and Mechanics*, trans. P. de Francia and A. Bostock, London and Boston, MA, 1951.

Le Corbusier 1955
—, *Modulor 2: Let the User Speak Next*, London, 1955.

Le Corbusier 1987
—, *Towards a New Architecture by Le Corbusier, Translated from the Thirteenth French Edition with an Introduction by Frederick Etchells, London, 1927*, London, 1987.

Lehmann 1890
Lehmann, A. G. L., 'Über das babylonische metrische System und dessen Verbreitung', *Verhältnisse der Physikalischen Gesellschaft zu Berlin*, VIII (1890): 81–101.

Levi 1871
Levi, L., *The Theory and Practice of the Metric System of Weights and Measures*, London, 1871.

Loach 1998
Loach, J., 'Le Corbusier and the Creative Use of Mathematics', *The British Journal for the History of Science*, 1998, 31: 185–215.

Locke 1988 [1690]
Locke, J., *Two Treatises of Government* [1690], London, 1988.

Lorenzen 1966
Lorenzen, E., *Technological Studies in Ancient Metrology*, vol. I, Copenhagen, 1966.

Lotz 1982
Lotz, W., 'Sull'unità di misura nei disegni di architettura del cinquecento', *Bollettino del Centro Internazionale di Studi di Architettura Andrea Palladio*, XXI (1979–82): 223–32, figs 113–22.

Lough 1982
Lough, J., *The Philosophes and Post-Revolutionary France*, Oxford, 1982.

McLean McDonald 1992
McLean McDonald, D., *The Origins of Metrology*, Cambridge, 1992.

Manetti 1976
Manetti, A. di Tuccio, *Vita di Filippo Brunelleschi*, ed. D. de Robertis and G. Tanturli, Milan, 1976.

Manuel 1974
Manuel, F. E., *The Religion of Isaac Newton*, Oxford, 1974.

Martini 1976 [1883]
Martini, A., *Manuale di Metrologia*, Turin, 1883 (reprinted Rome, 1976).

Maskelyne 1787
Maskelyne, N., 'Concerning the Latitude and Longitude at Greenwich [. . .] late M. Cassini [. . .]', *Philosophical Transactions of the Royal Society*, LXXVII (1787): 151–87.

Matteoni 1980
Matteoni, D., 'La ricerca di una idea di proporzione: Il Modulor', *Parametro* (1980): 12–37.

Mavidal and Laurent 1879–1913
Mavidal, J., and E. Laurent, eds, *Archives parlementaires de 1787 a 1860: Recueil complet des débats législatifs & politiques des chambres françaises*, 2nd edition, Paris, 1879–1913, 81 vols, 1st series.

Mémoires 1788
'Rapport fait à l'Académie des sciences sur le choix d'une unité de measures par mm. Borda, Lagrange, Laplace & Condorcet', *Mémoires de l'Académie Royale des Sciences*, 1788 [1791].

Mercier 1933
Mercier, S., *The Waiting City: Paris 1782–88*, ed. and trans. H. Simpson, 8 vols, Philadelphia, PA, 1933.

Mersenne 1644
Mersenne, M., *Cogitate physico-mathematica*, Paris, 1644.

Michaelis 1883
Michaelis, A., 'The Metrological Relief at Oxford', *Journal of Hellenic Studies*, IV (1883): 335–50.

Michelson 1894
Michelson, A. A., *Valeur du mètre*, Paris, 1894.

Middleton 1982
Middleton, R., ed., *The Beaux-Arts and Nineteenth-Century French Architecture*, London, 1982.

Middleton 1999
—, 'Soane's Spaces and the Matter of Fragmentation', in *John Soane Architect: Master of Space and Light*, exhibition catalogue, Royal Academy of Arts, London, 1999: 26–37.

Mink 1995
Mink, J., *Marcel Duchamp, 1887–1968: Art as Anti-Art*, Cologne, 1995.

Molderings 1991
Molderings, H., 'Objects of Modern Skepticism', in *The Definitely Unfinished Marcel Duchamp*, ed. T. De Duve, Cambridge, MA, and London, 1991.

Mollien 1845
Mollien, Le Comte N. F., *Mémoires d'un Ministre du Trésor Public, 1780–1815*, 4 vols, Paris, 1845.

Moreau 1975
Moreau, H., *Le système métrique*, Paris, 1975.

Morin 1870
Morin, Le General, 'Notice historique sur le système métrique sur ses développements et sur sa propogation', *Annales du conservatoire imperial des arts et métiers*, IX, 1870, 575–640.

Morsolin 1894
Morsolin, B., *Giangiorgio Trissino: monografia di un gentiluomo letterato nel secolo* XVI, 2nd edition, Florence, 1894.

Naumann 1991
Naumann, F. M., 'Marcel Duchamp: A Reconciliation of Opposites', in *The Definitely Unfinished Marcel Duchamp*, ed. Th. de Duve, Cambridge, MA, and London, 1991: 41–82.

Neufert 1962
Neufert, E., *Bauentwurfslehre*, Frankfurt am Main and Berlin, 1962.

Newton 1717
Newton, I., *Opticks; or, A Treatise of the Reflections, Refractions, Inflexions and Colours of Light. The Second Edition, with Additions*, London, 1717.

Newton 1726
—, *Philosophiae Naturalis Principia Mathematica (Mathematical Principles of Natural Philosophy)*, 1686; revised 1713, and 3rd ed. 1726.

Newton 1999
—, *The Principia: Mathematical Principles of Natural Philosophy*, trans. I. B. Cohen and A. Whitman, Berkeley, Los Angeles, London, 1999.

Nicholson 1912
Nicholson, E., *Men and Measures: A History of Weights and Measures Ancient and Modern*, London, 1912.

Nietzsche 1882
Nietzsche, F., *Die fröhliche Wissenschaft*, Leipzig, 1882.

Nietzsche 1959
—, 'The Gay Science', in *The Portable Nietzsche*, trans. W. Kaufmann, New York, 1959.

Onians 1951
Onians, R. B., *The Origins of European Thought about the Body, the Mind, the Soul, the World, Time and Fate*, Cambridge, 1951.

Outram 1989
Outram, D., *The Body and the French Revolution: Sex, Class and Political Culture*, New Haven, CT, and London, 1989.

Paine 1945
Paine, T., *The Complete Writings of Thomas Paine*, ed. P. S. Foner, 2 vols, New York, 1945.

Palladio 1997
Andrea Palladio, *The Four Books on Architecture*, trans. R. Tavernor and R. Schofield, Cambridge, MA, and London, 1997.

Panofsky 1970
Panofsky, E., 'The History of the Theory of Human Proportions as a Reflection of the History of Styles', in his *Meaning in the Visual Arts*, Harmondsworth, 1970: 82–138.

Paucton 1780
Paucton, A. J. P., *Métrologie; ou, Traité des mesures, poids, et monnaies des anciens peuples et des modernes*, Paris, 1780.

Pérez-Gómez 1983
Pérez-Gómez, A., *Architecture and the Crisis of Modern Science*, Cambridge, MA, and London, 1983.

Pérez-Gómez and Pelletier 1997
—, and L. Pelletier, *Architectural Representation and the Perspective Hinge*, Cambridge, MA, and London, 1983.

Perrault 1993
Claude Perrault *Ordonnance for the Five Kinds of Columns after the*

Method of the Ancients, trans. I. Kagis McEwen, Santa Monica, CA, 1993.

Peterson 1984

Peterson, M. D. ed., *Thomas Jefferson: Writings*, New York, 1984.

Peyre 1949

Peyre, H., 'The Influence of Eighteenth Century Ideas on the French Revolution', *Journal of the History of Ideas*, X (January 1949): 63–87.

Philipp 1990

Philipp, H., 'Zu Polyklets Schrift "Kanon" ', in *Polyklet: Der Bildhauer der griechischen Klassik*, ed. H. Beck, Frankfurt am Main, 1990, 137–9.

Piazzi Smyth 1867

Piazzi Smyth, C., *Life and Work at the Great Pyramid*, Edinburgh, 1867.

Piazzi Smyth 1891

—, *Our Inheritance in the Great Pyramid*, New York, 1891.

Picard 1666

Picard, J., 'Mesure de la terre', *L'Académie Royale des Sciences: Histoire de, avec les Mémoires de Mathematique & de Physique*, Paris, 1666.

Pictet 1791

Pictet, M. A., 'Measuring an Arch [*sic*] of the Meridien', *Philosophical Transactions of the Royal Society* (1791): 106–27.

Poincaré 1946

Poincaré, H., *The Foundations of Science: Science and Hypothesis. The Value of Science, Science and Method* (1913), trans. G. B. Halsted, Lancaster, PA, 1946.

Porter 2000

Porter, R., *Enlightenment: Britain and the Creation of the Modern World*, London, 2000.

Prier 1790

Prier, M. (ci-devant Du Vernois), *Mémoire sur la nécessité et les moyens de rendre uniformes dans le royaume toutes les mesures d'étendue et de pesanteur; de les établir sur des bases fixes et invariables; d'en régler tous les multiples et les subdivisions suivant l'ordre décuple* [. . .], Paris, 1790.

Raper 1760

Raper, M., 'An Enquiry into the Measure of the Roman Foot', *Philosophical Transactions of the Royal Society*, LI/2(1760): 774–823.

Raven 1951
Raven, J. E., 'Polyclitus and Pythagoreanism', *Classical Quarterly*, XLV, new series 1 (1951): 147–52.

Riccioli 1704
Riccioli, J. B., *Chronologia et geographia reformata*, London, 1704.

Richer 1674
Richer, J., *Recueil d'observations faites en plusieurs voyages par order de sa majesté pour perfectionner l'astronomie et la geographie, par messieurs de l'Académie Royale des Sciences*, Paris, 1674.

Riggs Miller 1790
Riggs Miller, Sir J., *Speeches in the House of Commons upon the Equalisation of the Weights and Measures of Great Britain*, London, 1790.

Romé de l'Isle 1789
Romé de l'Isle, J.-B. L., *Métrologie; ou, Tables pour servir à l'intelligence des poids et mesures des anciens*, Paris, 1789.

Rorty 1989
Rorty, R., *Contingency, Irony and Solidarity*, Cambridge, 1989.

Rosenau 1976
Rosenau, H., *Boullée and Visionary Architecture*, New York, 1976.

Roy 1787
Roy, General W., 'Measuring Greenwich to Paris', *Philosophical Transactions of the Royal Society*, LXXVII (1787): 188–469.

Russell 2001
Russell, T., ed, *The Napoleonic Survey of Egypt: The Monuments and Customs of Egypt – Selected Engravings and Text (Description de l'Égypte)*, 2 vols, Aldershot and Burlington, VT, 2001.

Rykwert 1976
Rykwert, J., *The Idea of a Town: The Anthropology of Urban Form in Rome, Italy and the Ancient World*, London, 1976.

Rykwert 1980
—, *The First Moderns: The Architects of the Eighteenth Century*, Cambridge, MA, and London, 1980.

Rykwert 1982
—, *The Necessity of Artifice*, London, 1982.

Rykwert 1996
—, *The Dancing Column: On Order in Architecture*, Cambridge, MA, and London, 1996.

Sagan 1973
Sagan, C., *The Cosmic Connection: An Extraterrestrial Perspective*, New York, 1973.

Sagan 1974
—, *Broca's Brain: The Romance of Science*, New York, 1974.

Sagan, Sagan and Drake 1972
—, L. S. Sagan, and F. Drake, 'A Message from Earth', *Science*, CLXXV (25 February 1972): 881–4.

Sarton 1934
Sarton, G., 'Simon Stevin of Bruges (1548–1620)', *Isis*, XXI (1934): 241–303.

Sarton 1935
—, 'The First Explanation of Decimal Fractions and Measures (1585), Together with a History of the Decimal Idea and a Facsimile (No. XVII) of Stevin's Disme', *Isis*, XXIII (1935): 153–244.

Schelle 1913–23
Schelle, G., *Oeuvres de A.R.J. Turgot, et documents le concernant*, 5 vols, Paris, 1913–23.

Schilbach 1970
Schilbach, E., *Byzantinische Metrologie*, Munich, 1970.

Scholfield 1958
Scholfield, H., *The Theory of Proportion in Architecture*, Cambridge, 1958.

Schwarz 1969
Schwarz, A., *The Complete Works of Marcel Duchamp*, London, 1969.

Scott and Rothaus 1985
Scott, S. F., and B. Rothaus, *Historical Dictionary of the French Revolution, 1789–1799*, Westport, CT, 1985.

Sennett 1994
Sennett, R., *Flesh and Stone: The Body and the City in Western Civilization*, New York, 1994.

Serlio 1996
Sebastiano Serlio, *On Architecture. Volume 1. Books I–V of 'Tutte l'Opere d'Architettura et Prospetiva' by Sebastiano Serlio*, trans. V. Hart and P. Hicks, New Haven, CT, and London, 1996.

Shalev 1967
Shalev, Z., 'Measurer of All Things: John Greaves (1602–1652), the Great Pyramid and Early Modern Metrology' (1967), *Journal of the History of Ideas*, LXIII/4 (October 2002): 555–75.

Shuckburgh Evelyn 1798
Shuckburgh Evelyn, Sir George, 'An Account of Some Endeav-
ours to Ascertain a Standard of Weight and Measure', *Philosophical Transactions of the Royal Society of London*, LXXXVIII/1 (1798):
133–82 (The quotes in the text are from the abridged version of
the *Philosophical Transactions*, XVIII (1800): 300–12).

Snellius 1617
Snellius, W., *Eratosthenes Batavus, seu de terrae ambitus vera quan-
titate suscitatus*, Leiden, 1617.

Snellius 1731
—, *Ouvrages des mathematiques*, The Hague, 1731.

Sprat 1667
Sprat, T., *The History of the Royal Society*, London, 1667.

Stewart 1978
Stewart, A. F., 'The Canon of Polykleitos', *Journal of Hellenic
Studies*, XCVIII (1978): 122–31.

Stewart 1995
Stewart, I., *Nature's Numbers: Discovering Order and Pattern in the
Universe*, London, 1995.

Stinger 1985
Stinger, C. L., *The Renaissance in Rome*, Bloomington, IN, 1985.

Stuart Jones 1912
Stuart Jones, H., *A Catalogue of the Municipal Collections of Rome:
The Museo Capitolino*, Rome, 1912.

Süskind 1986
Süskind, P., *Perfume: The Story of a Murderer* (Zurich, 1985), trans.
J. E. Woods, Harmondsworth, 1986.

Taton 1953
Taton, R., 'The French Revolution and the Progress of Science',
Centaurus, III (1953): 73–89.

Tavernor 1998
Tavernor, R., *On Alberti and the Art of Building*, New Haven, CT,
and London, 1998.

Tavernor 2002a
—, 'Contemplating Perfection through Piero's Eyes', in *Body and
Building: On the Changing Relation of Body and Architecture*, ed. G.
Dodds and R. Tavernor, Cambridge, MA, and London, 2002: 78–93.

Tavernor 2002b

—, 'Measure, Metre, Irony: Reuniting Pure Mathematics with Architecture', *ARQ: Architectural Research Quarterly*, VL/1 (2002): 67–76; also in: *Nexus* IV: *Architecture and Mathematics*, ed. K. Williams and J. F. Rodrigues, Florence, 2002: 47–61. Available electronically at www.nexusjournal.com/conferences/N2002-Tavernor.html

Taylor 1859

Taylor, J., *The Great Pyramid: Why Was It Built? And Who Built It?*, London, 1859.

Téron 1801

Téron, J.-B., *Instruction sur le système de mesures et poids uniformes pour toute la République Française [. . .] par [. . .] teneur de livres et maître d'arithmétique*, Geneva, An. X (1801), 10 prairial.

Thiersch 1893

Thiersch, A., 'Die Proportionen in der Architektur', in *Handbuch der Architektur*, ed. J. Durm, vol. IV, no. 1, Darmstadt, 1893: 38–87.

Thorpe 1840

Thorpe, B., *Ancient Laws and Institutes of England, Comprising Laws Enacted under the Anglo-Saxon Kings*, 2 vols, London, 1840.

Tomkins 1996

Tomkins, A., *Duchamp*, New York, 1996.

Tompkins 1973

Tompkins, P., *Secrets of the Great Pyramid*, with an Appendix by L. C. Stecchini, 'Notes on the Relation of Ancient Measures to the Great Pyramid', Harmondsworth, 1973.

Totten 1884

Totten, A. L., *An Important Question in Metrology*, New York, 1884.

Trachtenberg 1986

Trachtenberg, A., 'A Tribute to Liberty', in *Centennial*, ed. M. Rosenthal, New York, 1986: 6–21.

Turin 1816

Parere della Reale Accademia delle Scienze di Torino alle misure ed ai pesi, Turin, 1816 (copy in the Library of The Academy of Sciences, Turin, DD VI 39).

Turner 1977

Turner, P. V., *The Education of Le Corbusier*, New York, 1977.

Ungers 1994
Ungers, O. M., '*Ordo, fondo et mensura*: The Criteria of Architecture', in *The Renaissance from Brunelleschi to Michelangelo: The Representation of Architecture*, London, 1994: 306–17.

Upton 1879
Upton, J. K., Report to the House of Representatives, *On the Adoption of the Metric System of Weights and Measures*, Washington, DC, 1879.

US Congress 1904–34
US Congress, *Journals of the Continental Congress, 1774–89*, Washington, DC, 1904–34.

US Congress 1922
—, *Senate Committee on Manufactures. The Metric System: Hearings before a Subcommittee of the Committee on Manufacture*, on S. 2267, 67th Congress, 1st and 2nd sessions, Washington, DC, 1922.

US House of Representatives 1866
US House of Representatives, *Report No. 62 by J. A. Kasson in the 39th Congress, 1st Session, of the House of Representatives*, Washington, DC, 17 May 1866.

Uzielli 1899
Uzielli, G., *Le misure lineari mediovale e l'effigie di Cristo*, Florence, 1899.

Vasari 1965
Vasari, G., *The Lives of the Artists*, trans. G. Bull, Harmondsworth, 1965.

Vitruvius 1960
Marcus Vitruvius Pollio, *The Ten Books on Architecture*, trans. M. H. Morgan, New York, 1960.

Voegelin 1948
Voegelin, E., 'The Origins of Scientism', *Social Research*, xv/4 (1948): 462–94.

Voltaire 1733
Voltaire, F. M. A. de, *Letters Concerning the English Nation*, trans. J. Lockman, Dublin, 1733.

Voltaire 1962 [1764]
—, *Philosophical Dictionary*, New York, 1962 [1764].

Waele 1997
Waele, J. de, 'Vitruvius en de Klassieke Dorische Tempel', in *Vit-*

ruviuscongres 1995, ed. R. Rolf, Heerlen, 1997: 25–38 (summary trans. R. Padovan).

Walzer 1974

Walzer, M., ed., *Regicide and Revolution: Speeches at the Trial of Louis* XVI, trans. M. Rothstein, Cambridge, 1974.

Warren 1899

Sir Charles Warren, 'The Ancient Standards of Measure in the East', *Palestine Exploration Fund Quarterly*, XXXI (1899).

Weil 1958

Weil, S., *Oppression and Liberty*, trans. A. F. Wills and J. Petrie, London, 1958.

Weil 1987

—, *The Need for Roots: Prelude to a Declaration of Duties Towards Mankind*, trans. A. F. Wills (1952), London, 1987.

Wesenberg 1975–6

Wesenberg, B., 'Zum metrologischen Relief in Oxford', *Marburger Winckelmann-Programm* (1975–6): 15–22.

Westfall 1980

Westfall, R. S., *Never at Rest: A Biography of Isaac Newton*, Cambridge, 1980.

Whinney 1958

Whinney, M. D., 'Sir Christopher Wren's Visit to Paris', *Gazette des Beaux-Arts*, LI (1958): 229–42.

White 1973

White, J., 'Measurement, Design and Carpentry in Duccio's *Maestà*', *Art Bulletin*, LV (1973): 334–66.

Wiener 1907

Wiener, L., 'Origin of the Metric System', *Nation*, LXXXIV (1907): 103–4.

Wilford 2000

Wilford, J. N., *The Mapmakers: The Story of the Great Pioneers in Cartography – From Antiquity to the Space Age*, London, 1981 (revised 2000).

Wilkins 1668

Wilkins, J., *An Essay Towards a Real Character and a Philosophical Language*, London, 1668.

Wilson Jones 2000

Wilson Jones, M., 'Doric Measure and Architectural Design 1:

The Evidence of the Relief from Salamis', *American Journal of Archaeology*, CIV (2000): 73–93.

Winfield and Winfield 1982

Winfield, J. and D. Winfield, 'Proportion and Structure of the Human Figure in Byzantine Wall-Painting and Mosaic', *British Archaeological Reports*, BAR International Series 154, 1982.

Wölfflin 1889

Wölfflin, H., *Zur Lehre von den Proportionen*, Basel, 1889.

Woodward 1972

Woodward, C. D., *BSI: The Story of Standards*, London, 1972.

Yates 1856

Yates, J., *Narrative of the Origin and Formation of the International Association*, 2nd edn, London, 1856.

Young 1794

Young, A., *Travels during the Years 1787, 1788 and 1789 [. . .] the Kingdom of France*, 2 vols, Dublin, 1794.

Zeising 1854

Zeising, A., *Neue Lehre von den Proportionen des menschlichen Körpers*, Leipzig, 1854

Zervas 1979

Zervas, D., 'The Florentine Braccio da Panna', *Architectura: Zeitschrift für Geschichte der Baukunst*, IX/1 (1979): 6–11.

Zupko 1977

Zupko, R. E., *British Weights and Measures: A History from Antiquity to the Seventeenth Century*, Madison, WI, and London, 1977.

Zupko 1990

—, *Revolution in Measurement: Western European Weights and Measures since the Age of Science*, Philadelphia, 1990.

Index